# Zest

# ZEST

ESSAYS ON THE ART OF LIVING

IAIN BAMFORTH

CARCANET

First published in Great Britain in 2022 by
Carcanet
Alliance House, 30 Cross Street
Manchester M2 7AQ
www.carcanet.co.uk

A CIP catalogue record for this book is
available from the British Library.

ISBN 978 1 80017 205 0

Book design by Andrew Latimer
Printed in Great Britain by SRP Ltd, Exeter, Devon

Supported using public funding by the National Lottery
through Arts Council England.

# Contents

*Preface*                                                    11

I. INKLINGS

On the Good Life                                             21
*What Leisure Really Means*

First Fruit                                                  31
*Botanising in the Garden of Eden*

On the Surface of Events                                     38
*Rereading the Book of Jonah*

Green, Red and Blue                                          48
*The World in 1572*

Grace and Violence                                           62
*Anecdotes from the Napoleonic Era*

Balzac *et Cie*                                              67
*The Novel after Balzac*

A Critical Romance                                           74
*Dostoevsky as a Literary Character*


II. HAPPENSTANCES

Picking Olives                                               83
*A Working Week in Apulia*

Kinds of Blue                                      90
*Some Uses of the Cyanometer*

Trees and Forests                                  97
*The Axe-Man Discovers Civility*

Praise for the Siesta                             105
*Done with Down Time*

A Just Appreciation of the Pineapple              110
*Some Social Aspects of Taste*

Marcel's Cup of Tea                               116
*Getting it Wrong about the Madeleine*

Getting it Right                                  121
*The Thinking behind Meaningful Work*

White Noise Static                                128
*On Ambient Sound Shapes*

Falling off a Star                                135
*Loving Lou in 1882*

A Very Little Ice Age                             143
*Impersonal Violence and Metal Recovery*


III. MUNDANITIES

Making Things Clearer                             153
*Word, Image, Pictogram*

Person in Question                                                  163
*Around Lisbon with Fernando Pessoa*

A Philosophy of Buttons                                             174
*Steven Connor Examines Some Everyday Objects*

The Pitch Drop Experiment                                           180
*On Slowness*

The Low Shores Where We Walk                                        185
*Postcards from Europe's Mystic River*

Doing the Locomotion                                                194
*Paolo Sorrentino's film* La Grande Bellezza

Where Are We Now?                                                   201
*Necrology for a Starman*

Pictural Propositions                                               207
*Wittgenstein and Photography*

Fiddleheads and Horsetails                                          217
*On the Sex Life of Ferns*

Saxony's Other City                                                 222
*Books, Bombs and Bach*


IV. VAGARIES

Zest                                                                233
*Tobias Smollett in the South of France*

Ultimate Islands                                           240
*Island-Hopping with Peter Conrad*

Room for Fetishes                                          248
*Redmond O'Hanlon's Travel Philosophy*

Polish Projections                                         254
*Ryszard Kapuściński Comes over All Ethical*

Music and Metabolism                                       263
*The Composer Slamet Abdul Sjukur*

Other Varieties                                            268
*A Compacted History of Decomposition*

Archipelago and Submarine                                  272
*Field-notes from Indonesia*

*For my wife Cornelia, the true botanist of the family*

\*

Throughout the perishing occasions in the life of each temporal Creature, the inward source of distaste or of refreshment, the judge arising out of the very nature of things, redeemer or goddess of mischief, is the transformation of Itself, everlasting in the Being of God. In this way, the insistent craving is justified – the insistent craving that zest for existence be refreshed by the ever-present, unfading importance of our immediate actions, which perish and yet live for evermore.

Alfred North Whitehead, *Process and Reality*

# Preface

One day I'll write the book that brings my life together. But life is short, and there are always other things to do—like earning a living, or painting a house. Readers of this collection of essays (and one or two essay-reviews I wanted to preserve), all written in the fifteen years since my previous collection, *The Good European*—which floated around the idea and ideal of Europe—are going to find themselves veering from the sex life of ferns to the philosopher Friedrich Nietzsche's one serious affair of the heart, from the fifty-three gradations of the colour blue to the less than fifty-seven varieties of a famous condiment, from Lisbon to Leipzig and visions of ancient Rome in a contemporary film to 'field-studies' in the region of the world once known as the Malay Archipelago. If they feel inclined to recoil at such a dizzy assortment, I can only retort that any alarm they might feel is misplaced: these are sober versions of what the poet Louis MacNeice called 'the drunkenness of things being various' and, as it happens, entirely of a piece with my own lived experience, eccentric as it might be—at least in the geographical sense. But coherence, as Montaigne suggests in his essay 'Of the Art of Discussion', is principally a matter of character, not of theory or logic.

In the afterword to *The Good European*, I mentioned Nietzsche's recommendation that his future readers, reading him against the grain, would have to be 'monsters of curiosity'. The thirty-odd essays in *Zest* are curious in the old Latin sense of 'paying careful attention to detail', from the word's root-sense of 'cure'. Michel Foucault picked up on this half-forgotten etymological connection in his 1980 interview 'The Masked Philosopher' in *Le Monde*, in which he suggested that for him—contrary to the stigma it has attracted in

Christianity, philosophy and even some kinds of science—
curiosity 'suggests something altogether different: it evokes
"concern"; it evokes the care one takes for what exists and could
exist; a readiness to find strange and singular what surrounds
us; a certain relentlessness to break up our familiarities and
to regard otherwise the same things; a fervour to grasp what
is happening and what passes; a casualness in regard to the
traditional hierarchies of the important and essential.' This,
then, might be a suitable quality to describe a physician with
a horror of prescription, which is how I occasionally describe
myself, and not always tongue-in-cheek.

The title of this book derives from my short, whimsical
account of the travels (mostly 'travails') of the now almost
forgotten eighteenth-century Scottish writer Tobias Smollett
and his wife in the south of France; and zest hovers in the air
of my realisation that the cultural fetish of the madeleine, that
plump little scallop of a sponge, distracts from the fact that
Marcel Proust's famous instant of involuntary recollection in
his grand novel *À la recherche du temps perdu* owed everything
to the volatile elements in the lime blossom tea which had just
moistened the morsel offered to him by his mother. The notion
that a smell or taste can bypass years of forgetting and set off
an explosion of recall is one I find very appealing, especially in
a civilisation straining under the clutter of its paraphernalia—
to use Steven Connor's word. It is the scent of time abruptly
restored, henceforth to linger. Zest is the piquant, outermost
rind of a citrus fruit, but it is also, in Dr Johnson's definition,
'a relish; a taste added', the topic of one of my Indonesian
pieces at the end of the collection. It is the sharp, heady,
almost metaphysical sense of meaningfulness that catches me
off guard in the indefinitely ongoing task of describing (and
redescribing) the living element in experience—the quality
alluded to in the book's epigraph by Alfred North Whitehead,
the mathematician who became an academic philosopher

late in life, and who claimed in his famous dialogues that 'the meaning of life is adventure'.

In *Zest*, the focus—if such a word is appropriate for a book with so many things in mind—is on the author as ideal. Although it makes only one passing reference to Socrates, he certainly stands behind its scenes as the pre-eminent 'life artist'. The German philosopher Friedrich Nietzsche—that most singular and nuanced self-made man—spent many years 'doing battle' with the figure whose example, as mediated by Plato, did much to establish the broad premises of the moral culture of which we are still a part, even if the modern forms of civilisation, as Balzac anticipated, have followed the money. Nietzsche's ideal was to be the 'poet of one's life', but he certainly didn't believe that the way to be such a person was to listen for the divine voice (*daimonion*) that kept Socrates in the light, striving to be virtuous. Nietzsche even accused the rationalist Socrates of having destroyed the myths of Homeric art: the stamp of understanding could only be prosaic. What Nietzsche did think praiseworthy was Socrates' dedication to philosophy as an 'art of living'—a concept developed by the French scholar Pierre Hadot in his pioneering work on the ancient traditions of practical philosophical activity. But Socrates is ironically silent about how he became who he was—and this is what makes him, as Kierkegaard realised, the exemplary role model for the art of living. Nietzsche's notion of self-empowerment ('will to power') is utterly foreign to Socrates, who understood his life as one of service to the gods, notably Eros, who drew him into conversation with others, questioning them all the while. Socrates didn't say what constituted the good life; he *showed* it. In short, there is no general rule that can be applied to produce the unrepeatable fact of being an individual (which means that all 'self-help' literature is fundamentally mistaken about its vocation, although there is lots of money to be made from offering bogus forms of solidarity). Any discussion of the art of living can only reflect on previous attempts—failed and successful—to embody it; and we should not forget that the very notion of a 'good life', one cossetted in material comforts (and then not so short) has become widespread in developed parts of the planet only in living memory.

It strikes me, then, that a similar kind of ironic reflexivity exists in the fact that every piece of writing stands at the mercy of its readers.

*

I would like to thank the editors of the following journals and periodicals in which some of these essays first appeared, although in some cases the entries have been substantially modified and enlarged since their original publication: *Parnassus* (New York), *PN Review*, *British Journal of General Practice*, *Times Literary Supplement*, *Quadrant* (Sydney), *Hidden Europe* (Berlin) and *Literary Review*. Particular thanks are due to the late Les Murray, Ben Downing, Alec Logan, Tom Fleming, Jim Campbell and Maren Meinhardt, and also to Christine Thayer, who worked with me in Indonesia; the book owes its final form to the perceptive advice of Andrew Latimer and Michael Schmidt, my editors at Carcanet Press. I miss the wide-ranging discussions I used to have on German literature with my father-in-law Christian Schütze, who died in 2018; and appreciate my regular *causeries* with friends in Strasbourg—Gregory Owcarz, Jeremy Garwood and Raymond Bach—as well as the convivial warmth and generosity of two French friends, Patrick and Monika Garruchet, now displaced to Switzerland, who introduced me to the spectacular Fextal, behind the house where Nietzsche spent his summers in Sils Maria. Their motto has always been Charles Péguy's: 'philosophy doesn't go to philosophy classes'. Last but not least, I am especially grateful to my designer children, Felix and Claire, who, disappointed at the rather dull baroque still-life I had in mind as a cover illustration, surprised me by coming up one weekend with their own very striking visual equivalent to the art of literary lemon zesting.

# Zest

*Essays on the Art of Living*

# I
# Inklings

# On the Good Life

*What Leisure Really Means*

> *…the organization of the entire economy toward the 'better'*
> *life has become the major enemy of the good life.*
> Ivan Illich, *Tools for Conviviality*, 1973

Nobody with intellectual pretensions, even the slightest, wants to be called a dilettante. 'Dilettante' is the very assassin-word of character and motive. It is a lexical curiosity—and perhaps more than just lexical—that related social characterisations such as 'dandy' and 'flaneur', all their solitary hauteur notwithstanding, evade social censure; not so 'dilettante', a term that suggests a mixture of privilege, arrogant superficiality and skittishness. The great G.K. Chesterton, for one, went to some lengths in 'On Lying in Bed' to avoid the taint of dilettantism, even though his essay's Oblomovian title rather suggests he was one of the genus. His late father, he writes, 'was in a hundred happy and fruitful ways an amateur; but in no way at all a dilettante'. He describes one of the characters in his Father Brown novels as a 'great dabbler', and again is quick to add that 'there was in him none of that antiquarian frivolity that we convey by the word "dilettante"'.

Antiquarian frivolity is perhaps what did for dilettantes. As Bruce Redford observes in his *Dilettanti: The Antic and the Antique*: 'from the early nineteenth century to the present, "dilettante" has been a deprecatory… term, connoting the sloppy, the second-rate, the superficial.'

It wasn't always so. The Society of Dilettanti, founded in 1732 in London, was a sympotic club established by gentlemen who had been to Italy and were 'desirous of encouraging, *at home*, a taste for those objects which had contributed so much to their entertainment *abroad*.' Modelled on earlier societies like the notorious Hellfire Club and the Virtuosi of St Luke, the Dilettanti—motto: *seria ludo*—were nostalgists for the Grand Tour, that early anticipation of the gap-year. If they couldn't stay on in Italy, it ought to be possible to introduce good taste to the burgeoning mercantile society of the British Isles. Two of the society's more successful campaigns were to introduce Italian opera into the United Kingdom and to set up the Royal Academy. British watercolour painting also owes much to the support of the Dilettanti. Meetings in London were a mix of connoisseurship and carousing, offering a potent brew of 'the Bacchic, the sexual, the classical and the sacrilegious'. The licentiousness of the Society repelled some figures who might otherwise seem to be obvious dilettantes: the virtuoso (i.e. 'man of diverse interests') Horace Walpole (1717–91), Fourth Earl of Orford—now remembered chiefly for having invented the word 'serendipity' as well as for his volumes of vivid and gossipy letters and the famous Gothic pile he owned at Strawberry Hill—kept his distance. 'The nominal qualification [of membership],' he advanced, 'is having been in Italy, and the real one being drunk.' But some Dilettanti became famous. There was Sir William Hamilton, envoy to the Bourbon court in Naples and the Two Sicilies, who collected and studied as many antiquities as he could lay his hands on, addressing letters to other members in London on phallus worship, the volcanic Phlegraean Fields near Naples, and contemporaneous archaeological findings in Greece. His distant cousin Gavin Hamilton was just as well known in Rome for his archaeological digs and recreations of antiquity, often under licence to the Pope. Bequeathed to the nation (or the Papal state), such personal holdings were to enhance the collections of many public institutions, not least the British Museum. Contemplating the last days of Pompeii is dilettantism at its finest. It is Hazlitt on the Elgin Marbles.

Dilettantism would acquire its current association with effeteness only as the nineteenth century wore on: dilettantes (and all those related social types who stole the show in the more theatrical eighteenth century) patently lacked the moral high seriousness of the Victorian legislator, social reformer or even plain businessman. The origins of dilettantism were too close to those of eighteenth-century libertinism, and dilettantes too fond of the republican tradition—the presiding officer at meetings of the Dilettanti wore a scarlet toga and occupied the Roman consul's traditional seat of office—for them to be trusted patriots at a time when that ambitious Corsican, Napoleon Bonaparte, was threatening to invade the British Isles and install one of his cousins as the new ruling monarch. The rise of the middle classes made the life of a gentleman-loiterer mightily suspect. Doing something for the sheer pleasure of it, which is the sense of the verb *dilettare* (Latin: *delectare*) from which the Dilettanti took their name, was a dubious activity when being moral was beginning to be seen as a strenuous business. This attitude had already surfaced at an earlier period in British history: Thomas Hobbes, remembering his puritan origins, insisted in his tract *On the Citizen* that 'anything that has no purpose is Vain'.

Like Hobbes, the Scots were never very keen on dilettantes, although they did provide a good model—in Henry Mackenzie's once-famous novel—of that related social type, 'the man of feeling'. Work had been embraced by sixteenth-century culture as an escape from the terror of not knowing whether one's soul was redeemed, while the peasants of an earlier culture had flocked to festivities as an escape from the very same work. Pleasure was ever after deeply suspect. Perhaps the only writer truly to emancipate himself from the grudgingly puritan aspects of the culture in which he was brought up was Robert Louis Stevenson, who even had the temerity to write a manifesto against the work ethic called

'An Apology for Idlers'. Stevenson makes it shockingly clear that loafing and dawdling are synonymous for him with a *heightened* perception of being in the world. 'Extreme busyness… is a symptom of deficient vitality; and a faculty for idleness implies a catholic appetite and a strong sense of personal identity. There is a sort of dead-alive, hackneyed people about, who are scarcely conscious of living except in the exercise of some conventional occupation.' He observes that the industrious deeply resent the presence of 'cool persons in the meadows by the wayside, lying with a handkerchief over their ears and a glass at their elbow'.

Compare Stevenson's remarks with the lines written earlier in the same century by that other product of northern Calvinism, Thomas Carlyle: 'Fundamentally speaking, all genuine work is religion, and every religion that is not work can go and live with the Brahmins, the Antinomians, and the Whirling Dervishes.' Carlyle was blunt in endorsing a sense of cultural and racial superiority that was tied to the belief that dedication to work provides a pedestal for some peoples and nations: imperial rule by Britain was still being legitimised (and idealised) many years later as a combination of hard work and self-sacrifice in Kipling's poem 'The White Man's Burden' (1899). But by the end of the nineteenth century, Eastern religions were being imported lock, stock and barrel to overthrow the dominant Christian view of things. In 1890, Oscar Wilde criticised the society of his day in his article 'The Critic as Artist (With some Remarks upon the Importance of Doing Nothing)', in which he referred admiringly to Chuang Tsu (Zhuangzi) and claimed his ancient teachings were proof that 'well meaning and offensive busy-bodies have destroyed the simple and spontaneous virtue that is in man'.

Dilettantism had other philosophical supporters. Although he was a contemporary of Carlyle, Arthur Schopenhauer was very clear about what he saw as a vulgarly exaggerated respect for the 'professional': he believed most city-dwellers were unable to conceive of working other than for gain. He defends the dilettante as a person of true moral seriousness: 'The truth, however, is that to the dilettante the thing is the end, while to the professional as such it is the means; and only he who is directly interested in a thing, and occupies himself with it from love of it, will pursue it with entire seriousness.' We acknowledge this implicitly when we call the fine arts the 'pure' arts. They have no social utility: they are gratuitous in the sense defined by Schopenhauer, and after him, by Friedrich Nietzsche.

Turn aside, take time, be still, go slow: those were the impish instructions of Nietzsche, in the preface to his early work *Daybreak*, where he remarked that he had decided no longer to write anything that did not reduce to despair 'every sort of man who is "in a hurry".'

One reason we still have a very Victorian respect for professionalism is that puritan values spawned our culture, and are so deeply ingrained within it that few even realise their principles are something functional—the kind of moral calculus that would have appealed to Hobbes. One reason for the reluctance to acknowledge these puritan values may be the 1960s' spirited attempt to redeem dilettantism—we have only to think of the ironic career of the 'bricoleur', first spotted in Claude Lévi-Strauss' *The Savage Mind*, and ever since an all-purpose imaginary hero for people in the humanities. W.H. Auden insisted in his jottings 'The Poet and the City' that 'among the half dozen things for which a man of honour should be prepared, if necessary, to die, the right to play, the right to frivolity, is not the least'; and Michael Oakeshott—who in many ways was the philosophical accessory to Auden's poetry—wrote in his essay 'On Being Conservative' that what we value most in life are essentially purposeless activities. That is their higher ethic. They are pursuits undertaken for their own sake. The concept of play was not a frivolous idea for Oakeshott, who died in 1990 and was spared the consumer society's full blazon of inanity; it was the very possibility of an outlook that refused to treat things (and people) in manipulative or instrumental terms. It is only the puritan who needs frivolity to come kitted out with some hidden didactic purpose, an attitude still common among earnest British politicians and American film industry nabobs.

What Schopenhauer had identified as the deep seriousness of the dilettante is accompanied by a perfect disinterest about outcome. In every case, his mindset is hardly likely to be congruent with that of the rational economic actor who always acts with an eye on how his actions are likely to benefit him. 'One thinks with a watch in the hand, even as one eats lunch while reading the latest bulletin on the stockmarket', wrote Nietzsche; 'one lives as if one always "might miss out on something".' Indeed, the word 'activity' is wrong-footed, because it suggests an active appropriation, an *effort*—the assumption that was drummed into philosophy by that northern protestant, Immanuel Kant. He saw philosophy as a 'Herculean labour'; it ought to be strenuous. Yet true contemplation, grasping the essential nature of things, was to be receptive to inspiration. And the fact that inspiration was so often effortless made Kant suspicious. Goethe, who knew a bit about creative vision and didn't care too much for the formulators of moral laws, asserted that 'absolute activity' of the Kantian type makes people hard-hearted, and unable to receive—it 'makes one bankrupt in the end'.

The ancients Greeks had only a negative term to describe what they were doing when they were not at leisure. Being at leisure, educating yourself (in the sense still current, albeit vestigially, in the German idea of 'Bildung'), was the very basis of their culture. It could even be said that for the Greeks leisure was an obligatory activity for anyone trying to live the good life. 'Men without leisure', mused that truly distinguished dilettante Count Harry Kessler in his book on the industrialist Walter Rathenau, 'are men without hearts or souls and this is the most dangerous hindrance to culture. Precisely their competence makes them dangerous. The ancient Greeks called such a man *Banausos* and had excluded him quite correctly, whenever the most important questions of politics, religion, or art were discussed.' The Greek distinction was absorbed into Latin: *neg-otium* became the term to describe the hustle and bustle of doing business. It was actually a perverse turn for the English language to take the positive term, *otium*, and make a negative adjective out of it, 'otiose', which means to serve no useful purpose. When Coleridge and Southey published the chapbook *Omniana, or Horæ Otiosiores* (*About Everything, or Leisure Hours*) with Longman in 1812, they saw nothing pejorative about conscribing it.

In his famous 1948 tract on the topic, the Thomist philosopher Josef Pieper insisted on reminding his readers that leisure is the foundation of any culture. It is work restored to its original, formative, sense-bestowing role. For Pieper, leisure is a kind of worship. It is an affirmation of life.

Yet the issue refuses to settle, at least in my mind. Ours is a highly technical civilisation, one that has exceeded all others in terms of the useful gadgets and contrivances it has invented; and we want to be helped, when in need, by people who are not just knowledgeable in their interests, but technically competent too. If you're facing coronary bypass surgery you want it done by a cardiac surgeon who has done thousands of venous grafts, not a venal surgeon with a merely general interest in the dynamics of the heart. But while becoming a cardiac surgeon requires thousands of hours of technical training, knowledge of the other kind of heart, the figurative one we are all supposed to possess, can be acquired by anybody, though it is sometimes very painfully won. The general fear (as in the long-standing debate about 'the two cultures') is that the amateur is already hopelessly disconnected from the specialised jargon of technical knowledge, and lost in an idiom that is either untranslatable into anything concrete or, worse, has no bearing on reality at all.

Schopenhauer's is an instructive case. Being able to rely on a substantial inherited fortune (like so many middle-class German intellectuals who were to make a cult of their inner need for freedom, including Karl Marx and Friedrich Engels), he was ultimately defending his own position. He was not obliged to work. And he was an outspoken defender of the autonomy of individual reason, the political programme for establishing which had first been set out by Kant. Indeed, Schopenhauer became celebrated (in the wrong sense) for having decided, in 1820, to set himself up as a university lecturer in Berlin and deliver a syllabus that coincided exactly with the schedule of Hegel's principal course. Hegel was by then the most famous philosopher in town, and Schopenhauer ended up lecturing to an almost empty amphitheatre; shortly afterwards he threw over his entire ambition of becoming a lecturer and returned to his study.

While the privately wealthy Schopenhauer was right to identify the (nineteenth-century German) university as a place where dilettantism could flourish, the ideal of the university as a community of scholars pursuing and passing on learning for its own sake is one that barely survives in our day. Vocational training is inimical to education, which is what a dilettante is after. Indeed, perhaps the current institution that best corresponds to the old definition of the university is the five-hundred-year-old Collège de France, in the heart of Paris; it offers public lectures by some of the world's most distinguished minds but has no student body at all and confers no degrees.

So perhaps the economic argument is a charge that can be levelled against dilettantism. However delightful its pleasures and unselfserving its ends, it encourages us to live off the capital in the manner of unreconstructed and superbly sensitive *grands bourgeois*—and not just the proceeds of our own trust funds but the accumulated delights and riches of the entire globe itself. It is as if we were called to consume the fruits of other people's efforts all day long while concealing from ourselves the social importance of production. Hobbes took some relish in mocking the aspirations of those who seek to own and enjoy things prior to the contracts of civil society. 'We would have our Security against all the World, upon Right of Property, without Paying for it... We may as well Expect that Fish, and Fowl should Boil, Rost, and Dish themselves, and come to the Table, and that Grapes should squeeze themselves into our Mouths, and have all other Contentments and ease which some pleasant Men have Related of the Land of Coquany.' He was describing that ancient fantasy of living in Cockaigne, the land of plenty relished by the tide of beggars and vagabonds who were our medieval ancestors, and who so often had to chew on stale, ergot-tainted bread and mouldy bran-mash if they wanted to eat at all. Piero Camporesi's *Bread of Dreams* relates all the Pantagruelesque wretchedness of an age in which thousands went hungry. The only surrogate for food was words.

That empirical check on the dreams of uninterrupted consumption was something that Hegel, who had read his Hobbes (and Smith) closely, absorbed into his philosophy of right, and his meditations on the mutual dependency of statehood and selfhood. If the essence of politics is not primarily to administer a given society but to represent its members to themselves individually and as a whole, then it is difficult indeed to imagine a polity and social ethics for a club of lubbers and self-pleasers. The effect of the global market—a shorthand way of saying that we have entered a dispensation where in order to consume we need to make or produce (and one that was already well under way in the rapidly industrialising Germany of Schopenhauer's day)—is not to introduce us to the upholstered solidity of *Weltbürgertum* but, as Marx said, to proletarianise us. Being proletarian means being bound to the work process. That ugly verb can be interpreted as the abrupt realisation that even if we personally don't ever have to get down and dirty, our material lives depend on vast impersonal structures relating us to the labour of tens of thousands of (mostly Chinese) people we are unlikely ever to meet.

Yet if our society persists in moving further into the total world of work—giving life a rigorously economic explanation, making ultimate meaning the issue solely of productivity and audit, and failing to see that the genuine desire to perfect a thing for its own sake is actually the mark of a true craftsman— then the only socially accredited dilettantes are likely to be the *retired*. And the present legions of retirees, at least in western Europe, are the generation that made common cause with the Situationist International in 1968, which was adamant that the economic and social forces of a consumerist society would merely allow citizens to recuperate in commodity form what the system needed as its raw material. And what did they do about it? Took to the streets, barricaded the Sorbonne, fought running battles with the police and urged the workers to go on strike, all for the sake of indolence and spiritual beauty.

It was the sweet life—what the French call *la douceur de vivre*—they wanted, not the good one. The terms are practically antonyms, though it (presumably) takes a dilettante to wonder if they should be.

# First Fruit

*Botanising in the Garden of Eden*

> *The philosopher of the expedition was not a man to be silenced*
> *by referring him to the Garden of Eden.*
>
> Wilkie Collins & Charles Dickens, *The Frozen Deep*

There is more than a whiff of what the philosopher David Hume, following Thomas Hobbes, called 'decaying sense' in the story about self-knowledge in the Book of Genesis. It is rumoured, for instance, that the apple—'a beautiful, banal, Eden-red apple' as Nabokov put it in *Lolita*—was actually an apricot, the only thing of any value to be obtained by Christendom from the disaster of the Crusades, in the estimation of the historian Jacques Le Goff. Could the apricot and not the apple (*Malus domestica*) be the fruit of the 'tree of the knowledge of good and evil'? Everybody knows that the climate in Mesopotamia, which is where the Garden of Eden is likely to have been situated, should it ever have existed as such, has always been too hot to allow the cultivation of apples: they are to be found on the cool hills of northern Lebanon, where the Romans grew them intensively, but not farther east.

There is a sticking point, however, with this revisionist account of the Creation: the apricot originally came from China, and was unknown in the Biblical lands until after the conquests of Alexander the Great. So perhaps it was another kind of fruit Eve offered to Adam, and not necessarily the pendulous fig, the leaves of which cover their genitalia in so many Renaissance paintings. As Gottfried Ephraim Lessing wrote in one of his epigrams, it could have been something as unremarkable as the grape, like the cluster Hermes dangles in front of the infant Dionysus in Praxiteles' famous sculpture—ready to be pressed and fermented into the finest bottle of Château Musar. Then again, some fundamentalist Christians wouldn't want you to have that much pleasure: they believe the tree of knowledge is now extinct, having been created by the Lord for the sole purpose of testing Adam and Eve. (They failed the test. 'It is very unhappy, but too late to be helped, the discovery we have made that we exist', wrote Emerson, spelling out the scoop. 'That discovery is called the Fall of Man.')

Ford Madox Ford had a bright theory that the tempting fruit was actually a pomelo, which he called a shaddock, after the English sea captain who in the seventeenth century brought it to the West Indies from the East. (In Indonesia, where it is known as *jeruk Bali*, it is cut into wedges and eaten with a little salt as a snack or appetiser.) Ford spent a lot of time in Provence, which he loved (and wrote a lovely book about). The locals, he noted, had never eaten of this 'pompous lemon'—which they fed instead to their pigs—and had therefore never fallen: they were living in Paradise. There have been times in my life when I might have agreed too that Provence was Paradise, but quite frankly the thick albedo and weight of the pomelo, or even of the related grapefruit, make it, for me, a visually unappealing orb of desire, however delectable the juice.

More appealing, surely, is the persimmon, one variety of which (*Diospyros lotus*) is known in English as the date-plum. It grows around the Mediterranean, and was held by the ancient Greeks to be 'the fruit of the gods'—hence its botanical name. It has also been identified with the lotus tree mentioned in *The Odyssey*: Homer's persimmon was a fruit so delicious that those who consumed it forgot about returning home to their families and merely wanted to hang about eating lotuses. This kind of narcosis is most famously depicted in Hieronymus Bosch's fantastic paintings, in which all the human figures are colourless, classless, almost sexless Adam and Eves: only the fruits are giant and voluptuous and spectacular, being the sensual appendages of those who have abandoned history for a world without consequences.

Perhaps the reader will have suspected at this point that for me too, fruit has a Biblical taste to it. Curiously enough, one fruit that was easy to find in the 'greengrocers' (fruit merchants) of my boyhood Glasgow—in season, of course— was pomegranates, imported from Israel in those pre-EU days when the United Kingdom still maintained trading links with parts of the world it had previously colonised. Because of my peculiarly Old Testament childhood (my parents were Plymouth Brethren who had decided to enter the spirit of the 1960s by withdrawing from the world around them in order to bring on the 'End-Time'), pomegranates were swollen with meaning. For me, sitting as a small child in a cold, unadorned meeting hall learning and listening to the Psalms, the pomegranate was redolent of all the softer verses of the Bible. It was exoticism with a rind, something fresh from the Creation that might just outlast the Apocalypse. If there was a first fruit, it surely resembled the pomegranate. When my mother bought me one as a treat (and perhaps surreptitiously as a Bible teaching aid), I liked it just for the effort needed to consume it: the pith and membranes were sour and astringent and had to be avoided, but the pulp—or aril—around each seed was utterly delicious. I especially liked to extract a cluster of ripe seeds, bite on it, and let the red juice trickle down my throat.

A more intriguing possible first fruit is the quince (*Cydonia oblonga*), which will rapidly fill any room with its subtle yet distinctive scent. It seems that the quince, which belongs to the same botanical family as the apple and the pear, may actually have been cultivated in the Land of the Two Rivers (Mesopotamia) before becoming common in more temperate zones. Certainly it had a special status in Greek and Roman rituals, where it was often associated with marriage. The Greeks called it 'chrysomelon'—the Golden Apple. Pliny the Elder even mentions one obscure variety that can be eaten raw, thus drawing attention to the problem facing anyone transfixed by its heavenly smell: the flesh of the quince is hard, sour and astringent. It is difficult to imagine Eve being tempted by a fruit she couldn't bite into. Astringency in fruits is the effect of tannins, and they need to be bletted (over-ripened) to get rid of it. The taste of persimmons, for example, can be dramatically improved by leaving them overnight in the fridge. Cooking quinces has the same effect: thick strips of quince preserve or quiddemy—as the once-popular Victorian book of nostrums *Herbal Simples* calls it, claiming to have found the term in one of Francis Bacon's writings—are a delectable confection: every autumn I make quiddemy myself, profiting from the quinces that grow in the Rhine Valley close to our house. In the neighbouring Black Forest, quince is also used to make a distinctive eau-de-vie, its distilled spirit hovering delicately above the clear burning shot of alcohol. Dualism, you might say, in a single draught. Cyril Connolly greatly admired the downy quince, and *The Unquiet Grave* contains half-a-dozen references to it. 'I behold in it', he writes, 'an emblem of the civilization of Europe with its hard flesh, bright colour and unearthly savour.' (His descriptions of fruit in general are almost ecstatic—'there are some fruits', he adds, 'which awaken in me feelings deeper than appetite'— though he attributes his corpulence to his craving for them.)

While Connolly lists all the fruits of temptation in his famous book, he doesn't mention one interesting fact about the culture of the Mediterranean basin: 'golden apple' is the Italian word for the tomato. Although strictly speaking a berry, and for culinary purposes considered a vegetable, the tomato is another heavenly fruit, a kind of succulent ovary, and perhaps the best thing to have come out of the Spanish colonization of the Americas (at least as far as frugiferous plants go). Because the tomato is a member of the poisonous nightshade family (it produces a toxic alkaloid in its leaves and stems), it was long regarded with the kind of suspicion that forbidden fruit ought to attract. Eventually the southern Germans yielded, and gave it the name it deserved: *Paradeiser*. The word is still to be heard in Austria, and in Serbia too. As the poet Charles Simic—an American who grew up in the Balkans and is as much a fruit-fancier as Connolly—writes, 'A God who frets over his tomato plants makes more sense than the one who says, "Please don't touch my apple tree".' Granted, but it would take an ingenious revisionist to have tomatoes growing in Eden before Columbus set sail.

If, like Simic, you've known the pleasures of eating a luscious sun-ripened tomato just picked from the vine (a pleasure which came relatively late to me in life), you'll be inclined to agree with him. There's no forgetting the day you discover how a tomato really tastes. Freshness is what counts. The same applies to the banana (one variety of which used to be called *Musa paradisiaca*). Bananas straight from the tree—especially those miniature varieties known in south-east Asia as 'golden bananas'—are redolent of honey, lemon and cloves. (I have never enjoyed the same taste-experience while eating a Cavendish banana in Europe.) Bananas were the first consumer article East Germans sought out when the Berlin Wall came down in 1989—why shouldn't they be considered a temptation too? The Toraja people who inhabit the mountainous parts of southern Sulawesi in Indonesia have a creation story which tells of a progenitor human couple who came to earth by sliding down a liana from heaven. When their Creator offered them the choice between a stone and a bunch of bananas as a source of nourishment, they understandably chose the latter. Thus they condemned themselves (and their descendants) to the fate of their chosen object: corruption and decay. The banana therefore has more claim to be a genuine first fruit than we might realise. In his entertainingly instructive overview of intercultural communication and translation *Is That a Fish in Your Ear?*, David Bellos notes that Albert Cornelius Ruyl, a trader with the Dutch East India Company who translated the Gospels into Malay, transformed the Biblical fig into the *pisang* or banana, having astutely concluded that where fig-trees don't grow they can't be ripe with meaning. He was in good company: in his famous fourteenth-century fantasy *Travels* Sir John Mandeville had already espied banana trees as figures of the Cross.

It was only when I got to work in that part of the world a few years ago that I encountered the fruit the great Victorian naturalist Alfred Russel Wallace called 'the most excellent fruit of the Indies'. He wasn't referring to the mango, wonderful as that particular fruit is. That a fastidious man like Wallace could come to appreciate the bulky durian—the very symbol of tropical lushness and rankness—is itself remarkable. This is his rapturous description of eating one in his classic *Travels in the Malay Archipelago*: 'The five cells are silky-white within, and are filled with a mass of firm, cream-coloured pulp, containing about three seeds each. This pulp is the edible part, and its consistence and flavour are indescribable. A rich custard highly flavoured with almonds gives the best general idea of it, but there are occasional wafts of flavour that call to mind cream-cheese, onion-sauce, sherry-wine, and other incongruous dishes. Then there is a rich glutinous smoothness in the pulp which nothing else possesses, but which adds to its delicacy. It is neither acid nor sweet nor juicy; yet it wants neither of these qualities, for it is in itself perfect. It produces no nausea or other bad effect, and the more you eat of it the less you feel inclined to stop. In fact, to eat Durians is a new sensation worth a voyage to the East to experience.' Eating

*Durio zibethenus* shifts the usually very precise descriptive prose of the natural philosopher into a lyric register.

The durian (from the Malay word *duri* meaning 'thorn' on account of its spiny mantle) is a fruit which brings the tell-tale odour of corruption right into the experience of consuming it. It can be smelt from yards away, a mixture of carrion, turpentine and rotten onions. 'No handguns; no durians' read the sign outside the entrance to my hotel in Davao, in the southern Philippines, when I worked in the city in 2010. Once you taste the durian, however, the offensiveness of its smell magically vanishes, along with the disapprobation you felt for those who could stoop to eat something so disgusting. Disgust interdicts far more immediately than mere distaste. It is a moral sentiment we normally link with flesh and the physical, with creep and slime and potential sources of pollution: its very idiom invokes the sensory experience of what it feels like to come too close to something threatening. It puts us inside the realm known as the *visceral*. Yet as the American legal scholar and writer William Ian Miller claims in *The Anatomy of Disgust*, 'to feel disgust is human and humanising'. The story of the Garden of Eden is all about how botany—and the natural world in the larger sense—was an aid to socialisation. Sharing a durian, and experiencing feelings of aversion and attraction in unison, Adam and Eve could have erected a social order out of the recognition that in many (not just sexual) circumstances, disgust really amounts to a dare to try.

While the durian, like the tomato, couldn't possibly have been the fruit of the Garden of Eden (it only became known to the world beyond Asia six hundred years ago), it would have made a first fruit of some distinction. Imagine Adam and Eve sitting down together to eat the flesh of a durian: it would have turned them, right there and then, into moral philosophers.

# On the Surface of Events

*Rereading the Book of Jonah*

When I was small and Biblical and made to realise that my Brethren parents saw no nuance in the matter of salvation—either you were swallowed whole by giant belief or spat out among the unsaved—I was irresistibly drawn to the story of Jonah's going down to the lower deck of the ship taking him from Joppa to Tarshish. He is trying to reach the latter place, which present-day historians believe to have been the city of Carthage or a port on a trading island in the western Mediterranean, perhaps Sardinia, in order to avoid the divine command to get up and go to the glittering capital of the Assyrian Empire, Nineveh—'that great city, and cry against it'. Nineveh lay overland, in the opposite direction altogether.

Like Adam in the Garden of Eden, Jonah is trying to hide from his maker.

Even as the wind starts to torment the haunted waters of the eastern Mediterranean, Jonah, who must have known that fish were more likely to climb trees than he ever get to Tarshish, decides to steal a quick nap in order to prepare himself for the possibly sterner trials ahead. Jonah goes to his sleeping quarters during what turns out to be an almighty bluster called up by the same Divine One, a squall so sudden and fierce even the ship itself has terrible visions, as the Hebrew original says: it thinks it's going to capsize. This little ship would have much preferred to stay in a harbour.

Going below deck in the middle of a tempest for a snooze is an egregious act; being able to sleep through the chaos and commotion of an impending maritime disaster marks Jonah out as much odder still. The Hebrew text keeps hinting that his 'going down' is a descent from conventional experience into something abyssal.

The only paying passenger makes himself conspicuous by making himself scarce: a precondition for surviving really bad storms is a collective effort to ride them out—'all must contribute their Quota of Exertion', according to Coleridge (who had a bit of experience with storms in the Mediterranean). If a ship is anthropomorphic, and this roiling sea a formless argument of (as we shall discover) higher-sphere attributions, then all hands are needed on deck. Indeed, the sailors are already bailing out the hold and heaving everything overboard—their Bronze Age goods along with the contents of their stomachs. Every single bit of extraneous ballast has been thrown to the waves. And Jonah sleeps on, in a stupor or trance, insensible to the tumult thundering around him. Either he's shamming dead, or trying to pass himself off as a philosopher.

That great precursor of the modern novel François Rabelais wrote a similar scene into *Gargantua and Pantagruel*. When Panurge encounters a storm at sea, in the Fourth Book, Rabelais leaves us in no doubt that his heroes wish they had been elsewhere too: 'Believe me, it seem'd to us a lively Image of the Chaos, where Fire, Air, Sea, Land, and all the Elements, were in a refractory Confusion' (in Sir Thomas Urquhart's translation). In their distress, Panurge and Pantagruel eventually call out for the assistance of all the blessed saints. Their lamentations go on for pages, a comic scene which Milan Kundera identified as the moment in which Rabelais's tale 'becomes fully and radically a *novel*'.

On Jonah's boat, the sailors have evidently made similar if more animistic assumptions. One: a raging sea and fierce winds can only correlate to the anger of a god. Two: if they make a great show of throwing material objects overboard, they may be able to assuage this god's wrath. Three: but whose god is it that's in a huff? Nobody knows. These sailors are a rum bunch, since every man is appealing, as the verse says, 'unto his god'.

Anthropologically speaking, this is how humans respond to a gathering menace: we cut peripheral losses in order to stave off the looming core catastrophe. In moments of crisis, people try to make themselves lighter. To rid themselves of ballast.

The entire cargo has gone, but it doesn't calm the sea. The helmsman wakes Jonah, and urges him to 'call upon' his god, like the rest of the crew, in order to avert disaster. In the very next moment—in that abruptly foreshortened way the Bible has of moving on the action—lots are being drawn (in what seems an attempt to divine the intentions of that blind goddess later known to the Romans as Fortuna) and Jonah is owning up to being a Hebrew, somebody who, for all his disregard for the fate of others, is actually in awe of Yahweh, the Lord God of the heavens, 'which hath made the sea and the dry land'. His admission certainly puts the wind up the rest of the men on board, because they now know that they are implicated in a bigger storm: one that has everything to do with Jonah's being on their ship. A similar drawing of lots to determine the sacrificial victim (for eating) on a shipwrecked boat appears in the macabre French traditional (and now children's) song 'Il était un petit navire', which may refer to the wreck in 1816 of the frigate *Méduse*, subject of the famous painting by Géricault.

Terrified, the sailors try to row the ship towards land, and make no progress. Oars have never been much use in a storm. The men can't swim either—but then sailors don't take swimming lessons? In this regression into total helplessness and inertia that menaces every emergency Jonah does the right thing: he *volunteers* to leave the storm-tossed ship: he knows he's the true cause of this commotion. He has the courage to be thrown overboard even though he lacked it to go to Nineveh. 'So they took up Jonah, and cast him forth into the sea: and the sea ceased from her raging.' Man overboard does the trick. The sea calms, and the crew—being now 'exceedingly fearful' of Jehovah—decide to offer up another sacrifice in their overwhelming gratitude to the Hebrew God. The nature of this offering is unspecified: there can't have been much left on board. Perhaps it was Jonah's luggage.

Out of sight, Jonah, as every child used to know, has been swallowed by a sea monster 'prepared' by the Almighty. This is both an act of mercy and a punishment. It is a delayed response—a kind of dream supplement—to his earlier attempt to find a moment of rest as the storm assailed the ship.

The philosopher Gaston Bachelard called this act of bodily assimilation 'the Jonas complex', and observed that the notion of the 'eater eaten' (and yet surviving the act of bodily incorporation) is a common theme in children's stories. Phantasies of eating and being eaten are related to curiosity about the big questions of whence we come and whither we go. Jonas gets to spend three days knocking about in a great fish, the smelly insides of which must have resembled the rounded hull of another boat—a Phoenician cargo ship perhaps, ribbed just like those famous caravels *Niña*, *Pinta* or *Santa María* many, many centuries later. He has been removed from the belly of a ship to that of a great fish, and its hold is so dank and imposing that Jonah calls it Sheol: the stench of the bilge is overpowering. Lost to the world, condemned to his own company, he addresses God with a plaintive psalm in which he can see 'the bars of the earth closing upon [him] for ever'. He asks to be delivered from this tenemented refuge. He has seen the dark inside of events, and he wants out.

And God has the fish vomit Jonah up on dry land.

When word comes again from the Almighty to go to Nineveh and tell its inhabitants that the city has forty days before it gets wiped off the map, Jonah drops everything and goes. Now the private person and the public office are one. A prophet has no ego, a prophet can't withhold, a prophet doesn't argue: he simply announces what he's told to say. He is a *loudspeaker*. When he gets to Nineveh—a kind of sea monster done up as a city—he discovers it is such a grand place that it takes three days to walk from the west gate to the east gate, as tallied by the punctilious Sir Thomas Browne: 'So that if Jonah entered at the narrower side, he found enough for one Daye's walk to attain the heart of the City, to make his Proclamation.' Jonah cries against the citizens, crying in the Bible being sometimes less an act of communication than a hoarse exultation—God is vexed! Just wait and see what's coming your way!

What happens is something altogether unheralded: the people of Nineveh listen to his message. They hearken, as the Bible says, to the five prophetic words. Like the sailors in the boat to Tarshish, the people of Nineveh are susceptible to Jonah's message. '[A]ll genuine Morality, all applied practical vivified Moral Eloquence, is essentially prophetic', wrote Coleridge. The whole city of Nineveh—under orders from the king—dons sackcloth and ashes, even the livestock is smeared with cinders; and as Jonah walks through the streets he can hear the citizens 'crying mightily' to God. This is not the same kind of crying as was heard earlier from his throat: this is something that spills out of people's mouths and resembles the phenomenon Socrates calls 'opinion' in Plato's *Philebus*. Opinion is something wild and fearful that can't be restrained.

The act of public penance works. When God hears the prayers of the people of Nineveh, he decides not to carry out his promise to level the city. 'And God repented of the evil that He had said that He would do unto them; and He did it not.'

Jonah understands that he has been made to look ridiculous. His vision has taken in water, lots of it, and sunk ignominiously—to revert to the imagery of his earlier adventure. And by the agency of none other than the one true God, who is in one of his less readable moods. All that business with the storm and sea monster was just a kind of joke! He even confesses to Jehovah that he suspected this might happen all along, which is why he had tried to slip away to Tarshish in the first instance. A disturbing question takes shape in the mind, ours as much as his. What kind of prophet can he be if the weight of his world-historical warning is annulled simply by people acting upon its threat? That makes his prediction something less than a first-order truth. A prophecy and its fulfilment—aren't those two sides of a performative event that has no front or back, no right or left, which is the same truth however perceived? As George Steiner once pointed out, a prophet's use of the future tense is 'merely tautological'.

Perhaps Jonah isn't a prophet at all but that modern thing: a *weather-forecaster*. But what on earth was he predicting? Did he even know? 'The expert is a man who has stopped thinking—he knows!', the architect Frank Lloyd Wright is reported to have said. Experts get it right but sometimes they get it wrong, and wildly wrong at that. It even appears as if the king of Nineveh—sitting in cinders, with all his advisors around him wearing grey—might possess more insight into God's intentions that his appointed prophet. And Jonah can hardly fail to have noticed that the Almighty himself is in flagrant contradiction of the law of direct reciprocal justice. Nineveh had been wicked enough to bring itself to His attention—and here it is, still glittering and splendid, its towers and flagstones intact, and all its debts cancelled. Surely the message from an angry, imperious God didn't come with a non-performance clause?

This dramatic change in Nineveh's fortunes so riles Jonah that he goes into a deep sulk. He camps outside the city walls. By merely hanging around he means to force Jehovah to wipe it off the map. (Rembrandt made a sketch of the scene in

1655.) Imagine! God commands him to proclaim the religion of impending doom—and then the doom doesn't happen! All his brother prophets, too, vowed Nineveh would become 'a desolation'. To be prophetic was to show how the great scroll of universal history unfolded from the Word, as the Book of Deuteronomy says—anything else was merely human conceit. 'When a prophet speaks in the name of the Lord, if the thing follow not, nor come to pass, that is the thing which the Lord has not spoken; the prophet has spoken it presumptuously; be not afraid of him.' Prophecy is a rebuke, as well as a declaration of things to come. Prophecy is as irreversible as time itself. How could he, Jonah, be wrong on such a key issue?

Jonah is exhibiting, as Elias Canetti wrote, 'the most repulsive and dangerous trait in a prophet': having foretold the most terrible events he *needs* them to come true. Being a prophet, as we have seen, has nothing to do with the private life: being a prophet is to exercise a public function. Any dark glamour the calling has comes from being able to say 'I told you so'—but in the name of the Lord. Someone wrote in the Talmud that whoever saves a life saves the world, but at this moment in time Jonah doesn't give a jot about other lives. He just doesn't want to be remembered as a phoney.

God asks Jonah if he is right to get angry at what hasn't happened. He seems to be trying to win Jonah round to the viewpoint that he, the Lord of all Creation, is an artist: somebody who doesn't have to believe that he is capable of doing whatever enters his imagination, but merely has to entertain it as a *possibility*. (Had Jonah suspected this, he could have reminded the Lord of all Creation that a religion without prophets is bound, in the fullness of time, to subside into a cult of universal happiness.) Not only is God an artist, it might be said, but He knows all about deconstruction: a prophecy can just as easily be conscripted to serve as the cradle of its not-happening.

Observing Jonah's discomfort as he sits sulking outside the city walls, at risk of sunstroke, God causes a miraculous gourd to spring up beside him to protect him from the heat and glare: Jonah isn't unappreciative of its shelter. This plant grows fast, miraculously fast. 'It grew faster than any plant outside Eden, by sinuous thrusts, putting out leaves like geese stretching their wings', as Guy Davenport has it, in his adaptation of the story. But the next day God withers the gourd: as straightforward a procedure as flattening a city. Now the desert wind blowing in from the east is so stifling it causes Jonah to faint from the oppressive heat. When he comes round he is even angrier: he tells Jehovah that he is going to be in a funk 'even unto death'. He wants to die not only because of his physical torment; he is in 'ideological' distress too, as Jonathan Magonet puts it. Such is the pride of prophets. God continues to reason with him, drawing an *a fortiori* argument out of Jonah's chagrin about the here-today gone-tomorrow gourd—'which came up in a night, and perished in a night'—and the rather more considerable matter of the fate of the city of Nineveh: 'And should not I spare Nineveh, that great city, wherein are more than sixscore thousand [a formulaic Biblical number indicating *very many*] persons that cannot discern between their right hand and their left hand; and also much cattle?'

The Everlasting is scoring rhetorical—and ethical—points off his prophet.

The critic Harold Bloom insists that the four chapters of Jonah constitute the drollest, most 'Swiftian' book in the Tanakh. He also wonders whether the compilers of the canon dumped the Book of Jonah among the other minor prophets (Hosea, Joel, Amos, Obadiah, Micah, Nahum, Habakkuk, Zephaniah, Haggai, Zechariah, Malachi, all of whose names I was once able to recite in correct order of presentation to my parents) in order to conceal its sublimely subversive farce. After all, the chronicler has just exposed the petulant Jonah as a false prophet, a prophet who does not embody truth, and cast doubt on the very efficacy of prophecy itself. Future prophets are going to have to bring glad tidings, at least as an optional extra.

The chronicler of the Book of Jonah certainly raises some incongruities. After his initial recalcitrance, Jonah is ultimately shown to take the whole business of a summons from the future more seriously than God himself. Having initially been presented as a rather sympathetic shirker who wanted to have nothing to do with the dubious glamour of being a prophet, he ends up embodying the very evil he threatens people with. Jonah, as that distinguished reader and writer Jorge Luis Borges might have said, finds himself trapped in the labyrinth ordinary beings call *time*. What we say about the future influences how it turns out: that is one of the folds peculiar to this labyrinth. We could even say that future events happen because we all have a universally shared conception of what the future *is*. In that sense, the future is always a fixed point in the present.

The chronicler further reveals a Jehovah who, to convince Jonah of his powers, withers a pumpkin. (Jerome is his translation indicates that the Hebrew word *qiqayon* translated in the Septuagint as 'gourd' actually refers to a kind of preternaturally rapid-growing, self-supporting plant 'having large leaves like a vine', something like the magically sprouting seed in the story of Jack and the Beanstalk; Everett Fox in his new translation of the book identifies it—following Henri Meschonnic—as 'a castor-oil plant'). The comedy of the scene is lost on Jonah. If displaying mercy means eliminating not the wrongdoing—an impossibility in any case—but rather the resentment attendant on a wrong, we never get to find out whether Jonah ultimately acquires generosity and fellow-feeling. That would require him to recover some of the insouciance he showed at the tale's beginning.

So where the Book of Job ends with Job—who has suffered the most terrible injustices—silent in adoration, the Book of Jonah ends with Jonah mired in perplexity.

It has been said that there is no humour in the Bible. Humour doesn't necessarily come in guffaws. We are left to consider the scene, as Jehovah spells out his reasons for sparing the inhabitants of Nineveh: although humans can't tell their right hand from their left the city is also full of 'much cattle' which merit consideration. Cattle are dumb and don't talk back.

Uniquely among the books of the Bible, the Book of Jonah ends with a question: it is the voice of God—Elohim or Yahweh, both names are present—asking why it should be impossible for Him to be moved by a charitable impulse towards the beings He has nurtured, especially if they lack common sense. It is an ending that teeters on ambivalence, in a book that is all about turnings: the God of the Law has learned to feel pity, although only a moment before He might just as easily have wiped a city off the face of the earth. It suggests a future where divine prophecy will be able to walk away from its implications, even as Jonah petulantly insists on a more statistically predictable universe.

# Green, Red and Blue

*The World in 1572*

Globalisation is often presented as if it were a purely contemporary phenomenon. It is more instructive (and perhaps more unsettling too) to reflect that globalisation has been under way for centuries, at the very least since the Pope started putting a girdle around the world in his annual 'Urbi et Orbi' address, and Luther started the movement called the Reformation, which the philosopher Hegel, for one, saw as the constituting event in the developmental process he defined in his *Lectures on the Philosophy of World History*. In classical Latin *orbis* was a disk; now the term could be understood to designate a sphere. What is special about our world is that the spherical phenomenon itself is now global: everybody on the planet *knows* we are related. We live in one world. Genetically we are a unity, and economics has given material significance to the interrelationship. Yet that unity is physically closed in a different way, even as we honour the abstract ideal of an open society or allow ourselves to be inspired with used to be called 'frontier spirit'.

Indeed, in some respects globalisation was more advanced in the past than it is now. Before the First World War, passports were not required for travel and borders were more permeable than at present, the vaunted Schengen Agreement notwithstanding. In terms of the crow's-eye view, things go even further back. Google Earth, for instance, has an ancestor, and one that in its time was just as revolutionary in reconceptualising the world. In 1572, the dean of the church St

ESSAYS ON THE ART OF LIVING

Maria ad Gradus in Cologne, Georg Braun, became the editor of a series of atlases that set new standards in cartography. It went by the name *Civitates Orbis Terrarum*, or *Cities of the World*.

Inspired by Sebastian Münster's encyclopaedic *Cosmographia* and its impressive Holbein woodcuts—one of the most widely read books of the era—Braun wrote the Latin cartouches and hired reputable artists and voyagers to contribute to the six volumes. Their travel sketches were turned into handsome copperplates by the Flemish artist Franz Hogenberg, and include some early urban studies by Georg Hoefnagel, son of an Antwerp diamond merchant who toured Europe in the mid-century, as well as by Pieter Bruegel the Elder. Braun died in his eighties in 1622, the only one of the editorial team to see out the publication of the final volume in 1617. The editors of this new edition, Stephan Fussel and Rem Koolhaas, aimed to track down the separate plates but were lucky enough to find a well-preserved complete edition of the original in a Frankfurt museum. Now the art-house press Taschen, one of the most successful new European publishers and perhaps not coincidentally located in the same city, has published in a spectacularly beautiful folio volume the entire atlas of five hundred and sixty-four plans, views and maps.

In 1572, the year of the book's first publication, Spain was the pre-eminent European power, and its territories on the continent extended northwards to what today is Belgium. The Duke of Alba was laying siege with Spanish forces to Haarlem: Calvinist rebels had already gained control of large tracts of Holland and Zealand, and set up the Dutch Republic. That year Spanish forces in Central America sacked the last remaining Inca city Vilcabamba. Wreckage was still floating up the Gulf of Patras from the Battle of Lepanto fought the previous year, a colossal naval engagement which gave the forces of the Holy League victory over the previously invincible Turkish fleet.

That same year Miguel Lopez de Legazpi had founded Manila, capital of what was to become the largest European possession in Asia. Elizabeth I, having been excommunicated from the Catholic Church, had overcome traditional Christian–Muslim antagonism and newly forged a trading alliance with the 'terrible Turks'—Suleiman the Magnificent had died only a few years before at a time when the Ottoman Empire was a power more formidable even than the Spanish—that was to be of capital importance for the future development of the British Isles. A large Ottoman army encroaching into Russia was decisively repulsed at the battle of Molodi. The Protestant reformer John Knox died in Edinburgh. Most of Europe was still reeling from the effects of the Reformation, with the wars of religion in France causing the upheavals that would lead to the state-power politics of the Thirty Years War and the widespread devastation of much of Central Europe, including many of the predominantly German-speaking cities depicted in the book: 1572 was the year of the Bartholomew's Day massacre, at the sounding of the tocsin in the church of Saint-Germain-l'Auxerrois in Paris. Michel de Montaigne had just retired from public life to begin the work of reading and writing which would come down to us as his *Essays*. It was an age in which trade and conquest were changing the world, and a new empiricism was afoot. Maps characterise that age of discovery more than any other document; the Romans, after all, had no word to describe something they didn't need. And it wasn't just the earth that was being mapped. The astronomer Tycho Brahe observed the supernova in Cassiopeia now catalogued as SN 1572; and travellers were expected not to slip capriciously into the realm of the miraculous, as so many of their predecessors had done, some of them even falling off the world's rim.

'What we need', wrote Montaigne, 'is topographers who would make detailed accounts of the places which they had actually been to.'

The medieval world of contemplation was already yielding, as that utopian projector and lobbyist Francis Bacon hoped, to the modern one of *application*. But the imagination is loath to let go of its fancies. Abraham Ortelius's famous 1570 map of the world shows a fairly exact North Atlantic Ocean, in which real islands are depicted along with imaginary ones. Some of those—Seven Cities, Brasil, St. Brandan, Bass and Mayda— would continue to figure on otherwise accurate atlases until the end of the nineteenth-century. European minds were still grappling with the novelty of the fact that God had allowed an entire fourth continent to develop over centuries in total ignorance of the divine Word: all the mapmakers of the sixteenth century, from Martin Waldseemüller onwards, had great difficulty coming to terms with Europe's reduced status as a mere peninsula jutting westwards from Asia as well as persuading themselves that the New World was not a projection out of the same, as the name 'the Indies' originally suggested.

## THE TRADE OF WALLED CITIES

*Cities of the World* confirms the efforts of the tireless Melina Mercouri, former Greek Minister of Culture, in her campaign to get Europeans to realise that Europe's most inspirational history is that of its cities: it was on her initiative that Athens was nominated as the first European City of Culture in 1985. Ironically enough, Athens does not figure in this book, being then under Ottoman control; to contemporaries it was a city of legend and hearsay and in its magnificence somewhat piebald, like the very English city described by Shakespeare in *A Midsummer Night's Dream*. And of course, there is no representation of Istanbul, depicted in 1559 by Melchior Lorck in his extraordinary panorama which, on twenty-one sheets of glued paper, shows all the details of the city from the heights of Galata on the European side of the Bosporus. Illustrations of the time pointedly avoided showing Christian buildings that had been turned into mosques, and insisted on using the old names: *Byzantium sive Constantineopolis*.

Some cities were far more important in the sixteenth century than they are now (though the continuing importance of Rome and Jerusalem, city of cities on the medieval T-O *mappae mundi* that inspired Dante's cosmology and set Mandeville off on his half-imagined travels, to a species hopelessly divided between the desire for entertainment and the need for salvation, is confirmed by the exquisitely detailed fold-out maps of the two). The terrible fire of 1574 which ravaged the Doge's Palace in Venice, itself a city perched on oak pilings atop the sea, is recorded, apparently by an eyewitness. The Tower of London still had a moat around it, fed by those 'ancient streams' the Walbrook, Tyburn and Fleet, and the city's northern outskirts started at the Bishopsgate. The grazing land of the Spitalfields would in time become the grounds of Bedlam, the notorious hospital for the insane, and, later still, the concourse of Liverpool Street station. As the eponymic character reminisces in W.G. Sebald's novel *Austerlitz*, 'I knew that... marshy meadows had once extended to the city walls, meadows which froze over for months on end in the cold winters of the so-called Little Ice Age, and that Londoners used to strap bone runners under their shoes, skating there as the people of Antwerp skated on the Schelde, sometimes going on until midnight in the flickering light of the bonfires burning here and there on the ice in heavy braziers.'

In 1572, Chester and Norwich were major English cities, the view of the latter indicating 'the place where men are customablie burnt'. There is an illustration of Henry VIII's colossal Renaissance palace Nonsuch in Surrey; it was demolished by Charles II a century later to pay off the royal debt. Barcelona is shown with a rainbow above the Collserola. The aerial view of Paris, as if from a Montgolfier, anticipates the much more famous Merian print of the city in 1615. Buda has yet to acquire Pest. Augsburg, home of the banking house of Fugger, has grown rich from the transfer of profits made from the Church's trade in indulgences; copper and silver from the German mines was travelling southwards to finance the peppers and spices being shipped north from Lisbon. Antwerp—where the Portuguese ran a branch of the Casa da India—outshines Amsterdam, but its recapture by the Spanish in 1585 dimmed its fortunes and allowed its rival to establish itself as the platform of Protestant Europe, and eventually of world trade. With a population of 12,000, Basle was a large trading city dominated by its patrician families, and an important centre of the early book trade: Erasmus of Rotterdam had died there in 1536. All of the Rhine cities were important centres of trade and crafts, as were Lübeck, Königsberg, Riga and the Baltic cities of the Hanseatic League. What would now be called supranational institutions—the other one is the Holy Roman German Empire—guaranteed the autonomy of these urban centres through the interdependence of trade.

This kind of civilisation would later be derided by nineteenth-century nationalists as 'particularism', but it has been reinstated, to some extent, under that modern supranational institution called the European Union.

EXTENDING THE PARISH

Braun's cities are veritable idylls. They stand out as jewels of red-roofed decency walled from the empty green fields and copses that surround them: here be (just beyond the horizon) Hobbes' state of nature. *Cities of the World* doesn't extend its purview to the 'blasted heath': the book is so city-centred that only the sketchiest details are given of the tilled land beyond the postern gates, even though every city of the time subsisted on the produce and harvests of the farms outside its walls. Hadn't the Romans buried their dead outside the gates in order to preserve the integrity of the *urbs* within? And Aeschylus written about the importance of Dike's scales in cementing the social fabric?

Masonry marks the limits of civility. Walls, as in Shakespeare's *A Midsummer Night's Dream*, can be hindrances to ambition, but they also foster mental and social cohesion, and a sense of belonging. It dawns upon the reader that Braun's 'world' is a gathering of cities, each a fertile oasis protected by its wall. They could almost be islands, these cities, registers of order and understanding in a sea of demonic disorder—self-enclosed, girded with sovereignty, perhaps even enchanted.

My own home on the northern outskirts of modern-day Strasbourg is situated in what was once the city's pleasure garden, and was on that account extramural: it is mentioned as such in Sebastian Brant's pre-Reformation poem *Das Narrenschiff* (1494), which relates the adventures of a ship of fools on their way to Narragonia, the fools' paradise. When Braun's book was first printed, Strassburg (to give it its German spelling) was still a free city of the Holy Roman German Empire; it was sometimes called Aurentina or Argentina, after its old Roman name of Argentoratum. The city was famous across the continent for its marvellous Gothic cathedral, now known as Notre-Dame de Strasbourg, which had been built by masons from all over Europe between 1227 and 1439: for centuries it was one of the highest towers in the world. Strasbourg's pleasure garden ('A notorious amusement resort near Strassburg', according to the commentary in Zeydel's 1944 English translation of the poem) was also the site of its market gardens, where the fields were rich with alluvial silt from the Rhine. But we are living at the end of an epoch: from as many as sixty independent farms at the beginning of the twentieth century, social and economic forces have brought about a dramatic change, and in the twenty years of my living here the number of gardeners selling vegetables and flowers directly to the public has dwindled from six to one.

Insofar as Braun's cities have identifiable structures, many of them are ecclesiastical and military. They are solid structures of stone and wood. This was an age in which the art of fortification was still highly prized, and the typical city was apt to look like some fantastic natural extrusion, a star-shaped dodecagon bright above a labyrinth of trenches and moats. Bastions and siegecraft were still topics that obsessed Uncle Toby two hundred years later in *Tristram Shandy*, although the exigencies of strategic planning had spread by his time from the city-state to the frontiers of the nation itself, the future *theatrum instrumentorum et machinarum*. Its ultimate contemporary symbol are the concrete white elephants of the Maginot Line, which can still be found in some of the aforementioned market gardens of Strasbourg: hundreds of metre-thick casemates look set to keep crumbling away for decades in the forests on the west bank of the Rhine.

Every church is identified in the book by the saint to whom it is dedicated. This was a time when the good place could still be imagined as a city run on perfect Christian principles (like Johann Andreae's *Christianopolis*, a utopian scheme printed in 1619 in Strassburg and modelled on Calvin's admired Geneva), although the religiously-informed suspicion of money and exchange had already started to yield to a new vision that would put mercantile values and principles at the very heart of the new world: commercial institutions, most notably the joint-stock company, which had developed from the corporation under Roman law, were giving Europe a commercial edge that would make itself felt for centuries. The seventeenth century would be dominated by the expansion of trade and what Fernand Braudel called 'the Dutch versus the Portuguese, or the art of the takeover bid'. The old class of utopia (More's humanist dream was published in 1516) allows only the perfect society—something More himself admits in his conclusion could not be brought about because of *superbia*, or the lust for possessions rooted in original sin—whereas a new class was already springing up in the books written by Europe's men of letters: the past, felt with sufficient nostalgia, could be a utopia too.

## HEEL, WHEEL AND KEEL

Yet if the fortification of cities was all-important—in the famous Lutheran hymn, the Godhead is a 'feste Burg'—half of all the cities of the time are open to the sea.

The age of projection had begun. If the primordial undifferentiated flux of the great waters held fears for humans in the pre-modern period (identities are lost at sea in Shakespeare's plays, and the Book of Revelations promises that at the end of time the sea will be 'no more'), they were overruled by the fact that so much trade took place by sea and canal. Waterways were more reliable conduits than travelling the dangerous and poorly sealed roads—Erasmus's many letters are full of complaints about the real hardships of being on the road: he never travelled for the pleasure of it. Fluvial navigation was slow and rude, but a good deal surer. And ploughing the dangerous salt in barques and galleons held infinite possibilities. The famous lion of San Marco, which stands on guard outside the basilica, hind legs on the waves and forepaws on the shore, is a reminder that Neptune and Mercury, the gods of navigation and commerce, had shared interests if imperial dominion of the oceans was ever to become a project of state. When you commit yourself to the sea, the commitment is total.

Plenty of activities are seen going on along the shorelines. A vivid, extemporised plate shows tuna being beached, slaughtered and cured at Cadiz, a quasi-religious annual event that can still be observed in early summer at the La Mattanza ceremony on the Egadi Islands west of Sicily (and in Roberto Rossellini's classic film *Stromboli*), though overfishing on an industrial scale has badly depleted tuna stocks. A vast collection of trading ships lies at anchor behind the breakwater in the Zuyderzee. Trade demands information and institutions, contractual relationships and individual enterprise: it is surely true to say that political liberalism emerged as a creation of sea-going city-dwellers, as a phenomenon of port-cities with the land stretching behind them and their sea-gates open. Amsterdam is poised to enter the age of the V.O.C.—the Dutch East Indies Company—and its colonial expansion as the capital of one of the most unlikely pilot nations, the lowlands which even to this day still have to reclaim themselves from the North Sea. And London isn't far behind. In 1550, the city had a population of 60,000; within a hundred years that number was to increase sixfold as its trading companies followed the Dutch example, and London began to dominate the hinterland as in few other European nations. Both East Indies companies would ship textiles from the west coast of India to south-east Asia, where they would be exchanged for pepper, nutmeg and coral; additional ballast for the trip home would be made up of rice, copper, sugar and saltpetre. Excess goods would often be destroyed to ensure total control of the spice monopoly. Meanwhile, Malta, Famagusta, Rhodes and Corfu, all depicted in the book, were still important trading posts for Venice and Genoa in the Mediterranean—but what was a map of an empire along the Mediterranean littoral compared to the prestige of one that extended to the shores of the entire habitable earth?

Several extra-European *comptoirs* and colonies are depicted: Mombasa is a village with red roofs in the European style. Calicut, an important Portuguese spice port on the pepper coast of India, is fringed with a forest of palms. 'I like a plantation in a pure soil', wrote Francis Bacon, 'where people are not displanted to the end to plant in others. For else it is rather an extirpation than a plantation.' Colonial expansion brought the dilemma of having to decide whether to assume the burdens of settlement or simply continue to live, like so many pirates and privateers, from the plunder of native riches. The natives, in these plates, blankly submit to their fate. In Cuzco, the former Inca capital, a colonial official is being carried in a baldachin by four natives of the country that would eventually be known as Peru.

## MAKING THE WORLD A SUBJECT

Braun, like the Spaniards who went to Mexico, was evidently convinced of the superiority of his own religion, even though Girolamo Benzoni, in his *Historia del mondo novo* (Venice, 1565), had already advertised the cruelty shown by the conquistadores to the native peoples of the Americas. In the quiet of his study, Montaigne wrote little about the virtues, and instead reflected on the propensity of the civilised for wanton acts of malice, especially in relation to those deemed savage. 'I find', he wrote, 'that there is nothing savage or barbarous about those peoples, but that every man calls barbarous anything he is not accustomed to.'

Braun's text offers nothing of this cultural relativism—or even an anticipation of the bureaucratic Byzantinism and *ordo cucaniensis* of our latter-day Europe. His world is morally severe and punitive: the plate of Seville shows a woman caught in adultery being humiliated by being stripped to the waist, coated with honey and led on a mule through the streets—a swarm of cruelly attentive bees makes up her train. Visitors to Cairo are instructed not to waste time with the 'idolatrous temples' or the pyramids, which look more like spindly obelisks and are wildly out of proportion in relation to the city of Cairo towards the north-east. Although the Alhambra fortress in Grenada is in Christian hands, the fact that 'the Turkish archenemy' still possessed lands in south-eastern Europe and had only recently been besieging Vienna was gall to the good man of the church: crescents are seen in abundance, with men in kaftans directing workers. Every step in the Ottoman punishment of impalement is gloatingly depicted in one plate. A Polish knight outside the Hungarian city of Győr welcomes a lady with two Turkish arrows projecting from the back of his tunic: his courtly attention to the lady and studied air of detachment from his own sufferings are surely meant to call to mind St Sebastian. He may even be a visitor from the modernist future, pricked by our critical barbs.

Of dancing in the streets or tavern-fuelled revelry there is not a trace. It is an odd historical irony that the coffee-house, that centre for intellectual debate and sedition, sprang up only in the wake of the rout of the Ottoman troops by Polish hussars at the gates of Vienna a hundred years after *Cities of the World* was first published: drinking coffee and eating croissants were a kind of backhanded tribute to the janissaries and viziers. Bauer, presumably, would have frowned at anything that smacked of a merely secular Eucharist. (And it is piquant too that Istanbul was one of the European Cities of Culture for 2010: although Turkey has lobbied unsuccessfully for years to gain political and trade representation within the European Union it is nevertheless accepted at the cultural level as being part of the continent.)

With the bird's-eye perspective adopted in many plates, the

book drives home the novelty of the new spatial arrangements that the caravels of trade and adventure were bringing back to Europe in their holds. Geographers were starting to colour the world in: green, red and blue might as well represent spirit, reason and imperium. Men are in movement, the slaves of their passions; the practical details of the bumpy horizontal ride are of a more pressing nature than the vertical passage from this life to the next. Georg Braun would hardly have been moved to commission his illustrations if he had felt that intramundane power relations were entirely stable beyond his bishopric. What may have bothered him as a representative of the Church is that while globalisation was going on at a subterranean level, cities were emerging as nodes of knowledge and custom, and acquiring power as the guardians of their own vernacular traditions: the mystical body of Christ was being portioned out into the mystical bodies of the nations which, in time, would come to believe their parochial ways of life could be those of a universal civilisation. Plato's metaphor of the 'ship of state', (*The Republic*, Book VI) takes on an entirely new dimension as Europe's cities slide from their moorings—so many elongated Noah's Arks—and extend themselves around the globe, even if their captains ('Masters under God') were not philosopher-kings. Ships, then as now, were the prime vehicles of globalisation.

The business and restlessness that Montaigne—himself the first intellectual window-gazer—recognised as novel characteristics of his contemporaries are evident enough in these plates. Their labours are the first moves towards the 'growth' that is the source of modern society's legitimacy: vertigo and the growth of cities have always gone together, as the legend of the Tower of Babel suggests. *Cities of the World* comes from the same century as Hans Holbein's famous painting *The Ambassadors* (1533), with its anamorphic skull slewed across the centre of the painting, or Albrecht Altdorfer's dizzying work in the Alte Pinakothek in Munich, *The Battle of Alexander at Issus* (1529), which shows an apocalyptic scene of two vast armies colliding in a landscape over which the viewer has been set high atop heaven to survey the entire panorama towards what appears to be the southern shore of the Mediterranean basin, including Cyprus and the mouths of the Nile and Red Sea: this is the first painting to show the curvature of the earth from a great height (*Weltlandschaft*). It is also the viewpoint that Ruskin took in *The Nature of Gothic*, instructing his readers to imagine the Mediterranean 'lying beneath us like an irregular lake'. That synoptic view of the battle provides the frame of reference that would be applied to future history, in which landscapes sunk dreamily in time and space are held up in the dazzling new light of analysis and the implacable therapy of order. It is, all told, a complete falsification of ordinary human perspective.

A long time before air travel, Europeans were already imagining the terrestrial globe as a sphere: the world in 1572 is already modern *terra cognita*. In the famous sonnet, written early in the next century, in which John Donne called on the Angels to blow their trumpets at the round earth's imagined corners, he is also to be heard asking his Creator to allow him 'to mourn a space'.

# Grace and Violence

*Anecdotes from the Napoleonic Era*

Heinrich von Kleist was no Orpheus, that mythological figure made famous by the poet Rainer Maria Rilke: he was opposed to all the qualities Orpheus stands for. He didn't tame living creatures or even the bare stones with his song; he evoked wildness and wilderness, most of all right in the heart of that second nature we call civilisation. Earthquakes glint out of a society on the edge of breakdown into ours: 'mythical, sacral, but also aesthetic violence took possession of his artistic fantasies'. And there is historical violence too. Nobody on the continent could fail to miss the effect of Napoleon's passage through Europe between 1806 and 1811; Kleist believed the Grande Armée—first given this name in 1805—had to be resisted by might and main ('mit aller Gewalt'). What seemed much-needed reform to some—and Kleist at least intellectually was compelled to register the unifying modernity of the French civil code, which in 1804 displaced many of the vestigial feudal laws of the European countries under Napoleon's control— was a guillotining of tradition to others. Judicial violence and the increasing power of the state as the sole legitimate wielder of force were Kleistian obsessions: he understood violence ('Gewalt') most intimately, in its root sense, as the exercise of power ('walten'): this is the stuff of his comedy *The Broken Jug*. And violence is present in a muted form even in the exactitude of his writing: it is the aesthetic-psychological violence of the modern hyperrealist who by looking at things too closely renders the commonplace strange and outlandish.

Even the anecdotes he published at the end of his career (and life) have, for all their scenic qualities, a violent turn or

ESSAYS ON THE ART OF LIVING

cutting edge. These short entertainments—starved of detail—
were purposely designed never to amount to anything as
ponderous as the biography of a Wilhelm Meister. An entire
life or career has been foreshortened into a decisive moment
that suspends development; and ditches a lot of dialogue too.
Stumps and amputations in formal terms, their content is, as
often as not, a trimmed broadsheet report of freak injuries or
deadly outcome consequent to trivial cause. Kleist salts his
evident descriptive assets down to little poison pellets.

Kleist wrote the way his character Penthesilea loves,
biting where he should have been kissing; and some of his
contemporaries (Friedrich Schlegel and Madame de Staël)
thought his suicide an attempt to achieve by violence to
his person the tragic effect he was unable to produce in his
writings. A career move, in other words. They surely knew
little of his writings: when he was buried in Potsdam in 1811
he was barely known at all as a writer in Berlin, other than as
the less than successful jobbing editor of its first boulevard
broadsheet, the *Berliner Abendblätter*. If violence offers a
solution to intolerable situations, it comes through the element
of surprise, its sweeping abruptness; but that uncontrollability
is precisely what makes violence explode in our faces too. Love
and gratitude are a different story; and we have the benefit,
unlike Kleist, of knowing where acceptance of the necessity
of violence led German history: Europe in the twenty-first
century seems opposed to final solutions of any kind (except
that finality known as the European Union).

At times, however, Kleist grasps the impossibility of driving
out violence with yet more violence, and was moved to theorise
about a quality Orpheus would instinctively have praised:
grace ('Grazie'). This violence–grace antinomy may have
come from his friend Adam Müller's first theoretical work
*Die Lehre vom Gegensatz* ('The Doctrine of Contrariety'); and
Kleist wrote about violence overcome in his famous essay on

the marionette theatre. Grace is beyond the scope of a merely conscious performance. It can be found in the promptings of the mind of God, in which not just all causes, but reasons too, are understood; it can—shockingly at first—be observed in the crude mechanics of a wooden puppet. It also emerges in the sub-story told by Herr C. in the same essay, of the performing bear in Livonia which, during a fencing match with the expert narrator, parries his every thrust effortlessly. The bear has no tactics: it simply looks Herr C. in the eye, blocks his intended blows with a slight shift of its paw, and makes no move at all when he feints. It can't be outthinking him, for it's only a bear. Grace is there too in the perfection of that essay, and Kleist didn't realise it. How could he? Grace touches human affairs without attendants.

Antinomies in Kleist's literary work are problematic, and perhaps even spurious as in his famous distinction between 'thinking' and 'doing'. As befits a 'poetic of contraries' in which there can be no progression without discord, as suggested by the Blake epigraph to Rüdiger Görner's *Gewalt und Grazie*, a book which offers an absorbing excursus on Kleist's little-studied appreciation of the contemporary British scene, in particular as mediated by the novels of Samuel Richardson and the individualist economics of Adam Smith (to whose laissez-faire precepts Adam Müller—a half-forgotten economic, political thinker and money theorist, as well as friend to many other German writers and philosophers, most notably Novalis—put up a form of social and political organisation along associational lines that would become known as corporatism: companies in Germany were from the first conceived primarily as public associations). Prussia had been the United Kingdom's only ally in the Seven Years' War, a mere fifty years before. At one time Kleist entertained the whim of invading the island as a soldier in Napoleon's army: in fact, he maintained a keen interest in the 'toil and bustle' of the industrialising maritime empire that was still holding out against his arch-enemy.

This interest—along with entanglements of violence and grace—informed one of his last journalistic pieces, a half-page anecdote published in Kleist's own broadsheet *Berliner Abendblätter* in 1810: it concerns a championship round between two prize boxers, 'a Portsmouth man' and 'a Plymouth man', who, 'in the garden of a public house', are about to settle their rival claim to public fame as champion boxer. An old-fashioned ding-dong: two seemingly distinct persons (although the similarity between their origins in 'Portsmouth' and 'Plymouth' rather telegraphs Kleist's intention) face off in a bare-knuckle fight. First the Plymouth man hits the Portsmouth man so hard in the chest he spits blood. 'Bravo', says the wounded boxer, a true gent. Wiping his mouth, the man from Portsmouth faces up to his opponent again and delivers him a crunching blow to the body with his right hand. Power in a boxing match, we are reminded, is generated from the ground up, so that the force generated by the feet and ankles travels all the way up through the body until it emerges—compounded by the unitary work of thighs, chest, shoulder and arm—from clenched fist. The spectators around the ring cheer the Portsmouth man as the winner while the Plymouth man, succumbing to his internal injuries, is carted off dead. Kleist then adds a typical *aber*: 'The Portsmouth man however is said to have died next day of a haemorrhage.'

Kleist appends no moral to this double-death, and hardly needs to: this truncated anecdote gives a new meaning to the rhetorical term *inter se pugnantia*. The abrupt manner in which the distinction between defeat and victory is quashed allows us to glimpse, through a rip in the curtain of history, the arena of conflict in Athenian tragedy that offers more ways to lose than to win, and sometimes no way at all to win—in contrast to the absolutist ethics inherited from Leibniz and Kant in which all endings are the right one, and history can only be a comedy. Kleist's fatal-outcome fable is a parodic commentary on his friend Adam Müller's theories of contrariety and reciprocity, and even on Hegel's more famous philosophical duel for status: master and servant are supposed to outdo each other *dialectically* in order to gain the upper hand while leaving life and consciousness intact—for otherwise there's no point to the battle for recognition: a dead opponent can't acknowledge your victory.

Kleist's dramatisation of two unnamed English pugilists engaging in a fatal bout of fisticuffs ends on a barely admissible game theory outcome to the competitive processes that were soon to dominate the mercantile economies of the next two centuries: a 'lose-lose' situation.

# Balzac *et Cie*

*The Novel after Balzac*

Readers have sometimes commented on the air of repressed fright which courses through Honoré de Balzac's letters. Fright isn't the first quality we associate with Balzac, at least not with his novels. Unlike most of the poets of the nineteenth century he was quite openly an entrepreneur (and in this to be followed by many other lesser novelists), capitalising handsomely on his writing talents in the burgeoning print market and profiting from their market value in a way unfamiliar to most writers before if not since. He had a 'commercial surface for exploitation', as he himself put it, and he remarked at one point in his life that what Napoleon 'did with the sword, I will accomplish with the pen'. Faith in creative energy is what they had in common. Auguste Rodin's stiff-necked, bullish, wraparound colossus, cast in bronze in 1930 and standing almost three metres high at the intersection of the boulevards Montparnasse and Raspail in Paris's sixth arrondissement, is a memorial of the proper Herculean dimensions. Big things fascinate simply by virtue of their size, and very big things are particularly fascinating. Writing was Balzac's total project, evidence of his passion for extension, as suggested by his putting all his principal novels under a single rubric: *La Comédie humaine*. Balzac had realised that heroes would henceforth have to be sought in the previously lowly realms of finance and commerce—in the marriage market and helter-skelter of the stock exchange, among scenes of fabulous wealth and abject destitution. He himself was constantly pressed by creditors and almost continually on the verge of financial ruin—for all that some of his books were great commercial successes he complained that his financial straits obliged him to work all hours. Eighteen hours a day wasn't out of the ordinary for Balzac. The air of repressed fright in his letters perhaps comes from his realisation that while he appreciates the tokens of worldly success he knows himself to be a man of letters perforce detached from the values of that same world. 'To be a man apart from the rest, one has to begin by really cutting himself off from them.' He wore a monk's robe for good reason: only he could glimpse the truths that had been laid out for his readers' attention, and which they in the privacy of their rooms would be obliged to view through his eyes. 'All his books', observed Victor Hugo in his famous eulogy at the graveside, 'form one single book, a vibrant, luminous, profound book, in which our entire contemporary civilisation can be seen coming and going, walking and moving around, with a touch of something disquieting and dreadful mixed in with what is real.'

It took a later (but not much later) writer, Marcel Proust, to realise Balzac's ambition 'to compete with the civil registry': the total novel would be possible only by recuperating every moment lost in the life of its protagonist to the potentially endless universe of meaning. Or to put it even more vertiginously: by entering into an infinite regress where the identity of the author as constituted is indistinguishable from that of his characters in the making. Proust's (necessarily) incomplete masterpiece was already on the horizon of all Balzac's doings. By discovering the novel, as Graham Robb suggests in his monumental biography, 'Balzac was discovering himself'. And the many writers who arrived as sometimes unwitting captives in his train.

Here is a man whose life was so caught up with the labour-value of writing—fuelled by cup after cup of mocca—that he loses track of his own circumstances: he and the other entrepreneurial Balzacs (the one who dreamed of planting pineapples, the one who considered dredging the Tiber for lost treasure, the one who thought of monopolizing the market for artistic masterpieces and selling them to the highest bidder, the one who wanted to import railway sleepers from Ukraine, the one who thought of panhandling for gold in Brazil, the one who intended to revive the ancient silver mines of Sardinia— and actually made the trip to Cagliari only to find they had been sold to someone else) are embroiled in a plot that shows no signs of coming to a conclusion. 'It's incredible how much I manage to produce', he told his mother in a letter. All he needed was twenty years' worth of paper. Balzac had been a printer for a while himself ('Imprimerie H. Balzac'), as *Illusions perdues* makes clear, but he showed no mercy to his editors. His manuscripts were a nightmare for typesetters (who often had to shoulder some of the unbudgeted additional costs): proof pages came back from the author with copious comments and corrections. In June 1843, Balzac even went to live in the printing works at Lagny to speed up the process, scribbling corrections on pages hot from the hydraulic press like a steampunk tyro. His computers were human ones. Indeed, his novels themselves draw out the material connection between the commercialisation of literature and the new and cheaper paper manufacturing processes of his time.

Balzac was, consequently, the first novelist to grasp the full force of the spell cast by money and its impact on society. No less than four of his novels are about inheritance struggles: *Le Cousin Pons*, *Eugénie Grandet*, *Ursule Mirouët* and *La Rabouilleuse*. 'Civilisation in the nineteenth century is money', wrote George Moore, 'and Balzac instinctively knew, or rather felt, that money would be the stake for which Christianity would fight its last great battle.' Paul Lafargue wrote of his father-in-law Karl Marx that he loved *La Comédie humaine* so much that he intended, once he had finished writing *Das Kapital*, to write a study of Balzac's great procession of individuals trapped in their social relationships. Marx never got around to finishing

*Das Kapital*, not to mention examining the full extent of the almost hundred novels published in Balzac's lifetime along with the dramatic works, literary and political journalism and the all-encompassing correspondence, but would certainly have agreed with his collaborator Friedrich Engels that more could be learned from them about French society under Louis-Philippe than from 'all the professed historians, economists and statisticians of that period'. Balzac even anticipated contemporary gender fluidity in his novel *Séraphita*, published in the *Revue de Paris* in 1834, a Swedenborg-inspired meditation on the hermaphroditic main character of the same name who has transcended ordinary humanity: Arnold Schoenberg was fascinated by this story, traces of which are to be found in his unfinished oratorio *Die Jakobsleiter*, which he started composing during the First World War to mark music's 'ascension' into the heaven of a new musical space.

Literary success for Balzac was like the curse he had imagined in his speculative fiction *La Peau de chagrin* (*The Wild Ass's Skin*), the novella which made him a household name in 1831 after his first real success: a scandalous treatise on the nature of marriage that had appeared the previous year and been reviewed by the author himself under the name 'Comte Alex de B—', proclaiming that he had achieved 'the stature of genius'. He renounced ordinary life to write as if he were a factory, and he the person doing all the shifts. He gorged on reality until his guts almost burst. Who else but Balzac would ever have thought that he needed to supplement his novelistic output with books on the minutiae of social intercourse? He followed up his *Physiologie du Mariage*, indexed by the Church for its critical views on that institution, with a set of observations on contemporary fashion and etiquette, *Traité de la vie élégante* (1830), a pioneering study of gait *Théorie de la démarche* (1833), and a kind of pseudo-scholarly manual on diet and stimulants *Traité des excitants modernes* (1839). All offer plunging views of the enormous changes that French society was undergoing in his time. Balzac had capital invested in his own reputation: the more he published, the bigger his acclaim and the more money he could make—'All my other passions were just a deposit for this one', he told his notebook around the time he embarked on his long, epistolatory relationship with his Polish admirer Eveline Hanska, which was to turn into another novel of sorts. Everything he wrote was desperately candid—'guerrilla journalism' in Graham Robb's words. 'Nobody could ever possibly imagine how clumsy, silly and STUPID that great man was in his youth', wrote Baudelaire. 'And yet he managed to acquire, to *get* for himself so to speak, not only grandiose ideas, but also a vast amount of wit. But then he NEVER stopped working.' And his other great admirer, Flaubert, was even more acutely ironic in his assessment: 'What a man Balzac would have been had he known how to write! But that was the only thing he lacked. After all, an artist would never have accomplished so much, nor had such breadth.' Balzac's writing life, in his own words, was 'suicide by hard labour'.

It could be that this mood of foreboding and distress is what makes for a good novel: one of the qualities which characterises utopian novels, and the category includes almost all of those so mistakenly called science fiction, is that they take place in a world in which everything has been thought out in advance— and still it goes wrong. This idea seems to find favour with Jim Crace: 'Fiction loves distress stories more than it loves success stories. It prefers divorce to long marriages, it prefers illness to health. Literature is about humankind in disarray.' Lashings of catastrophe, then. Indeed, Balzac said something similar: 'The only mission of books is to indicate the disasters produced by changes in ways of life (*mœurs*)'.

The novel, in other words, isn't a leisurely nineteenth-century experiment in graceful living, individual enterprise or rational morality but a panic document, not even able to account for its own doings and motives: 'you can't stop progress' isn't a statement of confidence in the future but the phrase the distraught conductor is shouting out on a runaway train. Balzac had to renounce anything which resembled a life of his own so as to create, in a furious tumble, the masterpieces of his middle years. 'I shan't be able to leave the house for several days', he wrote to one of his acquaintances in 1835. 'Forgive me, but I sense I've only a moment in which to do what I have to do… Some things in literature are like joints of meat; too much time, and it's overdone; too little, and the flesh is still bloody.' The living paradox for Balzac was how an author who was evidently and, in every respect, so much larger than life could represent it accurately on the pages of a book.

Events in that life often unfolded from what he himself had written. He is lazily considered a realist, but he was something much stranger than that. It turns out he was a visionary. Oscar Wilde wrote in his essay 'The Decay of Lying' (1891): 'One of the greatest tragedies of my life is the death of Lucien de Rubempré. It is a grief from which I have never been able completely to rid myself. It haunts me in my moments of pleasure. I remember it when I laugh. But Balzac is no more a realist than Holbein was. He created life, he did not copy it.' In one of the many books written about him, Léon Gozlan's *Balzac chez lui: Souvenirs des Jardies* (1862), he is reported to have corrected the misapprehension of the notorious François Vidocq, head of the Sûreté, in no uncertain terms: 'Ah! my dear Vidocq. So you believe in reality? How charming! I never should have thought you so naïve. Reality! You must tell me all about it. You've actually been to that wonderful land. Come off it! *We*'re the people who make reality.' Such is the archaeology, and even geology, of modern living. It is the work of a writer of self-fulfilling prophecies. 'Balzac, c'est les Alpes', wrote one of his greatest admirers, the dandy and journalist Barbey d'Aurevilly. It is reported that, on his deathbed in 1846, an invalid at fifty-one, with the hue and cry of Paris dying in his ears, he called out in his delirium for the ministrations of Dr. Horace Bianchon, the only physician who had the power to save him.

Dr Bianchon was a fictional doctor in his masterwork *La Comédie humaine*.

# A Critical Romance

*Dostoevsky as a Literary Character*

The enchanted strip of Europe that runs from Switzerland to the Upper Rhine is haunted by literary ghosts. Some of them have Russian accents. Waiting distractedly for the number 8 bus in Geneva a while ago, I was startled to notice the name 'Dostoevsky' on a plaque discreetly affixed, just above eye level, to the wall of the apartment block just behind the stop at Chantepoulet. This plaque marks the lodgings, between the tiny Anglican Church and the lakeside, where the writer and his wife worried over their daughter Sofia, who was to die in May 1868, at the age of three months, soon after she had been christened.

On the other, German-speaking side of Switzerland, Basle's Kunstmuseum still has the remarkable naturalistic painting by Hans Holbein the Younger of the battered cadaver of Jesus in the sepulchre (*Body of the Dead Christ in the Tomb*, 1522) which with its sunken eyes and undeniable post-mortem changes— the blue Christ—shocked the Russian novelist into one of his most tremendous passages in *The Idiot*, that great yearning for a world of lost absolutes and eschatological ideals. And further down the Rhine, at Baden-Baden, are the spas and gaming tables of the Lichtenthalerallee where, in the summer of the previous year, in the town he renamed 'Roulettenburg' in his make-or-break novel *The Gambler*, Dostoevsky met his rivals Turgenev and Goncharov and risked total and shameful destitution, cadging and pawning his newly married wife's valuables so that he could go back to his scenes of brief triumph and longer humiliations at the gaming tables and lose even more money. 'Dostoevsky had very muddled relations with morality', as the philosopher Lev Shestov noted. Gambling provided the opportunity to be an unscrupulous optimist and bet his entire grubstake on the sure prospect of magical future assets, although it may be thought that Dostoevsky was more truly addicted to the exquisite pleasures of losing—'that exhilarating sensation of falling which made him feel superior to the surrounding world and even somewhat pitying towards his fellow men'.

Dostoevsky is a writer who obsesses his readers, but few of them have been as obsessed with every aspect of his life and work as Leonid Tsypkin. Tsypkin was a distinguished immunopathologist and researcher at the Institute of Poliomyelitis and Viral Encephalitis in Moscow who published more than a hundred papers in the Soviet Union and abroad. The first instalment of *Summer in Baden-Baden*, his only major literary publication, first appeared in an émigré newspaper in New York a week before its author's death, on his fifty-sixth birthday, in March 1982. Having only barely survived the invading Germans in the war, and Stalin's anti-Semitic purges thereafter, Tsypkin, it seems, had decided to live in total literary obscurity. Censorship and political intimidations, however, are only part of the story. As Susan Sontag writes in her introduction, Tsypkin 'remained—out of pride, intractable gloom, unwillingness to risk being rejected by the unofficial literary establishment—wholly outside the independent or underground literary circles that flourished in Moscow in the 1960s and 1970s, the era when he was writing "for the drawer".' Even as Tsypkin, a Soviet Jew, was writing this novel of adoration he was also applying for an exit visa to leave the Soviet Union.

Tsypkin's book, then, is about literature (specifically Russian literature) as a kind of paradise, and the snakes that wind through the undergrowth of all paradises. It is less a novel or fantasy in the manner of J.M. Coetzee's *The Master of St. Petersburg* than an act of intense identification and empathy:

this is Dostoevsky from the inside out. Tsypkin's exact, sinuous, paragraph-long sentences use punctuation more as breath marks than for strictly grammatical reasons. He might be a *littérateur*, condemned to rake over the already written, but he does it with the same febrile punctilio as the late W.G. Sebald: his act of homage is really a romance, in a specifically critical sense. What used to be known as a novel's characters have ceased to exist as such and authors (and sometimes readers) are obliged to stand in for them.

Tsypkin dovetails the contemporary and the biographical: he has made the theme of the 'double', dear to Dostoevsky, his organising principle. Dostoevsky's life is so imaginatively vivid for him as to be inseparable from the grey details of his own life, as he sits in the tram and ponders—in a convoluted but tender passage which reminds us of Tsypkin's professional background—why it is 'only now in our declining years that we become so sensitive to the touch of a woman's hair and, sitting on public transport, surreptitiously try to let our cheek or bald patch brush against a cascade of female hair flooding down from somewhere?—and the more casual the touch, the stronger the feeling of contentment, as we can then, having purposely placed our skin against this cascade, try to convince ourselves that it is pure accident, and the more painful is the enforced parting from this cool golden flood pouring down from on high, heedlessly flowing over shoulders covered by a suede or denim jacket and transferring a charge of electrons to our ageing skin.'

The narrator, a Russian intellectual travelling to Leningrad on a train one late December in the 1960s, begins to read the reminiscences of Anna Grigor'yevna, Dostoevsky's former stenographer and second wife, twenty-five years the younger, on their life together in Germany. This four-year absence from Russia began in 1867—only months after she had helped him transcribe *The Gambler* in less than a month to meet his contractual obligations with his editor and creditor Fyodor Stellovsky—and marked the beginning of what his biographer Joseph Frank has called 'the miraculous years'. The diary has been borrowed from a relative, a copy rebound from tattered remnants that he has 'no intention of returning'. It soon emerges that he has read it so often he knows it by heart. For the true reader of Dostoevsky, the writer of this fantasia, is also Anna, his lover and wife. She is his coupling to the social order. She is the business manager whose acumen helped to make her husband a famous writer in his lifetime.

Fedya was not an easy or even particularly sympathetic man to live with. His debauches in the gambling halls obliged him to abase himself, back in their room in the boarding house, at his wife's feet, 'more often than not falling down on his knees before her, calling her an angel, begging her to forgive him for making her unhappy'. He has just been had by the now well-known phenomenon of 'gambler's ruin', when early success at the tables encourages a player to increase the amount being risked: mathematically, this always leads to bankruptcy. Anna invariably forgives him, but does think it 'odd that such a serious and clever man as her husband could cry'. Anna, in fact, seems to understand more clearly the true nature of reciprocity: that those closest to us merit our love because they alone can be expected to love us in return. Yet she clings to his exemplarity and genius as to a 'mast', a nicely nautical image which rears above the repeated imagery of their love-making, which has them swimming away together into a mystical landscape that resembles nothing either of them has ever seen before. Swimmers are people who intend to be born again. 'That night, when he went to kiss Anya, they swam away again together, rhythmically thrusting out their arms from the water and raising their heads to take in gulps of air—and the current did not sweep him away—they swam towards the receding horizon, into the unknown, deep blue distance, and then he began to kiss her again—a dark triangle appeared, upturned—its apex, its peak, pointing downwards, forever inaccessible, like the inverted peak of a very high mountain disappearing somewhere into the clouds—or rather the core of a volcano—and this peak, this unattainable core, contained the answer both terrible and exquisite to something nameless and unimaginable and, throughout his life, even in his letters to her, he maintained his incessant struggle to reach it, but this peak, this core, remained forever inaccessible.'

Memories of his period in the Siberian labour camps and his humiliation at the hands of the Saint Petersburg literary crowd come back to torment Dostoevsky, as he ascends in his crisis moments of pre-epileptic lucidity to a kind of mental Crystal Palace. Issues of exigency torment him, the modal category that describes the relationship between what is and what has been: Prince Mishkin's life, as Walter Benjamin wrote, must remain unforgettable even if nobody remembers it. The unforgettable will never be commemorated; it is the ontological ruin every conscious mind bears within itself. Dostoevsky keeps running into Turgenev who, with his lorgnette and suave manners, seems to be mocking him—a benevolent uncle who has spent too much time in Paris. He promptly accuses his fellow writer of betraying the idea of Great Russia. All his bile about European civilisation rises in his gullet. He is unjust to everyone, himself included. Nobody fits Nietzsche's famous aphorism better than Dostoevsky: 'Luke, 18:14 corrected. He that humbleth himself wills to be exalted.'

Yet the author—like Anna, without whose moderation and steadfastness Dostoevsky's greatest novels might never have been written, and whose efforts were crucial to his becoming Russia's first self-published author—is able to forgive his hero everything except one thing: the blind spot at the centre of Dostoevsky's moral vision. 'It struck me as being strange to the point of implausibility', writes Tsypkin, 'that a man so sensitive in his novels to the suffering of others, this jealous defender of the insulted and the injured who fervently and even frenetically preached the right to exist of every earthly creature and sang a passionate hymn to each little leaf and every blade of grass—that this man should have not come up with a single word in defence or justification of a people persecuted over several thousands of years—could he have been so blind? Or was he blinded by hatred?'

So Tsypkin's act of adoration is also a reproach: he himself was living through a totalitarian system that still held out the promise of overcoming the world made by capital which, with its loosening of traditional ties and fealties, so appalled and fascinated his subject, the most prophetically self-exposed writer of the nineteenth century. Tsypkin wasn't just writing for the drawer, or in the knowledge of how the recognition-hungry Dostoevsky's notorious pronouncements on 'the Jewish question' in his socio-political periodical *Diary of a Writer* in 1878 had played a part in deepening the later plight of the Jews in Soviet Russia. Tsypkin was going one further in the paradoxes of imitated uniqueness than his hero, and into the darkly specular realms of what John Bunyan might have termed 'the Abyss of Abjection'. Here a writer could brood on a form of authorial suffering the figure on the Cross doesn't prepare us for, because its aesthetic is even more paradoxical and anti-heroic than that of the Christian message: *anonymity*.

# II

# Happenstances

# Picking Olives

*A Working Week in Apulia*

In the second week of November my wife and I make our way down from the Upper Rhine to the heel of Italy, even though late autumn isn't the best time to travel from Central Europe to the *basso Salento*—the stiletto of the large southernmost province known as Apulia or Puglia. Air Berlin offers a once-weekly flight to Brindisi from Munich, and if you forget to book it there's the long-distance bus across the Alps and down the full length of the country to Lecce, which takes a full twenty-four hours. For four years in a row we've managed to fly south in November, and even though last year I had to make an emergency visit to my mother in Scotland, my wife kept the tradition going on her own.

Our reason for visiting Apulia out of season, aside from the fact that November still offers pleasant days and a temperature around 20° C, is straightforward enough. This is our annual working holiday: we go to help with the Mediterranean's major winter harvest—olives. Our host is Anna, formidable Italian mother-in-law of my German brother-in-law. (That makes my bond with her somewhat tenuous but Anna treats me just like family.) She migrated to Germany from the *mezzogiorno* in the 1950s, when jobs were scarce in her native region of Campania, married a taciturn Rhinelander called Hermann, and had five children with him in a little town in the Allgäu, where they spent all their married life. And twenty years ago, with their scanty savings, they bought a ruined masseria, one of those ancient fortified homesteads studded across the region, between Presicce and Santa Maria di Leuca, Italy's *finis terrae*, and did it up over a decade.

Anna is a relic of the old European peasant classes John Berger wrote about in his trilogy *Into Their Labours*—the salt of the earth, and someone who knows a lot about its savour too. I've learned many kitchen skills from her, not least how to make pasta from fine durum flour, and methods of preserving garden vegetables, from zucchini to pepperoni. She showed me once how to cook perfect *cotolette di melanzane*—long slivers of eggplant dipped in a mix of flour, parmesan and parsley and beaten egg before being fried—while we drank our way though a bottle of the local *primitivo*, a strong, peppery wine that somebody once described as 'a marriage of blackberries and tar'. Her five children were brought up on a shoestring budget; she sewed clothes for them and made money on the side with hand-painted porcelain dolls which she used to sell on their local market in the Allgäu. She has never entirely mastered German—and it can be a strain to sit with her sometimes, hanging on her every word in order to tune into her Italian way with those unmanageable northern consonantal clusters (she pronounces 'tiptop' 'tip-peti-top' and I only surmised from the context that the knobbly word 'ge-kno-be-lo' was her domestication of the German word for garlic, 'Knoblauch'). It didn't stop her minding all her children through school and into good jobs. And though she likes to read detective novels in the evenings in the only room of the masseria heated by a log fire, very little of Anna's vast fund of practical knowledge comes from books.

Given her lifelong socialist if not communist sympathies, it's perhaps surprising that she's even a modest *castellana*. In earlier times, the ground floor of a masseria would be tenanted by farmers and servants, and the upper level opened up in the summer for the visiting families from the big towns. Its Spartan fittings are accentuated by its imposing size. The thick stone walls render a November night distinctly chilly, although the garden still offers figs and pomegranates, and the ridge of

Indian fig cacti separating it from the small olive plantation of 220 trees flash their bulbous clown's-nose fruits, the *fichidinia*. Anna is able to turn these into a sorbet and impresses me even more by discovering edible wild greens everywhere she goes: rucola, fennel, wild asparagus spears.

This unmanicured region is a part of the country visited by Italians themselves, if not at this time of year: Eugenio Montale's famous poem 'Eastbourne'—which opens with the brass-band playing 'God Save the King' on the shoreline pavilion—may not be so much about the British at the beach as an Italian remembering the abyss off his own coast. 'La festa non ha pietà', runs a line of the poem—the holiday has no pity. It is a grim enough thought for bank holiday England, but it might better describe a November among some of the older olive groves in Apulia.

Olive trees are indifferent to moods of such bleakness, especially short-lived human ones: I took scores of photographs of mature individual trees that had wrestled into startling anthropomorphic shapes behind the tufa boundary walls. Olive trees live for many hundreds of years, and can even survive burning and other acts of wanton destruction. The French illustrator Gustave Doré was fascinated by their contortions too, and used them as models for the images of hell in his famous illustrations to *The Divine Comedy*. His instinct was a good one: the founders of all three monotheisms were awed by the olive tree and its singular produce. 'Christos', after all, means the 'anointed one'—anointed, that is, with chrism. Christ *is* olive oil, you could say, with a hint of balsam. Gerard Manley Hopkins caught the association in his poem 'God's Grandeur', where divine glory 'gathers to a greatness, like the ooze of oil / Crushed'. When Vincent van Gogh painted his beautiful *Olive Trees* in 1889, he knew that anyone looking at it would understand it to be haunted by the figure of Christ, although he appears nowhere in the work.

If you stand on the flat roof of Anna's masseria, you can catch the hard glitter of the Ionian Sea at the edge of the flat landscape. Not far away on the other side is the rockier Adriatic coast leading up to Otranto, the ancient *promontorium Iapygium* which figures in Greek as much as Italian history. The masseria itself sits four-square in a green wash of olive canopies that extend in all directions. Only a few Aleppo or parasol pines stand out among their serried ranks, along with the conical trulli—Apulia's version of the bothy. The air is still except for the odd stray dog, distant reverberation of a car or the radio playing on a tractor, and at weekends the occasional crump of a rifle as a hunter tries to catch a bird on the wing. The spent plastic cartridges of the hunters litter the paths; and it can feel distinctly unsafe to go for a constitutional when they're out in number on a Saturday or Sunday. But every hand is needed for picking, and entire families congregate in some of the groves; time is of the essence, since the olives have to be harvested at the turning point known as *invaiatura* and taken to the mill for cold pressing before they start to ferment.

Olives aren't so much picked (which would be a truly Sisyphean task) as combed or shaken. Broad circular diaphanous nets are spread out on the ground, and the branches given a good carding and heckling; they can be pruned too as the olives fall. Many farmers use machines, which do a brutally efficient job of shaking out the olives along with lots of leaves and extraneous debris. Combing branch by branch is hard work, but there is a genuine sense of accomplishment when the mass of greenish-purple olives is carted away to be weighed prior to pressing. All of which must be done within a matter of hours, in order to avoid oxidation; the oil is pressed out by a simple hydraulic or centrifugal device in a process that is more like squeezing juice from fruit than extracting vegetable oils from seeds or drupes. Hermann and Anna have never treated their olives, and their oil is premium-quality organic. In terms of yields, a tonne of fruit will produce about 200 litres.

Italy has long been famous for the quality of its olive oil, although the stuff has been adulterated further back in antiquity than anyone can remember: the great physician Galen comments on the practice as long ago as the second century. Tom Mueller's book *Extra Virginity* investigates the turbid goings-on behind a product that is trafficked globally: like drugs, but with fewer risks. Until 2001, European law made it permissible for any olive oil bottled in Italy to be sold as 'Italian olive oil', and various conglomerates have made fortunes by commanding premium prices for supposedly pure oils that were cut with inferior products from elsewhere in the Mediterranean (Spain is by far the world's biggest producer of olive oil, as it was in Roman times when Andalucia was the province of Baetica). Although there are some 5,000 mills in Italy, distribution is dominated by a few big companies. Italy still sells three times more oil than it produces. And you certainly get the impression, walking down to the Ionian Sea, that there must be a lot more to this oil business than meets the eye. Scraggy young trees have been planted too close together ever to allow them to mature or be worked on. Hectare after hectare stands empty of machine or person. 'EU subsidies', Anna adds scathingly, 'or maybe tax avoidance schemes'. The landowners get funds from Brussels to plant the trees, she explains, and the more trees, the larger the subsidy; but it's clear enough that when they were planted nobody ever intended to harvest them. In the old days, to own a cluster of olive trees was to be above the barest subsistence level, as suggested by a Cretan proverb almost as shrewd as the famous paradox: 'You can only call a man poor when he doesn't own an olive tree from which to hang himself.'

Industrial production methods and adulteration aren't necessarily a problem for people trying to sell the genuine *extra vergine* oil, who often have their own sales networks and contacts and remained unaffected by dumping prices at the supermarkets. At the local cooperative mill in Presicce, you can stand and watch the entire pressing process: the mechanical cold crushing and malaxing in drums that allow the oil droplets to agglomerate and separate from the wet pulp. And you are reminded that it is brute force—the force of several gravities, or what Emily Dickinson called 'the gift of screws'—that produces the precious fluid. (Nothing is wasted: the residue or pomace is taken to other mills to be heated and chemically treated with solvents in order to win inferior-grade oil for industrial applications.) In a few days, the entire harvest will have been processed. Oil has to meet exacting organoleptic criteria if it is to be labelled as *extra vergine*, a classification that permits only a very low degree of free fatty acids—acidity being an index of corruption. In fact, freshly pressed extra-virgin oil isn't smooth and gentle, but robust and peppery. It has a phenolic 'green bite' (due to the chemical oleocanthal) that can make you cough, although you would hardly know it from the way it is marketed. That is the second adulteration—of taste.

Last year was a good year for Anna and Hermann: they had a yield of about 700 litres. This year is uncertain. Unpredictable and irregular harvests have to be accepted if you farm organically: sometimes there are no olives at all if conditions aren't right in the spring. And then there's the continual logistical challenge of shifting the oil by road in the back of the family van, a couple of hundred litres at a time, over a thousand kilometres to the north. It seems to me that we, as guest pickers, reap the major benefit of all this communal effort; we return home with a couple of ten-litre alembics as a reward for our contribution to the harvest. That keeps us in olive oil for the year.

There is also the satisfaction of knowing that our own efforts have helped to produce what we consume. It's a simple but subtle pleasure, and one not without appeal in an age in which production and consumption are almost entirely uncoupled activities. Ivan Illich would have recognised (and commended) olive-picking as a 'convivial' activity, and therefore meaningful in itself. Besides, we all need to be a bit cannier these days. Mueller suggests in his book that most of the cheap olive oil bought in supermarkets today would have been regarded by the Romans, whose empire consumed twenty million litres of the stuff every year, as fit merely to be left flickering in their lamps.

# Kinds of Blue

*Some Uses of the Cyanometer*

> *J'écartai du ciel l'azur, qui est du noir...*
> Arthur Rimbaud, Délires II

Wandering around the Musée d'art et d'histoire on a visit to the Swiss city of Neuchâtel, I stopped for a while in front of the monumental painting *Effet de soleil sur les Hautes Alpes du Valais en face de la chaîne du Mont-Rose*, 1843–44. It was the work of Alexandre Calame (1810–1864), a Swiss painter who made Alpine scenes his calling card. White-capped mountains formed an extended backdrop to a range of bare brown slopes guarding an untroubled turquoise lake, with the entire upper half of the painting given over to a clear blue sky depicted in subtle gradations of that colour. It was the sky rather than the barren scene of rocks and mountains that caught my eye, and the empirically informed way in which Calame had rendered its nuances as the *bleu bleuet* became powdery and then deepened into ultramarine and cyan above the range of snow-covered peaks in the distance.

What the German poet and mining engineer Novalis called 'atmosphereology' had matured by the nineteenth century into meteorology—a new science that caught the public imagination. Every new science comes with its own instruments, and one that was popular in Calame's day was the cyanometer. It was an invaluable device for landscape artists too. This simple handheld analogue instrument registers the intensity of blueness of the atmosphere. It had been developed a generation before by the remarkable eighteenth-century Swiss geologist and inventor Horace-Bénédict de Saussure, and became well known enough for Lord Byron to lampoon it in *Don Juan* as an instrument for measuring the blueness of 'bluestockings'—the name of an independent and educated women's movement in eighteenth-century England.

Saussure's circular cyanometer had fifty-three shades from white ('zero degrees') to black ('52 degrees') to measure the blue of the sky, which Saussure believed was due to the agency of moisture particles in the air. Saussure, who is generally credited as being the first Alpinist, was enraptured by the distinctive blue of the sky above the Swiss mountains: it held 'in its grandeur and its dazzling purity, an element of death and infinite sadness'.

Intense blue—the blue of lapis lazuli, Egyptian blue (a copper pigment known to the Romans as *caeruleum*), even the glaucous blue of the goddess Athena—was always outside the ordinary. Like sacred things generally, blue could be dangerous to get too close to. In Derek Jarman's last film (and testament), a deep saturated blue not dissimilar to International Klein Blue—the deep expansive monochrome made famous by the visual artist Yves Klein who was otherwise famous for his 'leaps into the void'—fills the screen for seventy-nine minutes while a narrating voice describes Jarman's fear of enveloping blindness and impending death. This, we intuit, is all the transcendence the filmmaker anticipates in the time left to him as he moves beyond the 'pandemonium of image' into Universal Blue. It will not be the theophanic blue of Fra Angelico.

On 20 June 1802, during their extended tour of middle America, Cuba and what was then called New Granada, Humboldt and his French botanist companion Aimé Bonpland set off in frock coats and walking shoes to attempt an ascent of Chimborazo, the daunting glacier-decked summit at the end of the Ecuadorian Volcanic Arc, at that time thought to be the highest mountain in the world. An oil painting by Friedrich Georg Weitsch shows them, standing together with Indian guides and mules on a bare stretch of the altiplano at 4,000 metres, with an impressive view of the snow-capped summit a farther 2,300 metres above them. They were prevented from scaling the summit by an impassable ice-wall as well as their lack of proper climbing equipment: nobody at that time had ever scaled such heights. Contemplating the view at 4,000 metres, they were testimony to Burke's notion of the sublime: that it required the spectator to climb mountains and not just admire them from afar. Both men look composed and collected, when in truth they had been having difficulty breathing and were suffering some of the other effects of high altitude (nausea and vertigo). But Humboldt took out his cyanometer, and recorded the degree of blueness on Saussure's scale. It was 46 degrees, the darkest blue ever seen—twice the value that would typically be measured at midday on a cloudless day in the Mediterranean.

Though the cyanometer could measure the degree of blueness, there was still much speculation about *why* the sky should be blue at all. It was after all a question that had been tormenting philosophers, poets and small children since the beginnings of recorded history—an apparently naive question. It is one as vast as the world itself. Giambattisto Vico, in his influential work of speculative philosophy, *Scienza Nuova* (1725), claimed that pondering the sky was the primal event in human consciousness. It is certainly true that a blue sky stirs even avowedly godless imaginations. Relating the exaltation he felt getting up before dawn at that ambiguous but often magical moment the French call *l'heure bleue* to sit at the bay window of his Toulon house, the French historian Jules Michelet wrote about the steely clarity of the air when he could see (like a god) for miles into the distance. 'An intangible shade of blue—a blue the rosy dawn as yet respected and did not dare disturb, a holy ether, a sublimated spirit—made all Nature spiritual.'

Even the title of Ludwig Teick's *Das alte Buch und die Reise ins Blaue hinein* (1834) offers a sally into the wild blue yonder, 'ins Blaue hinein' being the German expression for an enterprise undertaken without an ostensible aim in mind. The only limit is a blue one. 'I have been doing some skying', as John Constable told a friend. Constable, one of its great painters, always paid special attention to aerial phenomena and the effect of light on landscape, repudiating the 'white sheet' technique in landscape painting that made the sky a neutral background against which objects stood in relief: 'Clouds moving very fast with occasional very bright openings on the blue', is scribbled on the back of one of his sky studies. He had been inspired by the cloud studies of Luke Howard, whose famous 1803 'Essay on the Modifications of Clouds' established the Latinate taxonomy still used today for their 'production, suspension and destruction'. Constable was being faithful to the medium Aristotle had called the 'transparent' (*diaphonos*) more than two thousand years beforehand. Ruskin told his students to make a careful study of the sky: its pure blue was not just a hue 'but rather a profound, vibrating and transparent body of penetrating air'. If a sense of cosmic harmony had evaporated, it had been replaced by nature as a kind of half-understood hermeneutics that needed deciphering, as in 'Tintern Abbey', where Wordsworth speaks of 'A presence that disturbs [him] with the joy / Of elevated thoughts; a sense sublime' dwelling in the ocean and the air and 'the blue sky, and the mind of man'.

Leonardo da Vinci had spent months drafting a book in which he recapitulated those two thousand years of thinking about why the sky is blue and enlarged them with his own observations. Centuries before Calame, he reached the conclusion that 'the blue air makes distant mountains appear blue', and applied this heuristic to his own landscape painting: a subtle admixture of blues allowed him to create an illusion of distance and objects set back from the foreground. (The most impressive works of classical Chinese painting are also devoted to rendering remoteness through moisture-laden air and the effects of precipitation.) As for a scientific explanation, Leonardo believed that 'minute, imperceptible particles' were attracted by solar rays which then 'seem luminous against the deep, intense darkness of the region of fire that forms a covering above them', which is not far removed from Aristotle's explanation in *On the Senses*. Leonardo even tried to capture an 'artificial sky' in a bottle, something Saussure tried to do in his time too, using a saturated solution of copper sulphate and ammonia.

In the decade of Calame's death, the Victorian natural philosopher John Tyndall—also a keen Alpinist—thought he had found the secret of the everlasting blue, and called his agent 'aequeous vapour'. He mixed the sky in a bottle too, and was able to confect a mixture of hydrochloric acid vapour and air that appeared blue in white light. Even Ruskin, who had little time for science, was impressed: he thought that producing a perfect blue in a tube was 'magic of the finest sort'. This is now known as the Tyndall effect. Tyndall held to the idea that particles in the air create the blueness of blue sky, but Ruskin's suspicion that molecules in the air actually scatter the rays of the sun's light differently according to wavelength was closer to the mark. It was a hunch confirmed by Einstein's paper on opalescence in 1910, which showed this scattering effect in detail, and incidentally confirmed the reality of atoms. Revealing that the colour of the sky is caused by gas molecules scattering the sun's light had led to a convincing piece of circumstantial evidence in favour of atomic theory. 'The sky cannot be blue if atoms are not real', as Paul Pesic points out in his book, *Sky in a Bottle*.

Sometimes we associate the blueness of the sky with the azure of the sea. 'This indefinite lucid blue pallor of the aquatic evening' as the Portuguese poet Pessoa put it (writing as Bernardo Soares) in his *The Book of Disquiet*. At such moments we might lose our bearings and fear we're drowning had Emily Dickinson not reassured us that 'The Brain is deeper than the Sea'.

Almost contemporaneously with Pessoa, the Austrian novelist Robert Musil gave expression to the overpowering sense of vertigo—a narcissism of purity—that afflicts the wayward adolescent protagonist in his 1906 novel *The Confusion of Young Törless*. The eponymous hero goes for a walk in the park and, lying in the grass, notices 'as if for the first time' a bottomless blue gap between scuds of cloud in the vault of the autumn sky. He is seized by anguish—by a blue funk. 'He felt it must be possible if only he had a long, long ladder, to climb up and into it. But the farther he penetrated, lifting himself up as he raised his eyes, the deeper the blue luminous background receded.' Infinity, which had seemed to young Törless a concept that had been thoroughly tamed and domesticated—and had even been made to do 'circus tricks' in his mathematics classes—had suddenly broken loose and gone on the rampage. His abyssal vision was the same one which Vico thought must have struck the 'giants'—Noah's descendants—who roamed the densely wooded earth after the Flood and turned their gaze to the prospect of the sky where the deity insisted on speaking in signs. It is also a precisely aerial enactment of Friedrich von Schlegel's definition of *Sehnsucht*, that 'vague feeling of deepest longing' which knows no limits, but rather 'climbing step by step, never ceases to rise further' (*Philosophy of Language and the Word*, 1829).

Törless hadn't found the ultimate lair of blueness. In 1934, the American naturalist and pioneering ecologist William Beebe described his descent off the coast of Nonsuch Island in the Bermudas with the inventor of the bathysphere Otis Barton to a record 3,000 feet below sea level. As the steel sphere of this cramped, creaking construction with its tiny porthole was winched into the deep, and the warm reassuring red glow of the terrestrial day disappeared, giving way to 'chill and night and death', he tried to describe what was left, a twilight shade that was paradoxically phosphorescent: 'It was of an indefinable translucent blue quite unlike anything I have ever seen in the upper world, and it excited our optic nerves in a most confusing manner [...] the blueness of the blue, both outside and inside our sphere, seemed to pass materially through the eye into our very beings.' It was only by shutting his eyes and opening them again that he could register 'the terrible slowness of the change from dark blue to blacker blue'.

Beebe was describing the cyanotic chill of subaqueous blue. Midnight blue. In a curious way, Goethe had anticipated his experience, writing in his *Theory of Colours*: 'The colours which approach the dark side, and consequently, blue in particular, can be made to approximate to black; in fact, a very perfect Prussian blue, or an indigo acted on by vitriolic acid appears almost as a black.' There was no way to verify whether that deepest blue emanated from the absolute zone of Saussure's degree 51, or whether it was a kind of dark light phenomenon generated by his own eyes. Nonetheless, in the confines of a tiny bathysphere, cramped and in mortal danger, it seems he had an intense experience of what Pythagoras knew as 'the unlimited'.

But perhaps there's something evasive about all these sublimations. Reviewing the work of the surrealist poet and painter Giorgio de Chirico in his essay 'Poetical Space' (1989), specifically the depthless blue skies in the surrealist paintings that made his name, the poet John Ashbery commented with his usual mischievous nonchalance: 'How satisfying to feel that one lives in these flattened spaces.'

# Trees and Forests

*The Axe-Man discovers Civility*

Last spring we called on a gardening firm to remove three Norway spruces that had been in our northern Strasbourg garden from the time we acquired the keys to the house in October 1994, when both the trees and our two children were small. In the intervening time, our children had become adults and left home; and the trees—which I suspect had been lifted as seedlings from the Rhine forest at the end of our road by the previous owner (and should never have been in a suburban garden in the first place)—had become giants, were undermining my wife's *potager* with their roots, and keeping our increasingly disgruntled neighbours in the shade.

It is no small thing to cut down large trees. Well, you might think it would be no small thing, but the three gardeners who came from a German firm across the border with petrol-driven chainsaws and tree spurs had lopped all the branches off the spruces, which were over twenty metres high, and felled the three trunks within an hour. The rest of their work day was spent collecting the debris and digging out the roots with a small hydraulic excavator which they somehow managed to drive over the fence on an aluminium pontoon and into the garden. Root extraction was as tough as its dental equivalent. The spectacle of our garden suddenly desolate and in disarray made me think of the warning signs that are common in the Rhine forest these days, as the municipal authorities attempt to restore it to something resembling its primordial floodplain ecology: '*Abattage d'arbres*'. As in English, the same noun is used to describe the felling or planned slaughter of animals, an indication of just how serious a business forestry is.

Seeing trees being worked on in French cities is a common site in late autumn, when the municipality sends out its workers in trucks with telescopic ladders to lop and prune (*élagage*) the branches of the plane trees back to stumpy crowns. Strasbourg's municipal works department employs sixty élagueurs to trim its 23,500 roadside trees (and there are at least twice that number in schools, cemeteries and other public grounds). Pruning trees shortens their lifespan considerably, from several centuries to about fifty years. That is the price to pay for having an aesthetically pleasing city: you can't have rows of massive chestnut trees—which are spectacularly beautiful in spring with their red and white blossom-sprays—adorning a busy street without having to trim off branches and prune back dangerous overhangs.

While I've never been terribly fond of formal French gardens, with their insistence on a display of mastery over nature ('Show a French gardener a tree and he will reach for his pruning saw', writes Hugh Johnson), I do admire their *allées*, those long cathedral naves of plane trees, or the famous roadside *arbres d'alignement* which once thrilled Cyril Connolly as he drove past them on his way to the Midi. And although the plane tree goes a long way back in French culture—being introduced in the mid-sixteenth century by the naturalist Pierre Belon, who also brought the cork oak, cedar and lilac with him from his travels in Asia Minor—for about twenty years the French have been proceeding with a wholesale abattage of these magnificent plane trees, on the pretext that their slant of light and shade plays havoc with the steering abilities of hapless motorists (which was how Albert Camus died with his publisher Michel Gallimard in 1960). A recent experiment in Norfolk has in fact shown that planted intelligently, with a kind of staggered narrowing of the distance between each tree, along with a tapering of the alley's width at the approach to a town, it is possible to create a stroboscopic visual effect that makes drivers reduce their speed involuntarily.

There were reputedly three million of these *arbres d'alignement* in France at the end of the nineteenth century; these days they number no more than a few hundred thousand. I was surprised to notice a French-style *allée* in Scotland recently. Driving my hired car back to Edinburgh airport recently from my mother's house in Kirriemuir, I took a shortcut to Perth and realised I was being guided along an avenue of oaks and maples standing like sentinels along the Meigle road, south of Alyth. These magnificent trees must have been planted over a century beforehand by somebody who wanted to introduce the French effect to what is one of Scotland's most fertile (and protected) areas. Dundee and its hinterland are dotted with arboreal projects.

Sara Maitland, in the periodical *The Author*, suggested recently that 'writers of both poetry and prose seem to have a strangely deep affinity with trees'. She's not mistaken; you can find writers leaning on trees almost anywhere you care to look.

Fresh in Paris as a young man from the provinces, Stendhal felt fortunate that his cousin's patronage had procured him a desk job at the Ministry of War. It was a dull job, although the bureaucratic habits he acquired were to see him through employment under two regimes. He became a familiar of two pollarded lime trees at the bottom of the Ministry garden, against which his fellow workers were in the habit of urinating. 'They were the first friends I made in Paris', he writes, 'and I felt sorry for them, clipped as they were.' He contrasted them with the limes of Claix on his father's estate in the mountains, although it would have taken more than linden trees to bring him back to Grenoble.

Stendhal was an amateur dendrologist all his life. In his *Souvenirs d'egotisme* he mentions visiting the trees at Richmond: 'Nothing equals this fresh greenery in England and the beauty of these trees: to cut them down would be a crime and a dishonour.' He commended the respectful attitude of the British to such wonders of nature and lamented that a French landowner would, at the drop of a hat, order the logging of five or six large and ancient oaks on his estate for the sake of extra revenue. And he would surely have deplored the scene in Goethe's novella where an additional torment for the suicidal young Werther is the arrival from the city in his little town of Wahlheim of the new parson's wife, who has 'pretensions to scholarship' and orders the felling of the ancient walnut trees in the manse garden so that she can have more light to read the latest works of Bible exegesis.

Mikhail Chekhov relates that when his brother Anton moved to his estate at Melikhovo, he planted many trees which he tended 'as though they were his children. Like Colonel Vershinin in his *Three Sisters*, as he looked at them he dreamed of what they would be like in three or four hundred years.' Walt Whitman asked himself in *Song of the Open Road*: 'Why are there trees I never walk under but large and melodious thoughts descend upon me?' And a more recent line in Karl Ove Knausgaard's *My Struggle* carries the same sentiment: 'These motionless, foliage-laden, air-bathing beings with their boundless abundance of leaves… For whenever I caught sight of them I was filled with happiness.'

Trees aren't always attended by a sense of openness and happiness. Indeed, it is the argument of the Stanford literary critic Robert Pogue Harrison in his book-length essay on the place of the human in nature *Forests: The Shadow of Civilisation* that, at a subconscious level, we resent trees for their antiquity, their antecedence to human consciousness, their brooding presence on the edge of settlement. Drawing from the genetic psychology of the eighteenth-century Italian philosopher and historian Giambattista Vico, Harrison traces the human dread of forests—massed ranks of trees in other words—to the origin myths of the classical sky-god who ruled Greece as Zeus and Rome as Jupiter, and whose announcement to aboriginal humanity was a lightning bolt directed into the canopy in order to produce a clearing, and open up the 'mute closure of foliage'. It was only then that humans could see the overarching sky as a medium and source of revelatory messages about our origins and destiny, and worship its blueness (and this idea of the clearing was an important one for the most influential of twentieth-century philosophers, Martin Heidegger). For religious and secular authorities alike, the tent-poles of the biosphere have been objects to abominate, rather than consecrate. The governing institutions of the West from the family to the law, Harrison contends, 'originally established themselves in opposition to the forests, which in this respect have been the first and last victims of civic expansion'. The French writer Léon Bloy insisted, in one of his novels, that 'one of the most characteristic signs of the petit bourgeois is his hatred of trees'. The reason for such petit bourgeois hatred may be that for all their bulk and fixity, tree species are also assiduous migrants (given enough time).

Vico's association is anthropologically sound. In the remaining tropical forests of northern Jambi province in central Sumatra, which I visited myself several years go, there is an indigenous hunter-gatherer tribe known as Orang Rimba: until about twenty years ago, when loggers and landgrabbers intruded on their habitat, these people had had almost no contact with the outside world, which was known to them as *Terang*—'The Light'. Those who lived outside their dipterocarp rainforest were identified with the primary quality that broke though the trees, and flickered and percolated down through the high canopy.

In the Old Testament, Yahweh commands the Hebrews to burn down sacred groves wherever they find them, perhaps recalling the decisive role that two trees in a garden played in the events of Genesis 3. The word for woods is, as in Isaiah 21, synonymous with 'uncultivated places'; and that must have been the conviction of the New World settlers when they contemplated the endless pine forests of New England. In fact, there used to be an etymological distinction (as with so many doublets in English): the word 'forest' is of Latinate origin, and signified the area outside the city gates; 'wood' on the other hand is of Old English provenance, and designates a place of wildness, which is how Shakespeare usually regards the vast tracts outside the city—except for the cultivated Forest of Arden(nes) in *As You Like It*. For Dante, living in a Europe that would soon be cutting down its trees to build caravels and carracks, the forest was demon-haunted and evil, an underworld out of which his protagonist has to extricate himself in order to become more aware of his own humanity; for Descartes, it was the very embodiment of confusion, a maze of custom grown up any old how that needed to be lit by the rectilinear beams of reason. In the century after his death, planned cities were called 'villes à la Descartes'. So when Roquentin has his climactic moment of 'nausea' in Sartre's novel about the contingency of existing things, it is precisely when he wanders into a park and is confronted by a gnarled old chestnut tree whose grotesque root system resists his desire to assimilate it into his very Cartesian consciousness.

Just like other living organisms, trees need cladding to protect them from their environment. Walking with my wife in the Black Forest just across the Rhine from Strasbourg, I was reminded, as, in the forest above Bad Petersal, we passed a birch tree that bore the date 17 May 1945 on a widening scar in its bark, that dense woodland, as well as being the preferred setting for most of the testing folk tales collected by the Brothers Grimm, actually offers a refuge and reprieve for people in crisis. That date was just ten days after the unconditional surrender of German forces after six years of a terrible war. Perhaps it had been carved by a villager seeking safety in the forest. The forest constantly figures in the accounts of persons who escaped their villages in Poland and Eastern Europe and survived there, beyond the reach of the Wehrmacht or local militias. Back in 1834, in his famous poem *Pan Tadeusz*, the Polish poet Mickiewicz had even mythologised Baublis, an ancient oak-tree inside which 'a dozen folk could sup'. Under those circumstances, the forest stood for safety and tradition; it was the modernity of the century outside that was terrifyingly suspect. For almost his entire career the artist Anselm Kiefer has been preoccupied with the image of dense pine forests, remembering that his own family sought refuge in the southern Black Forest during bombardments of his native town of Donaueschingen, even as he knows that the Nazis celebrated the sylvan in German history. The Nazi movement itself was even described, in its early days, as a 'fantastic forest' (E. M. Cioran)

In our dealings with trees, it seems that they too are subject to a dialectic that plays on their nature as individual beings— the longest living on the planet—and as a massed force, the former having something of a personality and the latter being the lair of forces which continually threaten human civilisation; unless of course the said civilisation makes urban life untenable, in which event forests offer something of the primitive nurturing protection they always have. Perhaps their figuring in the earliest Biblical story about the acquisition of knowledge is a reminder that the tree was just as important as its fruit: they were created on the third day, before animal and human life on the fifth and sixth days of Creation. The learned Simeon of Frankfurt even calculated that there would be eight hundred species of marvellous and odorous trees in Paradise, among which number would doubtless be the Tree of Life itself.

In the excavations left by the uprooting of the spruces in our garden, we planted a young pear tree and a quince. When I looked around the garden the other day as it started to come to life again in the spring, the quince tree, hardly a metre high, was developing fruit, little surreally golden light bulbs bearing the faintest hint of fluff, only a year after being put in the earth. The quince, I recall, was another aspect of nature that thrilled the flatly unimpressible Cyril Connolly. It would be our tree of golden apples; we just had to give it time.

# Praise for the Siesta

*Done with Down Time*

My father-in-law is a German journalist who still writes, well into his retirement. He may owe his energy, and the fact that he still writes well too, to a remarkable ability: he flops down on his couch in the afternoon, closes his eyes for fifteen to twenty minutes, and then gets up refreshed and alert, ready to rise in the trailing wind of ideas. He has done this throughout his professional life, and he swears by it. He calls it a *Nickerchen*; my French friends in the south talk about a *méridienne* (title of a familiar 1889 painting by Van Gogh of two peasants lazing in the lee of the haystack), whereas in English we take a *nap*, or the curious *forty winks*. Siesta is the universal word for this activity—from the Latin *sexta*: the sixth hour for sundial users—though it's perhaps rather exotic-sounding under a northern European sky. And while I've tried to acquire my father-in-law's clandestine ability of catching forty winks myself, I'm not a very dependable *homo siestus*, except perhaps on holiday in the south of France, when the sun, from midday to about 4 o'clock in the afternoon, drums on the shutters of the village of E---, population 512 (plus 4).

Across the river the cicadas endlessly chirrup a line from Virgil—*Sole sub ardenti resonant arbusta cicadis* ('Under the burning sun the orchard hums with cicadas')—as their midday report to the Muses, and a lizard on the brickwork tries to teach me the sign-language which, as Heinrich Heine observed on his travels in Lucca, makes it possible even for poets to converse with mute nature. 'A quotation is not an excerpt', wrote another poet, the Russian Osip Mandelstam in his great essay on Dante. 'Quotations are cicadas.'

A siesta frees us, as the Spanish poet Antonio Machado nicely put it, from the omnipresence of the world.

In Greek times, Hippocrates thought that sleeping after a meal moistened and propelled the food to all parts of the body; and Hippocrates' prestige was such that we still remember his recipes. The best-known classical siesta-taker was the cynic philosopher Diogenes, who is remembered by everyone because he lived in a tub. He was famously rude to Alexander the Great because the upstart emperor, who also happened to be Aristotle's most famous pupil, dared disturb him during his tub-nap in the city of Corinth. 'Anything I can do for you?' asked Alexander, whose hunger for power would famously take him as far as the gates of India. 'Get out of my sun', suggested Diogenes, who had already recognised the emperor as the very first modern man, someone whose overriding concern was to bag his place in that same sun. (It is noteworthy that our use of the word cynic reflects Alexander's reality, not Diogenes'.) Homer mentions in the *Iliad* that the respected older warrior Nestor was almost as touchy as Diogenes about not being disturbed in the afternoon, whatever Hector and the Trojans might be up to.

In China, the right to nap is enshrined in the constitution— factory workers in the famously productive land commonly have a nap after lunch, sometimes even on their workbench. Peru's military once had to quell an uprising because its government foolishly thought to ban siestas. Europe's class-struggle extended to opportunities for sleep: Paul Lafargue, Marx's son-in-law, wrote a tract called *Le droit à la paresse* (*The Right to Be Lazy*, 1883), demanding that the proletariat ought to work at most three hours a day with the rest of the time set aside for the pursuit of enjoyable things including siestas. And Friedrich Nietzsche—though no lover of the proletariat— agreed: anyone who didn't have two-thirds of the day to himself was a slave. He came to the following conclusion: 'The hardest-working of epochs, ours, doesn't know what to do with its work, its money, other than always more money, more work.'

What is really at issue is the notion of *leisure*, which for us has an escapist ring to it: for the Greeks, leisure was a wholly positive term (and it is telling that the Greek word for leisure has given us the word 'school'): leisure was when people undertook activities for their own sake. Only busybodies were destitute of leisure.

Compare that attitude to the time-and-motion studies of the American F.W. Taylor which swept across a Europe producing armaments as hard as it could during the First World War, where the methods of trench organisation were noted for future reference by the young Walt Disney and Ray Kroc, the founder of McDonalds. 'You give in to the noise like you give in to war', wrote the French doctor and novelist Louis-Ferdinand Céline after a fact-finding mission to the Ford factory in Detroit for the League of Nations; he thought Chaplin in his film *Modern Times* had caught all the frantic cretinisation of work on the assembly line (even though the film was a silent one). Having discovered how to manipulate matter, the second industrial revolution put its mind to managing humans. Fat chance of a siesta when a foreman had to drill the monotony of the assembly line into his workers! It was the machine that counted, and the machine never slept. Workers are merely soft machines.

Work became precisely quantified as output: time to produce one item. Yet assimilating time to money is a relatively new concept in the history of the human race: we *act* as if time were a valuable commodity, therefore we consider it *must* be so. Difficult then to imagine that cultures still exist, even today, where nobody runs out of it, has to set some aside (e.g. for a siesta) or is ever compelled to live on the borrowed variety.

The curious thing is, as the philosopher G.C. Lichtenberg said, long before the industrial revolution came to his hometown of Göttingen: 'People who never have time accomplish the least.'

Now, as we hurtle into the third industrial revolution, one seemingly bent on changing the nature of reality itself, the siesta's slightly furtive moment of hunter-gatherer repose has been rediscovered—by Americans. Being an aspiration as much as a country, America lives in thrall to the idea of tomorrow, and is rather gnostic about today: this is called the work ethic. It is still true, as sociologists have observed over the years, that, although the United States is one of the most affluent countries in the world, Americans remain poor in terms of leisure (where the typical holiday allowance is a paltry two weeks, and some companies such as Microsoft frown on employees ever 'taking their foot off the gas'). Put your time to *good use*, as the saying goes. A balance sheet is clearly implied.

It might seem a bit odd then that an American World Nap Association (WNO) can now be found on the net. It is apologetic about what it promotes, pointing out that for most Americans napping is still tainted by Sloth, one of the seven deadly sins. Roget's *Thesaurus*—now transatlantically compiled—categorises the word along with 'indolence, inactivity, loafing, procrastination, lethargy, slouching, vegetating', none of them exactly glowing recommendations. Not being busy is, for the puritan mind, the very source of vice: leisure, for the other-regarding egalitarian mind, smacks of privilege.

I now read that American creative management, which is paid a great deal of money to have bright ideas, has just had a brainwave: why not get workers to have a pause in the middle of the day? Gould Evans architects' office in Kansas City, for instance, has just installed a napping loft for its employees to combat the performance dip between 2 and 4 pm. They've got it wrong though, especially with the term 'power nap'. *Impose* a siesta on people and you destroy the reason for having one at all.

So next time you feel an urge to lie down for a few minutes after lunch, just do it. Paddle in the shallows. Don't feel metaphorically entailed. We are intermittent beings. Seeking a permanent high—living only on the summits, as Nietzsche didn't quite say—is a production-line aspiration. That goes for happiness too. Whereas napping in the valleys, as Diogenes realised, is the original *acte gratuit.*

But beware: pondering why individuals claim to be free when their freedom so closely resembles alienation may unfit you for work altogether.

# A Just Appreciation of the Pineapple

*On the Social Aspects of Taste*

*There had been an age
When a pineapple on the table was enough...*
Wallace Stevens

Columbus brought the pineapple (*Ananas comosus*) back from
the Caribbean to Renaissance Europe, where it caused a
sensation. For two centuries, Europe's horticulturists spent a
fortune trying to find a method of cultivating—in hothouse
'pineries'—the armoured, succulent king of fruits with its ruff
of spiny green leaves. Its bizarre, artificial-looking appearance,
which is due to its being a coalescence of individual berries,
inspired architects and craftsmen, and from the Georgian Era
onwards it was common to find gateposts, sculptures and even
earthenware bearing the corona of a pineapple. An oil painting
by Hendrik Danckerts in 1675 shows the monarch Charles
II being presented with the first pineapple grown in Britain.
A character in Mandeville's *Fable of the Bees* (1714) attributes
their cultivation to Sir Matthew Decker, president of the
East India Company, whose hothouse garden in Richmond
was famous 'for the Production and Culture of the *Exotick*'.
Alexander Pope's gardener was using giant stoves to grow
'ananas' by 1734. While for the American colonies the more
easily freighted fruit was commonplace enough to become a
symbol of hospitality, it remained the ultimate luxury item in
London, so coveted by the mercantile classes that specimens
could be 'rented out' as décor for the evening. It was the barely
attainable something you hoped the guests would be tactful

enough just to look at and admire.

Dr Johnson was of a mind to have a word with the covetous: 'The pineapple thrives better between the tropicks', he writes in his *Further Thoughts on Agriculture* (1756), and he goes on to counsel the reader not to envy such finicky and unnecessary privileges. 'Mankind cannot subsist upon the indulgences of nature, but must be supported by her more common gifts. They must feed upon bread, and be clothed with wool; and the nation that can furnish these universal commodities, may have her ships welcomed at a thousand ports, or sit at home and receive the tribute of foreign countries, enjoy their arts, or treasure up their gold.'

By 1850, the global reach and faster ships of the British Empire had made the pineapple that little bit less grand and inaccessible, and costermongers would sell 'a taste of paradise for just a penny a slice'. By the end of the century, pineapples had even lost their resemblance to the pine cone: once cut and cored, this whim of nature fitted the shape of a steel can.

You wouldn't necessarily expect pineapples to appeal to philosophers, who have on the whole a reputation for austerity; on the other hand it is quite fitting that a natural object as startling as a pineapple should attract the attention of fine minds. One of the most interesting and earliest philosophical references to the pineapple occurs in John Locke's *Essay Concerning Human Understanding* (1690), in which he asserts the impossibility of knowing the taste of pineapple before it has been in the mouth. 'We see nobody gets the relish of a pineapple, till he goes to the Indies, where it is, and tastes it.' Until then, the person who (like Locke himself) tries to imagine how pineapple tastes cannot have a 'new', first-hand appreciation of it. This was a key moment in the history of ideas: taste (a complex idea) was understood as the direct effect of experiencing the sensory nature of a fruit (a simple idea) on the requisite taste organ, as well as an aesthetic concept rising above its rude origins in the mouth.

One would expect a poet to be properly attuned to his perceptive faculties. John Keats could indeed wax eloquent about the materiality of fruit, if not the pineapple. In a letter written to his friend Charles Dilke on 22 September 1819, he breaks off to exclaim: 'Talking of Pleasure, this moment I was writing with one hand, and with the other holding to my Mouth a Nectarine—Good God how fine. It went down soft pulpy, slushy, oozy—all its delicious embonpoint melted down my throat like a large beatified Strawberry. I shall certainly breed.' (The best commentary on this exclamation is an unrelated entry in the famous scrapbook of Keats' slightly older contemporary, the German philosopher Georg Christoph Lichtenberg: 'He could say the word "succulent" in such a way that when you heard it you thought you were biting into a ripe peach.' We don't know who 'he' was but it might almost have been Keats.)

As Locke had suggested, if we seek to convey the taste of an unknown fruit we are bound to describe it in terms of known fruits. Keats relishes his nectarine, but compares it for Dilke's sake to a strawberry. There is a gulf between having a sensation and describing it: the poet moves inwards to the raw feel of the fruit while directing his description outwards to the qualities he thinks will appeal to his interlocutor. He has to describe those qualities in terms that merge his inner state with what his friend will already be in a position to understand, and appreciate. Dilke has previously tasted other fruit, perhaps even a nectarine, and can at least construct a *something* in his mind. Even then Keats' description flirts with the ineffable. (I have had the same difficulty trying to describe the quiddity of the delicate mangosteen, which grows only in tropical countries and doesn't travel well, to those of my family who have never tasted one.)

Those who were among the first to taste the pineapple—including the diarist John Evelyn, who sampled one portioned by King James II in 1688, and for whom it was redolent of 'the Quince and the Melon'—resorted, like Keats, to describing one fruit in terms of others. Joseph Addison and David Hume repeated Locke's strictures about the alimentary nature of taste: instead of the pineapple, the former took as his example tea which, before the Industrial Revolution transformed the British into a nation of tea drinkers, still had exotic connotations; the latter, a hogshead of wine. (Hume also has a passage in *A Treatise on Human Nature* on the difficulty of forming 'a just idea of a pineapple, without having actually tasted it'.)

Hume, of course, was less interested in the limits of language than in the empiricist claim that simple ideas are derived from impressions, which come about from the stimulation of the 'proper inlets to each sort [of object]'. And these simple ideas are precisely what cannot be brought across verbally. Words are sounds, and can excite no simple ideas in us other than those proper to sounds. Although he never intended so, Hume joins the language sceptics, for whom language is inherently inadequate to experience—all first-person experience, that is, and not just the description of sensations.

On the other hand, it is perfectly obvious that taste is a social experience, and inextricably part of our nature as language users. People love to taste things and discuss what they perceive with those standing next to them. We seek confirmation or negation. Oenologists—who tend to be more florid in description than Keats and lack his original charm— typically exhort casual imbibers to go out and sample wines for themselves, preferably in company. Knowledge comes through acquaintance. Tasting is a social activity. And no opinion is wholly authoritative. Once you accept that, you're ready to discriminate between different tastes of the same thing, or determine how they might differ depending on when, how and where they are eaten. A fresh pineapple might even taste differently from a tinned one. And then you're ready to appreciate what are truly culturally acquired tastes: whisky, bird's nest soup, even Vegemite.

It was another philosopher who banned the gustatory from our general appreciation. To the best of my knowledge, Immanuel Kant—that sober figure in Königsberg—never ate a pineapple (although presumably he could have, Königsberg having been the principal port for eastern Prussia). Nevertheless, he nourished a kind of Johnsonian worry that taste, the agency of aesthetic judgement—which he did so much to categorise in his seminal *Kritik der Urteilskraft*— might revert to its organic origins. Distance from the object that triggers appreciation of its beautiful qualities is a crucial aspect of Kant's thinking, a consideration so obvious to him that he never draws out its implications. There is of course something very Protestant and self-denying about keeping your distance from a delicious fruit such as the pineapple. Smell and taste, which thrill the body, are more likely to produce pleasure than knowledge. They also require proximity to the object of sensation, while sight, the most noble of the senses, is able to 'take in' an object without any kind of empirical considerations at all. What counts for Kant is keeping aesthetic judgement disinterested and impartial; he must therefore rely on a notion of taste which hovers above experience as pure metaphor and avoids any admixture of sensation. It is, oddly enough, an imperialist's vision of aesthetics. Locke at least recommended going to the Indies to get the 'relish' of a pineapple. Empiricism is sometimes charged with not knowing that it is an ideology; Locke however assumes that the object of sensation—a pineapple—can only be properly experienced in its natural setting. His brand of empiricism was sensitive to its own assumptions.

Kant wanted to emancipate the tongue. But then he never thought it worthwhile to linger like Keats over the description of a raw sensation, and his idea of taste could express the pleasurable and agreeable ('das Angenehme') only as a *metaphor*. And the result was that for over a century good taste had precious little to do with things that actually taste good. Even today, studies of taste avoid the gustatory: you might have expected something different from a Frenchman, but Luc Ferry's *Homo Aestheticus: The Invention of Taste in the Democratic Age* (1990) entirely avoids mentioning the gastronomic origins of taste: he is interested solely in artistic pleasure uncoupled from the senses and the body itself. Taste is an organ of the mind, in the best Kantian manner. As Joseph Litvak commented, this makes us 'gourmets', able to apply discernment only when we are least aware of the ancient confusion between eating and knowledge.

The curious thing is that somebody who had spent a lifetime on a desert island eating pineapple and no other fruit would not understand what his rescuers, with a wider experience of eating fruits, attributed to the selfsame fruit he had been eating in solitude all those years. The taste of a pineapple has to be related to other tastes, to other people's eating experiences, and even to taste in the exalted, Kantian sense; it needs them all for its just appreciation.

# Marcel's Cup of Tea

*Getting it Wrong About the Madeleine*

Early summer is a heady moment in the life of a French city. It is the time when the lindens—*Tilia europaea*—come into bloom, and the subtle scent of lime blossom wafts down the avenues and boulevards. Every year my wife goes out on her bike along Strasbourg's canal walks with her scissors and a large bag, and gathers a cloud of these flowers. She brings them home, and spreads them out on a piece of muslin in the sun for a few days to let them dry out completely, and then they get stored in paper bags: a handful of the dry leaves, stalks and fluff are taken out of our larder when we have guests and wish to offer them a non-alcoholic *digestif* before they go home. The flowerheads are steeped in hot water for five minutes and then discarded: this is the source of the pale yellow infusion that has guests sniffing as much as voicing their appreciation.

I thought about lime-blossom tea when I finally got past the hypnagogic first fifty pages of *A la Recherche du Temps Perdu* this year, about which a disgruntled reader at Ollendorff—one of the publishing firms that turned down his manuscript—grouched, 'I fail to understand why a man needs thirty pages to describe how he tosses and turns in his bed before falling asleep'. I'd been trying for about a quarter of a century to read the *incipit* of Proust's masterpiece, one of the most erotically disconcerting passages in literature, as it happens, but also a heavily soporific stretch of writing that worked on me like a benzodiazepine. 'For a long time I used to go to bed early to read Proust, but I kept dropping the book', would be my version of that famous opening sentence. Proust's narrator hesitates deliciously on the borderline of wakefulness and sleep, going under several times only to pop up again in a backwash of the conscious life. Soon he is experiencing his famous epiphany, when the full flood of his seemingly forgotten (and pampered) childhood in Combray returns to him.

It all happens because his mother offers him a cup of tea, which he ordinarily doesn't drink. But he changes his mind, and she sends for one of those 'gateaux courts et dodus appelés Petites Madeleines', with their characteristic seashell shapes. In his low mood, he raises to his lips a spoonful of tea in which he has soaked a morsel of the cake. Suddenly a shudder of pleasure runs through him, and he enjoys an access of what he calls 'this potent joy'. The sight of 'the little scallop-shell… so moistly sensual under its severe, religious folds' hadn't suggested anything in particular. Of the classic five senses only taste and smell—'more fragile but more enduring'—are able to detect the spirit of a life hovering over what it has to leave behind, in time. Now he is able to remember in intimate detail a lost era of his childhood: Sunday mornings at Combray—'silence, sonorous, perfumed, and limpid'—when his aunt Léonie used to offer him the same thing, a bit of cake soaked in tisane, as a treat. This is the first of several *moments bienheureux* that lifts the narrator's mood—and indeed the giant tide of Proust's novel itself. 'The whole of Proust's world comes out of a teacup', wrote Samuel Beckett in his study of the novel, 'and not merely Combray and his childhood.'

The madeleine de Commercy, a simple cake first made in Lorraine in the eighteenth century, is now Proust's talisman, a visual cliché that sticks to his name (the PM of 'Petites Madeleines' even spells his initials in reverse!) and gets sold by the dozen to tourists in Illiers, the Normandy village that has added Proust's fictional Combray to its own name. But I have to disagree with Marcel; by far the most interesting thing about the madeleine is visual: its scalloped shape, and the association of that shape with Botticelli's Venus and the pilgrim trail to Santiago de Compostela. A friend who recently visited—well, being Irish, she went on an actual pilgrimage to—Illiers revealed to me that the local church is dedicated to St James: he is the patron saint of Santiago too, and his traditional emblem, the scallop, is often worn around their necks by pilgrims on their way to Galicia.

It seems surprising that Roland Barthes didn't do one of his classic debunking essays on the confectioning of involuntary memory—especially in view of what can be read into the shape of the madeleine. Some psychoanalytically minded critics think the madeleine a synecdoche for Proust's mother. As one wrote: 'Hardly food, eating the madeleine cake is closer to sharing a kiss... To eat the madeleine cake is to eat the mother... The madeleine is a "woman-cake".' In point of fact, the narrator is so absorbed in his own experience he doesn't even bother to tell us whether Maman sitting nearby shares his sensations as she nibbles on her own bit of cake dunked in tea.

I must confess that I'm rather agnostic about the madeleine's ability to resurrect a childhood in all its magic. It's just a simple Genovese sponge cake—sugar, flour and eggs, sometimes with ground nuts folded in with the butter. I've sampled a few madeleines over the years, steeping them in various kinds of fluids too, and I must say there was very little about the eating experience to trigger an epiphany.

Earlier this year, reporting on an exhibition of Proust's manuscripts at the Morgan Library in New York, Colm Tóibín confirmed my suspicion. 'Visitors lining up to see the word "madeleine" as it appeared in Proust's handwriting for the first time are in for a shock. What appears in a 1910 draft of *Swann's Way* is the banal word "biscottes," easy to spot in the manuscript. Soon Proust will find that this word will yield to another word that will open many doors for him in his narrative. But not yet. It is as though a draft of *The Great Gatsby* had, at first, a hero called Jones and Daisy was originally called

Anne. Or the first draft of *The Old Man and the Sea* had the old man merely fishing for mackerel. Or that Molly Bloom, at one point in the composition of *Ulysses*, ended her soliloquy by saying "Maybe".'

*Biscottes*! You mean dry toast? Rusks? Those grilled slices enjoyed by infants and old people down to their gums, as well as Italians for breakfast?

So I began to wonder about the chemistry of Proust's sunburst of involuntary memory. In fact, I had a kind of epiphany myself when I realised, whipping up the egg yolks, melted butter and castor sugar, that madeleines are made more interesting if lemon zest is worked into the cake mix before baking. Lemon zest contains terpenes, fragrant ethereal oils such as limonene, nerol and terpineol. And where else do you find these volatiles? In lime-blossom tea, of course, along with various alkanes, phenols and esters. The tea has been used in European folk medicine for centuries for its sedative, antispasmodic and mildly astringent properties (due to its tannins).

So it's not so much the madeleine as the lime-blossom infusion—*un bon tilleul*—that offers the narrator his moment of joy. Volatiles from linden blooms are aromatic compounds with a low boiling point that allows them to waft out of teacups towards the olfactory bulb in the nose: they convey everything suggested in Verlaine's phrase 'un peu d'ombre et d'odeur'. Proust hints as much himself, when he describes Françoise, the maid, preparing the tisane for his aunt Léonie, whose bedroom always seemed to the young Marcel to have a woody, medicinal smell. Shaken out of the papery little package in which they had been prepared by the pharmacist (another fetish object for the French), the leaves 'resembled the most disparate things, a fly's transparent wing, the blank side of a label, a rose petal, which had all been piled together, crushed or interwoven like the materials for a nest'. These were the sprigs of real lime trees, the narrator goes on, which he could see suspended from the trees in the Avenue de la Gare when coming in from Paris on the train and the 'rosy, lunar, soft gleam that lit up the blossoms among the frail forests of stems from which they hung like little gold roses'. (For the American poet Amy Clampitt, who knew her botany, they resembled 'bell-pulls'.) And it was into this boiling infusion, so redolent of faded blossoms, that his aunt would dip a piece of madeleine, and hand it to him, pre-digested as it were. 'In that moment all the flowers in our garden and in M. Swann's park, and the water-lilies on the Vivonne and the good folk of the village and their little dwellings and the parish church and the whole of Combray and of its surroundings, taking their proper shapes and growing solid, sprang into being, town and gardens alike, from my cup of tea.'

Proust, as Ortega y Gasset wrote in a tribute to the author a year after his death, is an atmospheric writer: everything in his writing aspires to be particulate and airborne, an ambience that could just as easily incapacitate him, as the asthmatic author knew all too well. His experience of involuntary memory is the mind's attempt to fill the lungs with fresh air. The nose is clearly the primary sense organ in all that. Proust's personages even have something vegetal about them: they receive, like plants, what the atmosphere of his treelike novel brings them. Proust had a true sense of smell, even if he also had an advertising man's instinct for the branded vector product whose odd name is going to prevent you ever forgetting it.

My father-in-law, the journalist, once caused consternation in German gastronomic circles by suggesting in the paper he worked for, *Süddeutsche Zeitung*, that the country's famous anaemic white sausage shouldn't be taken seriously since it's really just a vehicle for mustard ('Die Weißwurst darf man nicht ernst nehmen, sie ist traditionell nur ein Senfträger'). Something similar could be said about the madeleine: it's a sponge for a very literary kind of aromatherapy.

# Getting it Right

*The Thinking behind Meaningful Work*

If there is a guiding thought behind Richard Sennett's *The Craftsman*, a digressive series of reflections on his life's work as a social critic, it is the maxim 'making is thinking'. This brings him directly into conflict with his old teacher, the philosopher Hannah Arendt, who erected a division between the world of animal needs—unreflecting work for beasts of burden— and the higher world of *homo faber*, of those who reflect on art and work, and even draw moral conclusions from the activity. That division started with Plato: in the *Symposium* he separated those divinely inspired by the daemon, i.e. poets and philosophers, and all those 'wise in any other regard, whether in the realm of arts and sciences or manual labour', whom he called 'banausic'. This separation between the higher and the vulgar spheres was elaborated into a metaphysics by the neo-Platonists, some of whom made a distinction between the purely contemplative supreme Intelligence or First God and the inferior demiurgic Second who acts to form and direct the world. This attitude practically compels the philosopher to become a recluse, detached from anything resembling an economy, and even suggests, as Plato did at times, that any civic engagement by a philosopher is corrupt—certainly a corrupting pursuit for the philosopher himself.

As a pragmatist, Sennett believes this to have been a serious philosophical error with important ethical and political consequences. It isn't only that it demeans those who do manual labour, it suggests that thinking comes *after* making, and that it starts from what is highest and derives from that Platonic reality everything lower: it is a justification for the kind of politics that gives status to expert elites and technocrats (ours), and in which the word 'benchmark' is nothing more than an empty signifier.

Some of the most eloquent pages of his book are devoted to that great Victorian sage John Ruskin, who spent much of his life defending the old idea of the economy as a husbanding of resources against the new idea of maximum output for minimum effort, and writing well-intentioned if somewhat high-minded addresses for the edification of self-educated working men. His prose has 'an almost hypnotic tactile power, making the reader feel the damp moss on an old stone or see the dust in sunlit streets'. Thinkers from William Morris to Karl Marx broadly sympathised with Ruskin's argument, and defended craftsmanship as a middle ground between (personal) autonomy and (external) authority. A certain archaic nobility still attached to an activity that went back to the ancient Greeks (other than Plato), who thought that manual skill or *techne* was the only sphere in which human brings could aspire to anything resembling perfection. (Yet the god of the craftsmen was limping clubfooted cuckolded Hephaestus, 'proud of his work if not of himself'—and his ugliness is surely another marker of his banausic status.)

With the accelerating industrialisation that made Britain 'the workshop of the world', Ruskin began a long lament for the trades recalled in some of our commonest surnames— Mason, Cartwright, Smith, Glover, Cooper, and so on. Karl Marx, in his analysis of capital, observed that the division between manual and intellectual work is itself a great source of degradation, since the former obliterates the human need to reflect on what we are doing. His vocabulary challenged the dehumanised proletariat (initially only an economic term) to understand itself as the true matrix of humanity, and gave work an anthropological, even semi-religious dimension: battle lines were being drawn for future civil war. But class consciousness put the emphasis on the wrong term. The unprecedented conflict that arrived was a war between nations, not against capital. With the industrial-scale slaughter of the First World War, when the machine seemed finally to have triumphed, the word 'craft' lost its stuffing and became a term of mockery—a pastime for harmless eccentrics and incorrigible traditionalist: the Italian futurist Marinetti, who had welcomed war as 'the world's only hygiene' (along with important figures in the anarchist movement such as Bakunin), deplored Ruskin's 'morbid dreams of primitive rustic life'. The electrification of the new Soviet Union in the 1920s was only the most blatant example of the new worship of the machine, and perhaps the last of its more terrible revolutionary manifestations was the purging of Cambodia in the 1970s under the stated Khmer Rouge project of 'taming a man to become a machine'.

Sennett does not believe craftsmanship has disappeared in the twenty-first century. It has found other communities of workers 'who embody some of the elements first celebrated in the (Homeric) Hymn to Hephaestus'. In line with his conviction that the work of the hands informs the work of the mind (a topic brilliantly explored, as he acknowledges, in Raymond Tallis's recent philosophical work, although even the title of the latter's book *The Hand: A Philosophic Inquiry* idealises what for Sennett are most fully *bimanual* activities), he reinterprets how we ought to understand the Enlightenment. *The Encyclopaedia, or Dictionary of Arts and Crafts in thirty-five volumes*, edited by Denis Diderot, son of a master cutler from Langres, sought to show its readers how to *do* things. His illustrious A–Z was not so much one of ideas but of craftsmen at work in the material world: maintaining beehives, preparing hemp, grinding wheat, repairing shoes, or making paper—these were all activities that contributed to the proper functioning of society.

Craftsmanship is focused on getting a thing right. It is an absorbed ethical child's play extended into adult life—*homo laborans* is also *homo ludens*. It is essentially humble, in contrast to many of the key projects of modernity: Sennett dislikes Le Corbusier's hyperrational planification projects of the 1920s but has a soft spot for Frank Gehry's computer-designed Guggenheim Museum in Bilbao, the sleekly clad lines of which surely mark it out as an ostentatious piece of modernist expressivism rather than as a genuine craftwork. The craftsman doesn't create imaginary worlds like the modernist artist in competition with God; he cultivates skills that allow him to *discern* potential meanings already present in the world. This discernment—with its careful attention to details and particulars—can even be seen as intrinsically reactionary insofar as it eases up 'the march of progress', slowing it to a pace at which new techniques can be properly absorbed or adopted. A craftsman will rarely do the same thing twice: each situation requires an accommodating, adapted, intelligent response that depends on correct appraisal of the problem in hand. He knows that failure is always a possibility and, as Ruskin insisted time and again, imaginative freedom cannot be understood unless it makes room for imperfection. Craftsmanship has—as the non-craftsmen like to say—*added value*: 'Learning to work well enables people to govern themselves and so become good citizens.' Pursuing excellence in a craft tradition may actually a specialist's way of being happy—it is what Aristotelians call 'flourishing'.

Indeed, if this is Enlightenment it is the fire being taken from heaven by prior arrangement with a reputable courier service (and one version of the Prometheus myth actually has *him* lifting the fire from Hephaestus' forge.)

\*

Sennett might not be an orthodox Marxist, but he certainly believes that the labour process shapes consciousness. It takes, he tells us, about 10,000 hours of apprenticeship (6–10 years depending on hours given over on a daily basis) to become accomplished at any given skill, a discovery that discountenances the young knight Walther in Wagner's *Meistersinger* opera, which is imbued with the pageantry of guilds and their spiritual role in the medieval city—a notion that was taken up by Walter Gropius in his manifesto for the Bauhaus (1919), the name of the school an update of the word Bauhütte, a medieval German term for a guild of masons and decorators.

If that assumption holds, Sennett has a deep problem with making it explicit how the joy of experiencing a vernacular craft can be converted into a civil polity. The very nature of the activity works against its abstraction, as Michael Oakeshott, who is surprisingly absent from the book, pointed out in his famous essay 'Rationalism in Politics' (1962), in which he makes a cogent distinction between practical and theoretical understanding (or *episteme*). Forms of craftsmanship (medicine, for instance) which have fellow humans as plastic 'material' embrace both, yet the irony is that practical reason is tacit: it can only be grasped through doing. It cannot be abstracted from the occasion of its performance. It creates its own sense of temporality—time needed for the task in hand (a notion completely destroyed by the chronometric band-work of Taylor and Ford). Oakeshott in a footnote to his essay cites an episode in the teachings of the Chinese philosopher Zhuangzi where a wheelwright patiently explains to a duke, who is initially enraged by his impudence, why the instruction he is assiduously seeking in a manual is worthless: 'The right pace [for making a wheel], neither slow nor fast, cannot get into the hand unless it comes from the heart. It is a thing that cannot be put into rules; there is an art in it that I cannot explain to my son. That is why it is impossible for me to let him take over my work, and here I am at seventy still making wheels.' Sennett's example of this mute art is the situation of the seventeenth-century violin-maker Antonio Stradivari, whose two sons, though both quite competent craftsmen, never managed to equal the quality of the instruments their father had produced in the very same workshop with the same resonant spruce wood from the Val di Fiemme, near Venice. Expertise at that level seems to require a special kind of affinity between craftsman and material. It was surely in recognition of the difficulty of transmitting skills that the professional relationship between master and apprentice in the high age of the medieval guilds took precedence over the natural relationship between father and son.

Sennett offers hundreds of similar examples and insights to captivate the reader. His distinction between all-purpose and fit-for-purpose tools is particularly intriguing. He takes as his example the screwdriver, flat-edged *vs.* Phillips-head: the former acts as a stimulus to imagination and can 'without hesitation... be described as sublime—the word sublime standing, as it does in philosophy and the arts, for the potentially strange. In craftwork, that sentiment focuses especially on objects very simple in form that seemingly can do anything.' Ivan Illich, another surprising absentee from Sennett's book, said the same thing in his *Tools for Conviviality* (1973), but observed that our imaginations have been industrially shaped to 'conceive only what can be moulded into an engineered system of social habits that fit the logic of large-scale production': Illich regretted that such simple tools had lost their hold on the imagination.

But I suspect the legions of people with tasks at the management level (a noun that is ironically derived from the Italian verb *maneggiare*: to handle, especially tools, and further back from the Latin word *manus*: the hand) are likely to be deaf to Sennett's explanation of why the present-day workplace— dismissive of guild rules and hardly run on egalitarian principles either—is hostile to craft. As 'knowledge workers', they are not likely even to understand what is wrong with such a trendy phrase. Sennett (who is no Romantic and quotes with evident approval William Carlos Williams' Imagist slogan 'no ideas but in things', a still influential blast against all poetic 'soul talk') puts in a good word for Linux system developers as public craftsmen, but scepticism is called for: how or even where do you draw the line between form and function when describing the gadgets of a digitised high technology (mobile phones, tactile gloves, Home Reality Engines) that are, more and more, living, buzzing bundles of semiotics? Is it still possible to talk of work done for its own sake, i.e. for the ritual service it renders those who perform it, when, for the average technocrat on 'flexitime', what exists as a practice is hardly knowledge at all? As management knows, activities formerly regulated by the hand have now given way to intrusive fingers ('digital' derives from the Latin *digitus* or 'finger').

What ultimately characterises the crafts, or indeed the great professions, Oakeshott suggests—choosing a word that appealed greatly to Nietzsche in his last lucid days—are their *nuances*; tradition is 'pre-eminently fluid'. Its perceived rigidity is all in the rational mind. Sennett dares to contemplate the astounding prospect that the entire political philosophy engendered by the Enlightenment, and which serves as a template (the word is carefully chosen) for every contemporary action, may be founded on a misconception with regard to human knowledge. Our economy's exclusive obsession with productivity and growth suggests he may be on to something. The real danger in an economy obsessed with quantity is not just loss of quality: it is also loss of the ability to distinguish what is good, and therefore worth attending to.

# White Noise Static

*On Ambient Sound Shapes*

'Interior and exterior silence are necessary in order to hear the Word', Pope Benedict told the massed pilgrims in St Peter's Square on 7 March 2012, in the last of his catacheses on the personal prayer of Jesus, specifically on Christ's silence on the cross. He hardly had to point the lesson—'our age does not, in fact, favour reflection and contemplation'. In a civilisation attended by constant noise, the Pope had to tell his audience not be afraid of silence, for when they feel 'a sense of abandonment' in the stillness of a prayer, they should be confident that 'this silence, as happened to Jesus, does not signify absence'.

Of course, it isn't just the divine Word that can't be made out in such Golgotha moments. It can be difficult to hear somebody talking right next to you. Ambient multivocal noise may put your teeth on edge. Sometimes you can't even hear yourself thinking, as the phrase goes. For it is a strange paradox that while we are able to feast uninhibitedly with our eyes, the ability to hear can be stopped by extravagant sound. External noise can even shut out the internal conversations we are having in our heads. 'The shock from a bursting shell will scatter a man's thoughts as the iron fragments will scatter the leaves overhead', an American Civil War soldier once wrote.

Having spent quite a bit of time recently in some of Asia's larger cities, which can be exceedingly noisy (and most of the noise comes from the reverb of hundreds of Honda, Suzuki and Yamaha scooters stealing in between the pick-ups and minibuses and amassing their canned thunder until the lights turn green at the next interchange), I've had occasion—even

behind the double-glazing of air-conditioned hotel rooms—
to meditate on noise. Those are the only places that afford you
the luxury of being able to meditate on noise. But how do you
meditate on something that is out to obliterate you?

When I think back on it, most of my nightmare moments
as a traveller have been associated with noise: I recall a
particularly tense night when, after travelling all day in a
boneshaker of a regional bus through the Cardamom Hills
to reach the city of Madras (now Chennai), I opted to bunk
down in the nearest hotel room: what I didn't realise was that
it was directly above the central bus station for the entire
Tamil Nadu region. I simply hadn't anticipated what might
be happening underneath, starting at 4 a.m. It is reported that
the night-time noise level in present-day Mumbai, a city of
over 20 million (and therefore even larger than Chennai), is 63
decibels, climbing to 78 during the day—and the decibel scale
is a base-ten logarithm, so the relative difference in sound
intensity is far greater than it might seem.

I also recall moments of deep repose elsewhere in those
travels, when a sonic bubble closed over me and it almost
seemed possible to experience the planet turning on its axis:
a year in the Australian outback with my wife and our young
son at the beginning of the 1990s provided not only nightly
displays of the Milky Way in high definition, free of the urban
light smog that makes it impossible to see any detail beyond a
few common constellations in our northern cities, but also the
ripples of quietness of inner Australia. All those Australians
who crowd along the littoral (which is nearly the entire
population) simply don't know what they're missing.

Noise seems so much a product of modernity—the
unwanted, out-of-place, disruptive sounds generated by our
seemingly insatiable need for mobility and communications—
that it's hard to believe ancient civilisations could suffer the
effects of noise intolerance too. The story of the Flood as told in

Genesis is well known, and God's reason for wanting to put an end to humankind. The P version: 'The earth was exceedingly corrupt and filled with violence.' The J version: 'Now when the Lord saw how great the evil of humans was… he was sorry that he had made humans on the earth, and he was pained in his heart.' He vows to wipe them out, and it is in one of those odd and inexplicable moments of divine tender-heartedness that Noah is given the opportunity to build and caulk his zoo-raft. Tablet III of the Atrahasis Epic, a four-thousand-year-old Sumero-Akkadian flood story taken up in the much better known Gilgamesh Epic, offers another explanation for the flood. Enlil ('Wind-Lord'), the elder god of breath, tells the council of the other great gods: 'The noise of humans has become too loud, their constant uproar is keeping me awake.'

There was no distance between Enlil and the plenum: the ambient noise level was all presence. He was suffering from a kind of hyperacusis—the modern discovery that noise and thought are incompatible.

Perhaps the noise that disturbed Enlil was the cellular noise of burgeoning life itself. Everything in the universe gives off noise: it is the random background conversation of atoms. There is even a phenomenon called thermal noise, which is generated by electronic devices. Infrasound is registered by barometric instruments when a volcano explodes, well before we hear the audible explosion. Many other natural phenomena can generate infrasound, such as calving icebergs, lightning and avalanches; and it is thought that through their susceptibility to infrasound animals were able to detect the 2004 Indian Ocean tsunami long before the event became apparent to humans. At the other end of the scale, ultrasound—which we associate with diagnostic techniques and echolocating bats—is also generated by winds of ionised plasma that rise up in the atmosphere with the northern lights. The French surgeon René Leriche once coined a famous phrase about 'the silence of the body', but place a person in an isolation tank—in other words remove all external sound sources—and bodily processes begin to sound alarmingly loud: bowels churn, breath rasps, saliva gurgles, teeth tap, even eyelids flicker perceptibly. Nothing, as the poet Edwin Morgan testified, is not sending messages. A man he admired, the composer John Cage, wrote performance pieces that recruited universal sounds, and made listeners acutely—and sometimes uncomfortably—aware of their origins in silence. 'A sound is the very first movement of the unmoveable', asserted the even more mysterious composer Giacinto Scelsi, 'and this is the beginning of creation.' His ominous sounds create giant cavernous rooms for the imagination, whereas noise is creation's lo-fi stochastic hum. Noise is the 'parasite' that limits the minimum signal level to which a radio receiver can respond: this is why radio telescopes, which scour the expanding universe for the whisper of the stars, have to use low-noise amplifiers cooled by liquid nitrogen. (And we now know that even super-massive black holes emit bubbles of inaudible sound through the galactic clouds around them—at 57 octaves below B flat in the middle of a piano keyboard, to be precise.)

What may really have disquieted the Mesopotamian gods was that humans, if the ancient tablets are anything to go by, had discovered self-consciousness: where once their minds had been quiet, now they were filled with an unceasing inner gossip, or what Meister Eckhart would call 'the storm of inward thought'. Silence is only ever a seeming.

And, frankly, the Akkadian god Enlil hadn't heard anything yet in terms of anthropogenic noise. John Ruskin interrupts Letter 20 of his *Fors Clavigera* to bemoan the shrieking and din of the ships docking close to his hotel in Venice. 'My friends—', he opens his letter, 'You probably thought I had lost my temper and written inconsiderately, when I called the whistling of the Lido steamer "accursed".' He breaks off his letter to go and see whether a large new steamer is coming in from the Adriatic, but it turns out to be 'a little screw steamer... not yet twelve yards long, yet the beating of her screw has been so loud across the lagoon for the last five minutes.' He rhapsodises to a passage in Isaiah, and halts on a parenthesis: 'Steam-whistle interrupts me from the Capo d'Istria, which is lying in front of my window with her black nose pointed at the red nose of another steamer at the next pier.' The roaring and whistling of various ships goes on for some time (and Ruskin too) and is so deafening he thinks it would be impossible to 'make any one hear me speak in this room without an effort'. High-pressure blasts resound across the lagoon—four, five, six, seven, and he stops counting—but not before observing that all these noises go through his head 'like a knife'. All told, Henry David Thoreau had a similar reaction to the locomotive whistle he heard at Walden Pond in 1853. Noise had yet to be recognised as part of that modern syndrome we call *stress*, and it is only very recently that governments and international bodies have recognised that noise might be an environmental health problem and not just a nuisance. Occupational health experts have published many studies that show increased levels or morbidity and mortality in high noise settings, and there is even an organisation (The World Forum for Acoustic Ecology) dedicated to keener awareness of sounds and space. Noise and pain have one thing in common: they shut you in a solipsistic way into your own self, like bad dentistry, and the body turns into a sounding board.

Ruskin would have known that the Great War was evil simply by the fearsome whistling shrieking thundering noise it made, day and night, without a pause. 'You can't communicate noise', Robert Graves told an interviewer in 1971, reminiscing about his experiences in the Battle of the Somme. 'Noise never stopped for one moment—ever.' Robert Musil, writing his long novel *The Man without Qualities* during that war, elected to describe the Vienna of 1913, then one of the great metropolises of the world, in terms of the juggernaut sounds that were transforming it into the support line of the trenches that would soon be dug all over Europe. 'Hundreds of noises wove themselves into a wiry texture of sound with barbs protruding here and there, smart edges running along it and subsiding again, with clear notes splintering off and dissipating.' In that same 1913, Luigi Russolo, a leading Futurist, had written a famous manifesto—*L'Arte dei Rumori*—advocating a new kind of machine-age music in which the actual tones and timbres of the performance would derive from the rhythms and configurations of urban-industrial life: he believed, apparently in all sincerity, that modern humans had evolved a greater capacity for more complex sounds. He wanted a MUSIC OF NOISE.

The first concert of Futurist music took place in April 1914, and incorporated his 'Convegno d'aeroplani e d'automobili' ('Meetings of Airplanes and Automobiles'): it caused a riot. Though Russolo couldn't record anything in those days, noise would go on to find its place in the repertoire. He had discovered that individuals could display their sense of being modern by converting the pain of impersonal aural torture into the fiction of personal power. The electroacoustics of *musique concrète* would follow, along with the performance theories of art-noise practitioners. And modern rock music discovered psychoacoustics, which turned out to be a less cerebral kind of Futurism with lots of feedback. By combining noise with rhythm it is possible to empty bodies into a communal celebration where participants quite happily surrender their individuality to the audio god of integrism.

Robert Musil hadn't heard anything yet either, come to think of it. I was rudely reminded of Enlil's conjuration and Musil's frighteningly spiky sound-shape in a supposedly soundproofed hotel in one of the great Asiatic cities of our contemporary Babel. There was no refuge even with a pillow over my head. The very framework of the hotel seemed to be reverberating, as though I were bunked on a cargo ship. Subterranean echoes conveyed the six categories of sounds as classified by Russolo: 'roars, thunderings, explosions, hissing roars, bangs, booms'. I had let myself in for it though: my head was still ringing from the blare of the basement bar in which I had thought to ease my solitude for a while, with its galactic lighting and voluptuous *shamhats*. Karaoke's decibel heroes, it seemed, had been let loose there and were still torturing me, although I was four storeys above them.

Rhythmic noise, I decided, must be the real god of global exchange: it forces us into a state of total material sympathy, where the thinking self has no choice but to follow the body. And some people are even able to celebrate it by dancing.

Silence is more mysterious. It speaks only if you know how to enter it. Silence is dense. John Cage's celebrated pieces took away the formal structures of music, its emotional contrasts and developments and atmosphere, and asked listeners not to absorb whatever they thought the exterior might be saying, but instead to create their own wide spaces and connections. Ludwig Wittgenstein said he liked the idea of a silent religion. I wonder what he would have made—and John Cage for that matter—of the doings of the American musician and biophonist Bernie Krause, who since 1979 has been archiving sounds from the natural world. More than half of the 4,000 hours of his field recordings are all that remains of the original inhabitants of those abodes, whose silence grows even as our din expands.

# Falling off a Star

*Loving Lou in 1882*

'Tell me what stars we dropped from to meet up here...'

This fall from heavenly bodies (and soft landing) was Friedrich Nietzsche's opening gambit in his attempt to sweep the precocious Louise von Salomé (born in St. Petersburg as Luíza Gustavovna Salomé and known to all as 'Lou') off her feet when he met her in St. Peter's Basilica in Rome in April 1882. 'Von welchen Sternen sind wir uns hier einander zugefallen?' Lou must have startled at such a staged sentence: it teeters on the comic rather than the cosmic. In his fine translation of Nietzsche's letters (*Selected Letters*, 1969), Christopher Middleton draws attention to the 'archly ophidian' phraseology of Nietzsche's letters in the 1870s—noting that it often 'conspires to conceal, rather than reveal, his feeling and thought'. Not just his letters then.

Nietzsche, thirty-seven years old but a sexually inexperienced and even slightly prudish man, to judge by the comments he makes about women in his writings (which otherwise and especially regarding matters of the mind lacked any kind of prudery), had previously made the acquaintance of Lou only through the letters sent him by his independently wealthy younger friend Paul Rée, a philosopher who also had a romantic interest in Lou. 'Give my regards to the Russian lady if that makes sense: I yearn after this kind of soul', he had written to Rée a month before meeting her, expressing his desire to meet a 'intelligent and educated young person' who might even consider marriage, although it would have to concord with what he planned on doing 'in the coming decade'. His influential patron and supporter Malwida von

Meysenbug, who lived in a grand house, the villa Mattei, in the via della Polveria close to the Colosseum, had also written to Nietzsche about Lou, telling him that she was a remarkable girl and an extraordinary creature, 'who seems to have reached in her philosophical thinking the same conclusions as you, namely a practical idealism unconcerned with metaphysical *a priori*...'

Not long before, Nietzsche had used the same exalted astral imagery to talk about friendship, as suggested by entry 279 of *Die fröhliche Wissenschaft*, 'Sternenfreundschaft' [Star friendship], which Lou later thought must have been a reference to Rée—whose naturalistic ideas and aphoristic style of writing he often commended as 'Réealism'—though Nietzsche most likely had in mind his old mentor Richard Wagner. The entry ends on this wish: 'Let us then *believe* in our star friendship even if we should be compelled to be earth enemies'. Creativity was another force he associated with the galactic: art, he wrote, meant giving birth to a dancing star. Heavenly bodies exerted a gravitational pull on each other without leaving their orbits, much as one singularity might inspire another, and perhaps even bask in its glow: although Nietzsche cherished his solitude, his letters show how much he appreciated—and was appreciated in turn—by his friends and correspondents. He was hardly a perfected ego indifferent to the fate of lesser bodies.

In the event, evidently startled by his remark about star-shaped destinies and interstellar travel, the twenty-one-year-old Lou summoned just the right degree of unflappability in front of her distinguished would-be suitor, and pronounced the marvellously bathetic phrase: 'I've just arrived from Zurich'.

What Nietzsche could not have known about Lou—born in Dostoevsky's 'most deliberate city in the world' to parents of Huguenot and German and Danish descent, the only girl after five brothers and apple of her father's eye—was that nearly all the (older) men who had come into contact with her, beginning with her mentor in the city on the Gulf of Finland, Hendrik Gillot, a Dutch pastor who provided her with a solid grounding in theology, literature and modern philosophy (see her novel *Ruth*), and continuing with his friend Rée, had wanted to marry her on first sight: it was to be a lifelong repeating pattern. It was surely this self-possession, especially in the company of men, allied with her cultivated intelligence and rather virile beauty, that made her irresistible. (It was only in her mid-thirties, from 1897 to 1900, that she consented to an *affaire passionnelle*—with the fledgling poet René Maria Rilke, whom she insisted on calling Rainer. In their case the age difference that she had experienced with Nietzsche was almost exactly reversed: Rilke was fifteen years younger than Lou.)

And what Lou could not have known about Fritz was that this was the second time he had implicated a male friend in his dealings with a woman he considered 'of generous enough mind' for him to contemplate marriage. Six years before, Nietzsche had recruited his friend Hugo von Senger to act as a go-between in asking for the hand of Mathilde Trampedach, an attractive twenty-one-year-old he had met in Geneva (letter of 11 April 1876). She turned him down, and eventually married Hugo. This triangular structure of friendship and rivalry can also be seen in his attraction to Wagner's wife Cosima, who had scandalously left her husband, the conductor Hans von Bülow, for the composer. (Her first husband, who remained dedicated to Wagner and his music, conducting the first performance of *Tristan and Isolde* in Munich in 1865, in spite of knowing about his wife's adultery, is reported to have remarked—realising history had cast him as King Marke—that if a woman is compelled to choose between a man and a god, it is entirely understandable when she opts for the latter.)

Late spring and summer of 1882 were to be taken up with Nietzsche's attempts to form a kind of intellectual workers' commune with Lou and Rée, with Vienna or Paris as possible destinations, and waiting impatiently for the first copies of *Die fröhliche Wissenschaft* from his publisher in Chemnitz. They even considered asking Lou's repeatedly outflanked mother, also called Louise, if she would be their chaperone in order to banish gossip in the German expatriate community in Italy about their shacking up together in a '*wilde Ehe*', rumours of which were already doing the rounds after Nietzsche had arranged for that famous 'bondage' photograph, taken in Jules Bonnet's studio in Lucerne, of the two men not very convincingly pulling an open cart while Lou brandishes a whip behind them. When Nietzsche's mother Franziska saw the photograph in September (thanks to his sister) she thought it scandalous, and told her son that he had dishonoured his father's grave ('daß mich meine Mutter eine Schande für das Grab meines Vaters genannt hat', he told his friend Overbeck). In truth, the two philosophical bullocks' relationship with their female flogger was more trinitarian (*heilige Dreieinigkeit*) than *ménage à trois*.

Lou in any case was unenthusiastic about any prospect of marriage, having already turned down Nietzsche's proposal, delivered by Rée, within weeks of their first meeting ('I consider myself obliged to protect you from the general tittle-tattle by offering to marry you…'), and again when they made an ascent of Sacro Monte di Orta in northern Italy. Nietzsche described their joint walk to the top of this medium-sized mountain, a famous devotional ascent, as the most exquisite experience of his life. What they said to each other on the climb is not known, other than that Nietzsche returned believing he had found his first disciple. He wrote to her a few weeks later: 'Back in Orta, I conceived a plan of leading you step by step to the final consequence of my philosophy—*you* are the first person I took to be fit for this.' They had become intimate, at least on the level of ideas. It was rumoured that they had kissed on the mountain, but when Lou wrote about the climb later in life to a friend she could no longer remember whether they had or not.

Whatever the role Nietzsche was dreaming up for 'Frl. L.', his plans were upset in the late summer of that year by the meddling of his sister, Elisabeth ('Lisbeth'), intermittent housekeeper for her brother during the nine years of his Basle professorship; she had decided after meeting Lou in Leipzig and Bayreuth that her brother was about to fall prey to a 'loose' girl—a thing she would never allow. She accused Lou of running down her brother behind his back, of flirting with every man she met, even of sporting 'false breasts': padding to make her slim figure even more desirable. Elisabeth became Lou's deadly enemy, and Nietzsche's loyalties were torn. (Elisabeth was also scandalised and humiliated by the gossip circulating at Bayreuth after the revelation that Wagner had written to Nietzsche's personal doctor, Otto Eiser, to inform him that he thought the cause of her brother's frequent headaches and incapacitation to lie in 'excessive masturbation'.)

Nietzsche never made clear his true feelings about Lou, even to himself, though the line in his letter of 27 June to Lou suggests they ran deep: 'I had to be silent, because I would have keeled over at the mere mention of you.' A few weeks earlier, he had told her in another letter (23 May) that when he was quite alone, he would say her name—'often, very often'— just for the sheer pleasure of hearing it. The two of them did manage to spend three weeks together in August in the village of Tautenberg, in Thuringia, where they went for long walks and had day-long conversations in spite of Elisabeth hovering in the background. Long lists of dicta and precepts have been preserved from their time together: Nietzsche was clearly *tutoring* Lou. One of his aphorisms from this period suggests that he might have been having second thoughts about the three of them living together: 'Bei jedem Gespräch zu dreien ist einer überflüssig und verhindert damit die Tiefe des Gesprächs' ('In every threeway conversation one person is too many and thereby prevents the conversation being a profound one'). Nietzsche was made aware of the fact that his friend Rée was more deeply entangled (if non-sexually) with Lou than he had hitherto supposed: in their letters she was the little snail ('Schneckli') to his shell ('Hüsung'). In fact, Lou kept a diary for Rée all through the summer, in which she remarked that Nietzsche's nature was 'deeply religious' and in its disdain for the transcendental had been thrown back on itself and become 'a heroic force'. 'We shall live to see that he will emerge as the promulgator of a new religion, and then it will be the sort that recruits heroes as its disciples'—an anticipation of *Zarathustra*, which Nietzsche was to start writing the following year and which he claimed would not have been possible without his meeting her—'the most intelligent of all females'. For all the intensity of these conversations, and the closeness of their thinking, she felt that 'in some deep dark corners' of their natures they were worlds apart—and that some of Nietzsche's recesses were very deeply hidden indeed. 'It is strange, lately, the thought went through me with a sudden force, that some day, we could even confront each other as enemies.' She was enacting Nietzsche's own separation of the spheres in 'Sternenfreundschaft'.

By December 1882, the infatuation was over. A letter—never sent but preserved as a draft along with several other scribbles—shows that, at least as the year closed, he bitterly rued his eight-month entanglement with Lou, and used the most belittling terms (some of them his sister's slurs) to slander her. What had happened? A full month before, Lou and Rée, after spending several weeks with him in Leipzig, had abruptly left for Berlin: there they rented an apartment with separate bedrooms and a salon, which soon attracted a host of eminent philosophical figures. Nietzsche felt betrayed when he learned about it later: it was now apparent that his potential disciple and good friend Rée had merely been playing along with his idea of an intellectual trinity while drawing up his own plan for a life under one roof with Lou. Nietzsche took himself off to the Italian resort of Rapallo in some distress: at the end of the year, he was having suicidal thoughts and taking large doses of opium to dull the pain of separation. Yet he wrote to his sister, defending Lou in strong terms against her now several detractors, who numbered not just her but also Ida Overbeck, wife of his closest friend from his Basle days, and his confidante Malwida: 'it was previously impossible for me to visit the Overbecks in Basle because I had not forgiven Frau Overbeck for her sordid and derogatory opinions about a [creature] who I had told her was the only kindred nature that I had come across in my life.'

Nietzsche never saw either of them again. Lou and Rée continued to cohabit chastely in a *mariage blanc* until 1886. The following year, to Rée's puzzlement and distress, Lou married the linguist and central Asian specialist Friedrich Carl Andreas; their marriage would also be celibate and tolerant, but it perdured until Andreas's death in 1930. Lou wrote to Nietzsche to tell him of her engagement but he chose not to reply, informing Malwida von Meysenbug in a postscript to a letter (12 May 1887) that 'one must avoid people like her, who have no reverence'. In 1885, Paul Rée had published his book *Die Entstehung des Gewissens* (The Emergence of Conscience), a theory of morals derived from Darwin's theory of natural selection, with which Nietzsche took issue in his own *Zur Genealogie der Moral* (1887). The same year Rée decided to study medicine, and in 1900, the year Nietzsche died, moved to Celerina in the Upper Engadin—not far from Sils Maria—to provide medical care for its residents. A year later, he fell to his death, aged fifty-one, on the Charnadüra Gorge near St. Moritz. Whether he slipped or took his life has never been established.

It remains nonetheless true that Nietzsche, this great psychologist of human motives *in general* ('out of my writings', he boasts in *Ecce Homo*, 'there speaks a psychologist who has no equal') had little insight into his own personal needs ('a *non-observer* of his own person', surmised Paul Valéry), and ultimately seems to have felt humiliated by his year of loving Lou. 'Consider me, the two of you, as a semilunatic with a sore head who has been totally bewildered by long solitude', is the revealing comment he makes in a letter he *did* send them that December. Nietzsche was unable to decide whether Lou was a real soul-sister ('it is not possible for two people to be more closely related than we are', he had revealed to his friend Overbeck), or a simply an especially cultivated member of the opposite sex best kept at arm's length. But he set 'Lebensgebet' ('Prayer to Life'), a poem she had written as a student in 1880, to an arrangement of his own 'Hymnus auf die Freundschaft' ('Hymn to Friendship'), the only musical composition of his own he later wished to preserve. A line in a letter addressed to his sister Elisabeth in March 1885—after she had told him about her impending marriage (against her brother's wishes) to the anti-Semitic adventurer Bernhard Förster—looks back on his relationship with Lou and Rée: 'When I have been most angry with you, it is because you forced me to relinquish the last human beings with whom I could speak without Tartuffery. Now—I am alone. With them, I was able to speak without a mask about things that interested me. I was completely indifferent to what they thought of me.'

Perhaps not so completely indifferent. An aphorism by the Austrian poet Ilse Aichinger, written (as far as I know) without reference to Nietzsche, seems a perfect foil to the events of 1882. 'Vielleicht erkennen wir einander nur richtig in einem Licht von Abschied.' – Perhaps we recognise each other properly only in a valedictory light.

# A Very Little Ice Age

*Impersonal Violence and Metal Recovery*

In February 2012, with a sub-zero front from the Urals hanging
over Central Europe for two weeks in a row, Strasbourg's
canals froze over, a phenomenon I had observed only once
before in almost twenty years. Instead of a smooth *patinoir*
glaze, the surface of the normally placid Grand Bassin, one of
the arms of Vauban's massive star-shaped defensive structure
guarding the approaches to the city, had been ruffled by the
easterlies even as it froze, and taken on brashly agonal postures.
Ice can be a dramatically sculptural substantiation of its liquid
medium. Over the next few days the jaggedness was reinforced
by the ice-breaking tug which forced its way around the city
in order to ensure at least a few hours' open transit on the
Rhone-to-Rhine canal for the occasional barge—as well as for
the swans, which gathered at night in tight dark pools close to
the bank where the water was warm enough to be still lapping
at the quay. The eerie moonlit stillness of the scene reminded
me strongly of Caspar David Friedrich's compelling paintings.

   One painting in particular; and it is a terrifying depiction
of the primal power of nature. Friedrich's painting *Sea of Ice*
(*Das Eismeer*, 1824), which hangs now in Hamburg, depicts
a shipwreck in the polar ice: you have to look hard to find it
but a ship's stern, with the name HMS *Griber* inscribed upon
it, is just visible in the right midground against a pressure
ridge that has shattered the rest of the hull. It is less an event
than a kind of grudging acknowledgement that one has taken
place: rescue or salvage is not even remotely feasible. This is a
boat being crushed to death. 'To make any thing very terrible,
obscurity seems in general to be necessary. When we know the

full extent of any danger, when we can accustom our eyes to it, a great deal of the apprehension vanishes', wrote Edmund Burke, in his famous 'Philosophical Enquire into the Sublime and Beautiful'. But nature knows no catastrophes. Friedrich's shipwreck resembles a boat only to the same symbolic degree as the stacked pieces of driftwood in Cy Twombly's bronze cast *Winter's Passage: Luxor* (1985) resemble the Egyptian funeral barque that freighted the dead across the Nile to the Temple of Osiris at Abydos: the poet David Shapiro pointedly called Twombly's pieces of museum debris 'toys for broken adults'.

In Friedrich's painting another menacing *stamukha*—the Russian term for these large pile-ups of deformed sea ice has been universally adopted by glaciologists—rears against the horizon. Were it not for the shipwreck, this might well be a study of purely natural phenomena: of the elastic instability of sea-ice rubble fields, which Friedrich would have been able to see whenever the Baltic Sea froze over in the winter. 'The ice was all around: / It cracked and growled, and roared and howled', in the words of Samuel Taylor Coleridge's ancient mariner. It is said that Friedrich had been inspired by reading William Parry's account of his North Pole expedition in 1819, in which his two ships were locked for weeks in Arctic pack ice (but had not been subjected to the disaster of Friedrich's painting). His painting's radical monumentality—as an uncompromising exhibition of the laws of nature—and the unmistakable sense it conveys of a world glacially indifferent to human aspiration, were evidently themes compelling to the artist alone: the painting remained unsold on the death of 'the taciturn man from the North' in 1840. But Friedrich knew something intimate about ice: his younger brother had drowned in a frozen lake in their childhood. When it was first shown in Prague in 1924, the painting bore the prosaic title *An Idealised Scene of an Arctic Sea, with a Wrecked Ship on the Heaped Masses of Ice*. It has also, and more pointedly, been called *The Wreck of Hope*.

Friedrich was a near contemporary of Hegel, and what he wrote about his paintings sometimes sounds as if it had come straight out of *The Phenomenology of Spirit*. 'Art is infinite, but the knowledge and skill of all artists are finite.' To get close to the divine, the artist has to expand his consciousness, to become 'profound'. In the year Hegel died, 1831, Friedrich's friend Carl Gustav Carus, a medical man, friend of Goethe and art theorist whose speculations on an individual-transcending collective unconscious were to have a marked influence on the theories of Carl Gustav Jung, published *Nine Letters on Landscape Painters*, in which he suggested that for Friedrich 'painting was a kind of divine calling'. Landscape was a luminous expression of the divine; and the same divine essence was present in the artist's soul. The symbols in that landscape seem to be a natural part of it; not least boats, the ultimate symbol of life as a journey. Windows represent the life beyond; bare trees our actual spiritual life; only in the mountains is the true fatherland.

In fact, Friedrich's painting of a shipwreck among the suspended agitation of the ice floes signals the moment when a German artist provided a pictorial representation that subverted Kant's notion of the 'mathematical' sublime—think of Etienne-Louis Boullée's architectural projects in the 1780s for museums and libraries, where the imagination strains to accept what reason insists will march into the infinite—with the dynamic sublime: the apprehension of the raw power of nature. It is a negative moment, a space between concert and conflict, between two ways of experiencing the world, one which finds satisfaction in formal order and another which admires the dynamics of unstoppable process—half-crystal, half-monster. 'In that which we are accustomed to call sublime in nature there is so little that leads to particular objective principles and forms of nature corresponding to these that it is mostly rather in its chaos or in its wildest and most unruly disorder and devastation, if only it allows a glimpse of magnitude and might, that it excites the ideas of the sublime' (*Critique of Judgement*).

The painting's hallucinated scene of piled-up shards and ice floes buckling and jutting into the sky over a flat travertine expanse of pack ice could, it strikes me, be an allegory of German sentence structure: the impacted strata of subordinate clauses, regular inflections, prepositions on a mission, genitive attributes and dangling prefixes—the whole thing marooned in a landscape formed by late Proto-Indo-European gender shifts. German always sounds to me like something archaic being tensed in the press of history. One of the masters of its violent tension was the enigmatic writer Heinrich von Kleist; and it is altogether appropriate that he, as editor of the cultural broadsheet *Berliner Abendblätter*, and another Prussian patriot in those giddy Napoleonic times, should have alerted the German public in the twelfth folio of his paper (13 October 1810), to Friedrich's painting *Monk by the Sea* (*Der Mönch am Meer*): Kleist thought that the radical sense of monotony and boundlessness of the painting which was cut off only by the picture frame made the viewer feel 'as if [his] eyelids had been cut off'. Kleist could think of nothing better than sitting alone at the edge of the sea under an overcast sky, looking out over the endless expanse of water. 'It is essential that one has come there just for this reason, and that one has to return.' Friedrich is the artist who comes closest to Kleist in the shapes of his creation. Some of his politically symbolic landscapes were even inspired by his reading of Kleist's ferociously patriotic drama *Die Hermannsschlacht*, which he told friends had moved him greatly.

A pendant to Friedrich's ice-sea painting is Paul Nash's oil *Totes Meer* (displayed like Twombly's sculpture in the Tate Gallery), which the artist worked on for months in 1940. Nash has the curious distinction of being one of the few artists of real note to cover both world wars, having been sent to Ypres twice in 1917—a similarly lunar landscape is evident in his *Caterpillar Crater*, 1918. His homage-pastiche depicts an eerie gun-metal grey moonlit scene of wrecked German aircraft dumped in a clearing, and is an obvious echo of Friedrich's seascape. What the German painter had depicted as the awesomeness of Nature as it crushed a solitary human construct has become an unstable frozen sea of human-built debris gashing the entire forefront of Nash's painting—'all lunar mashed metallic celery' as the poet Jamie McKendrick described it. Nash's painting was based on his discovery of over a hundred acres of former grazing land near the Morris car factory in Cowley, Oxfordshire, which the War Office had turned into what it called the Metal and Produce Recovery Unit: these wrecks were to be recycled for their alloys. Nash liked airplanes—he called them 'beautiful monsters' and 'killer whales'—and was notorious for pestering the War Office for documentary material; the spectacle of hundreds of torn and battered Heinkels and Messerschmidts heaped on top of each other over such a vast tract of land must have exerted a powerful tow on his imagination. By implication, his 'dead sea' holds all the anfractuous carcases of Romantic aspiration—British visionary along with German transcendental—in a composition of utter desolation. Nash described the scene thus: 'The thing (the salvage dump) looked to me, suddenly, like a great inundating sea… the breakers rearing up and crashing on the plain. And then, no: nothing moves, it is not water or even ice, it is something static and dead.' Destruction is enormously simple. Especially when an artist with a coolly British sense of scepticism turns to one of the precursors of the Romantic movement—whose countrymen were at that moment trying to bomb his island-nation into submission—and makes an inventory of a stack of ruined shards. In reality, it must be presumed that the wrecks of many British planes were mingled with the German ones: Nash has pointedly chosen to keep them out of his painting.

Friedrich searched for sublimity in landscape, or at least sought to allow landscape to speak of God. The problem is that God seems to have withdrawn from the Creation, for Friedrich backlights his paintings in such a way as to suggest that the figures standing motionless in them are perpetually homesick for something beyond the vanishing point—a lost land. And most of his paintings seem to be an invitation to the person looking at them to take up position, at a second remove, behind his beholders: *Woman at the Window* (1822) is a painting of his wife looking out from an interior space through a half-opened window on to a river—for all we know it could be one of the rivers of the underworld. We are allowed to see her back and pleated skirt; that is all—a *Rückenfigur*. This was to be a constant of Romantic era painting, as Friedrich's famous *Wanderer above a Sea of Fog* shows, right up until Vilhelm Hammershøi's 1902 *Interior (with young woman seen from behind)*. If the face of God is habitually never revealed, it would seem the faces of ordinary humans are not to be seen either, including surrogates for the artist himself, and may only be inferred. Friedrich's black silhouettes, including those of his capuchin monks, seem to have lost any firm sense of what it means to be embodied in the flesh.

That is why there is something troubling about this painting of the ice sea. It attracts me, even though I find its sublimity sinister. Nobody understood the stilled chaos of Friedrich's painting enough in his own time to appreciate it fully; or perhaps at some level everybody understood its violence all too well and wished to turn away from its implications. The twentieth century that some experienced as 'the dark age of the sublime' (the expression comes from the Dutch architect Lars Spuybroek) had its origins in Romanticism. The modern appreciation of the sublime has something of the blitzkrieg about it, as Longinus anticipated with his description of it 'flashing forth at the right moment and scattering everything before it like a thunderbolt'. But there is something missing in this scene of cosmic violence, as there is something missing in Friedrich's *Sea of Ice*: the growling and roaring of the fractured ice. Coleridge, visiting Germany in 1799, put his finger on the missing element: 'there are sounds more sublime than any sight *can* be, more absolutely suspending the power of comparison, and more utterly absorbing the mind's self-consciousness, in its total attention to the object working upon it'.

It may be that Friedrich himself, who never abandoned his calling as an artist, didn't understand its symbolism entirely either; and that the painting had to wait for its parodic reinstatement in the hands of Paul Nash. Only then could its meaning become wholly manifest. Art, I tell myself again, is a strange kind of disaster archaeology.

# III

# Mundanities

# Making Things Clearer

*Word, Image, Pictogram*

> *To suppose that clarity proves anything*
> *about truth is perfect childishness*
> Nietzsche, *Will to Power,* 538

A clear view of things, that was what counted. When René Descartes asserted as a general rule of his *Discourse on the Method* (1637) that 'the things we conceive very clearly and very distinctly are all true' he was proclaiming one of the articles of the coming rational faith. Not only that, he was boosting sight as a metonym for thinking itself. He was not alone. Twenty years before, Galileo's *The Starry Messenger* (1610), a book that had revealed for the first time details of craters on the moon, four of Jupiter's satellites and many new stars, also provided a statement of intent: in the future, speculative theories about the universe would have to be tested against the evidence of the eyes—by empirical observation. Almost one-third of Galileo's book comprises images and diagrams integrated within the text. The modern era was going to be a flat one: of maps and grids and networks. Its workings—at least—would be obvious. Clarity also girded the three principles of pragmatism, as outlined by the American polymath Charles S. Peirce in his famous *Popular Science Monthly* paper, 'How to Make Our Ideas Clear' (1878). Peirce was even more forthright than Descartes: 'A clear idea is defined as one which is so apprehended that it will be recognized wherever it is met with, and so that no other will be mistaken for it. If it fails of this clearness, it is said to be obscure.'

Between the wars, there was great interest in the issue of clarity, not least since it was generally felt that for want of perspicacity about motives Europe's nations had 'glided, or rather staggered or stumbled' (Lloyd George) into the disaster of 1914–18. The famous Bauhaus institute in Weimar was set up to bring sobriety to pre-war ornamentalism. Sans serif typefaces, including Helvetica and Arial, were championed by the modernists because of their clear, unfussy lines. Ludwig Wittgenstein felt a major source of our inability to understand situations was that 'we do not *command a clear view* of the use of words'. For Wittgenstein, the cause of our lack of understanding was grammar itself; and the latter part of his career was an ambitious attempt to correct its parallax effects. The Vienna Circle, with which he was tangentially involved, was on the whole less glum: one of its members Otto Neurath (1892–1945), had the distinction of being the Secretary of the Austrian Association for Housing and Allotments as well as the driving force behind Isotype—a graphic language for displaying quantitative information using easily comprehensible icons. Since quantitative information meant, to a large extent, economic and political facts and correlations, it may come as no surprise at all that Neurath was obliged to leave Austria. He died as an exile in Oxford, in 1945, but not before founding the Isotype Institute, which carries on his work. Much of the effort to standardise the visual display of statistical information in serious newspapers and journals, to produce universal pictograms for display in airports and public places across the globe and even to produce a standard signage for the British motorway system, can be traced back to the impetus of Isotype.

On the other side of the Atlantic, probably the most charismatic and certainly most visible proponent of clarity in the contemporary field of information design is Edward R. Tufte. Born in the war years, Tufte taught at Princeton University's Woodrow Wilson School in the 1970s as a political scientist, which resulted in a densely technical publication, *Data Analysis for Politics and Policy* (1974), downloadable from his site. The following year, he was asked to prepare a statistics course for a party of visiting journalists. He found the existing literature paltry and 'grimly devoted to explaining the use of the ruling pen'. The materials he designed for this course, with the participation of the celebrated statistician John Tukey, became the drafts of his first book *The Visual Display of Quantitative Information* (1982). It appeared after he had moved to a new post as professor of political science, computer science and statistics at Yale University. Unable to find a publisher willing or even able to produce the book to his specifications, Tufte took the bold step of mortgaging his house and moving into self-publishing: the book as a physical object—*his* book—was going to reflect the intellectual principles governing its conception.

That was the beginning of the Graphics Press, with only one author on its list. It was a classic garage start-up operation but, as anyone who has handled one of Tufte's books will realise, his books meet exactingly high design production standards. They are beautiful objects. With the help of a professional book designer Tufte was able to integrate graphics into the text: it was less of a revolutionary move than it might seem, but startling enough at the time to ensure a wide readership for his titles. Tufte has a keenly ironic sense of how early texts such as Galileo's had far fewer qualms about placing word and image together than those of Victorian historians, whose snobbery about the prestige of the Word lasted long into the twentieth century. The following books—*Envisioning Information* (1990), *Visual Explanations* (1997) and *Beautiful Evidence* (2006)—were all successful, and made Tufte that unlikely thing: a star of the information age. He has even been called 'the Leonardo da Vinci of data'. At his own count, almost 2 million copies of his books are in print, which must make Tufte one of the most successful self-publishers ever.

A decade after leaving Yale his fame has also been swelled by the popular one-day seminar 'Presenting Data and Information', delivered to large audiences since 1993: those who attend his 'gig' describe it as the closest scientific presentation gets to revival preaching. At $380 a time it has also made him a rich man. Tuftisms are now to be found in such august organs of the press as the New York Times and Wall Street Journal, although Tufte's notions of what constitutes a good chart or graph began to influence the way they displayed information decades ago. In recent years, he has even been called up by policymakers to get a grip on the deluge of data flowing out of government departments as they attempt to set up websites providing graphic testimony of their activities. He is quoted by engineers, financial analysts, software constructors and design students alike.

If he is the secret king of information design, it is largely because he stamped his name on what he prefers to call 'analytical design'. It is not—*pace* some of his American admirers—anything like a new intellectual domain: it is part of the cognitive science groundswell that spilled out of the famous post-war Macy Conferences. These conferences also provided early computer science and cybernetics with their theoretical underpinning: evidence-based medicine is a later product of the same style of thought. Tufte is a true child of the information age and its idolatry of the factual. His interest in the 'fit' between seeing and thinking, and his conviction that design architecture should assist analytical thinking about evidence, show that his own thinking still bears the traces of his early training. Undaunted by the increasing scale of the digital universe—it has been estimated that the data size of the Internet is about 500 exabytes ($500.10^{18}$ bytes), with a monthly traffic of at least one-tenth that figure—Tufte became one of the first persons to understand that there was common ground between designers making graphics for mass consumption and scientists who want to convey their findings through imagery.

Why bother so much about visual presentation? Tufte's zealotry is surely related to the fact that only in science does the term 'model' reverse the sense given to it in normal speech. A model is a thing (usually person) worthy of imitation. In science, however it is the model that sets the predictive pattern. The hierarchy of relations is reversed. The model—often mathematical, sometimes graphic (think of Feynman diagrams in quantum physics), perhaps even a scaled reproduction—is an idealisation providing a synoptic view of relations within a system, parts of which can be replaced with other elements. Starting out as an abstraction of the phenomenal reality of nature, the scientific model is now the matrix of functional relations against which nature is tested. The model is— ambiguously—the product of what it originates. Kenneth Clark expressed the thought elegantly: 'It is often said that Leonardo drew so well because he knew about things; it is truer to say that he knew about things because he drew so well.' (Only in respect of that understanding does Tufte merit the hyperbolic epithet 'the Leonardo da Vinci of data'.)

Tufte has always advocated parsimony in design, and some of his terms ('Tuftisms') are characteristic of his confident style. 'Chart junk' is his Bauhaus-inspired term of derision for elaborate design schemes that obfuscate, one incriminating factor commonly being a poor 'data-ink ratio', where the graphical detail is out of proportion to the amount of information being conveyed. Data visualisation is not necessarily an aid to knowledge: it can as readily obscure or disrupt what is already known. If the thinking task is to understand causality, then the design task is—as Wittgenstein might have said—to *show* causality. A comparative chart calls for a different display set; multivariate analysis yet another. Like

Noam Chomsky, whose theory of language posits a universal grammar with a fixed innate principle behind all languages, Tufte believes in the universality of certain cognitive tasks: he calls them 'forever knowledge'. The underlying principles are universal, 'like mathematics, the laws of Nature, the deep structure of language—and are not tied to any language, culture, style, century, gender, or technology of information display'. Accordingly, he takes pleasure in making his books feel deliberately old-fashioned, with their attention to quality and style: he even feels himself that they have something 'Japanese' about them.

This belief in the truth of perfect communication may have its Utopian aspects, Utopia being the future place that has long shimmered at the edge of the Enlightenment project; it makes Tufte a fierce opponent of moral and intellectual relativism. In *Beautiful Evidence* he embarked on a full-out campaign against PowerPoint: 'I thought that too many PP presentations were… about power and marketing'. The cognitive style of PP is corrupt, he believes; it 'turns information into a sales pitch'. It is 'fiction'—not a word of praise in Tufte's vocabulary. Tufte even suggested that PowerPoint was a 'co-conspirator' in the space shuttle disaster in 2003 when Columbia burned up as it re-entered the earth's atmosphere. Following his analysis of NASA's slides, he concluded that its presentation style prevented engineers from entering results in scientific notation, and that its information density was anyway too low to stimulate effective thought. At fault was 'the PP design style, which uses about 40% to 60% of the space available on a slide to show unique content, with remaining space devoted to Phluff, bullets, frames, and branding'. His thirty-page counterblast 'The Cognitive Style of PowerPoint'—a good place to encounter his work—is now available as a stand-alone offprint. He is not the only person to regard the widespread use of PP in American primary schools (not to mention across the board in corporate and government meetings) as another, somewhat more slowly evolving disaster. Tufte is still a paper enthusiast.

The virtue of a good graphical display is that it allows the viewer to see trends, patterns or other structures that might otherwise have passed unperceived. We all might have information at our fingertips, but we are also surrounded by 'non-information', the unceasing digital doings of what the first professor of sociology at Harvard dubbed, none too approvingly, 'quantiphrenia'. The signal-to-noise ratio of our culture has, if anything, tended to boost the noise quotient. Tufte is not dismayed. 'There is no such thing as information overload', he likes to say when he begins his courses, 'only bad design.' His own contribution to sorting out the wheat from the chaff is sparklines, which he introduced in *Beautiful Evidence*: they are 'data words'—small, high-content, simple graphics that allow the reader to follow movement of a parameter over time, with additional contextualisation being provided by a band indicating normal range. A stack of sparklines allows several different variables to be visualised, as well as rapid comparison of their possible significance. They can be inserted in the line, being scaled to the same font size. Interspersed words and images are a new feature of digitalization: in the old analogue texts, pictures and illustrations came at a premium. Sparklines appear in the sports section of the New York Times and on the Financial Times shares pages. And yet, perhaps the most elementary, slightly paradoxical message to emerge from Tufte's mission is that computer technology and other modern 'enhancements' have little to do at a fundamental level with the development of ideas; their flashiness can sometimes inhibit thought.

The annotated map of the dwindling of the military forces assembled by Napoleon for his fateful 1812 march on Russia, prepared by the French engineer Charles Joseph Minard in

1869, has been reproduced and commented upon so often in Tufte's writings that it now seems to crop up in every discussion of his work. Tufte claims Minard's presentation is one of the finest statistical graphics ever made, and one that exemplifies all the fundamental principles of good analytical design. He describes this one-page narrative as 'War and Peace as told by a visual Tolstoy'.

Minard's map is certainly an immediately comprehensible document of slaughter and suffering: it shows the successive losses of the *Grande Armée* in Napoleon's Russia campaign of 1812, with a broad tan flowline indicating the size of the army as it crossed into Russia in June, as well as the approximate geographical route taken to the capital. Of the original 422,000 troops, only 100,000 reached Moscow in September, which the Russians had deserted and stripped of supplies. After the largely wooden city went up in flames, the retreat back to Poland in October is shown as a dwindling black band. Following the desperate passage of the frozen Berezina when 22,000 men died in two days, Napoleon's army numbered a paltry 10,000 when it reached the Nieman river—where the campaign had started—in December. Tufte greatly overstates the interpretative power of what is, it must be admitted, a beautiful piece of draughtsmanship in which several variables are presented in a common visual field. The plummeting Réaumur temperature line along the bottom of the map is perhaps too tendentious, since it suggests Minard subscribed to the view that the *only* explanation for his terrible losses was the excuse advanced by Napoleon himself: the arrival of 'General Winter'. The icy weather certainly dwindled his lines, but it was far from being the only cause for the tattered numbers of soldiers: starvation, desertion, typhus (especially) and suicide all played a role in events too. Dominic Lieven's *Russia against Napoleon* makes it clear that the Russian tactic of avoiding pitched battles and harrying the enemy was highly effective over the several months of the campaign. Very few foot soldiers, it is safe to presume, returned from Russia: these were times of upheaval, as Stendhal told his sister in a letter out of Königsberg after having been part of the retreat himself, 'when a horse meant life or death'.

For all his old-fangled enthusiasm for the virtues of paper, Tufte describes his own driving ambition as a desire to escape 'Flatland', the present hypersurface (computer screen for most people) that we are condemned to inhabit insofar as we depend on technological means to represent the three-dimensional world around us. About the time he began working on *Beautiful Evidence*, Tufte took up sculpture. Oversized installations made out of porcelain and steel, or even scrap metal, his works loom over the landscape of Cheshire, Connecticut, in the torqued manner of Richard Serra: the search for fundamental relations goes deep in Tufte's imagination. Not only is 'Flatland' the title of a popular satirical fable by the Victorian writer E.A. Abbott, it is also the term Thomas Mann reserved for the familiar mundane world from which his hero Hans Castorp is transported to the pure introverted air of the mountain sanatorium in his novel *The Magic Mountain*. That kind of rarefied space-time indulgence is presumably not what Edward Tufte is after, although a note of self-satisfaction creeps into the later books.

After all, it is only because we are compelled to live in the exotically alien country of Flatland, with its radical flattening and levelling, that we need specialised geometers like Tufte to tell us what is real and what is only apparent. Balancing purity of expression and the demands of reality, getting them to 'fit' has always been a difficult task. Tufte's writings breathe the whole aerodynamic atmosphere of modern technology— his books could only have been possible in the marketplace of ideas that characterised the late twentieth century. 'Where is the Wisdom we have lost in Knowledge? / Where is the

Knowledge we have lost in Information?' intones the chorus in T.S. Eliot's *The Rock*. Tufte hovers between those latter two levels, but says nothing about the first. I wouldn't want to impugn his belief in universals, but it does seem as if Tufte overdoes the timelessness. Information design has a history too.

# Person in Question

*Around Lisbon with Fernando Pessoa*

As Fernando Pessoa would tell you: there is no better time to visit Lisbon—'luminous Lisbon'—than winter, when the sun is slant, the light weak and diffuse, the streets mostly empty, and the rain gusting in from the Atlantic Ocean sleeks the pavements with a fine skein of rain that turns them mother-of-pearl. Visitors who favour leather-soled shoes have to be careful when they walk the seven hills of Lisbon though. Many of Lisbon's roads are still paved, and many of its sidewalks too, with slick and shiny granite cobbles. You have to be especially careful if you're carrying one of Pessoa's books in your hand.

Not only did I have one of his books in my left hand, the all too appropriately named *The Book of Disquiet*; I was ill-advisedly trying to open a pop-out map of the city of Lisbon with my right. All I had to do was flick my wrist, and all of Lisbon would open out before me, in a kind of historical reconstitution thanks to the magic of origami; or so I thought.

Obviously I was rather eager to observe the universe at a slight angle to it, like Pessoa himself...

\*

Lisbon's air is 'a hidden yellow, a kind of pale yellow seen through dirty white. There is scarcely any yellow in the grey air. But the paleness of the grey has a yellow in its sadness', according to Bernardo Soares, putative author of *The Book of Disquiet*.

Bernardo Soares was Pessoa's alter ego, an assistant book-keeper who lived in a rented room and worked for a textile trading firm in the same street, Rua dos Douradores, one of the drabber streets in the bustling commercial district of Baixa—'I know: if I raise my eyes, I'll be confronted by the sordid row of buildings opposite, the grimy windows of all the downtown offices, the pointless windows of the upper floors where people still live, and the eternal laundry hanging in the sun between the gables at the top, among flower-pots and plants.' Not much happens in Rua dos Douradores except for the occasional sound of someone practising scales, squalling arguments between family members and the endless meteorological rearrangements overhead. That was how Soares liked it.

The description of Soares (whose contribution to *The Book of Disquiet* eventually superseded that of a gauche 'office worker', also of Pessoan acquaintance, called Vicente Guedes), and the circumstances of his life, as laid out in the preface to *The Book of Disquiet*, sound very similar to those of Pessoa himself, who often ate lunch in a café on the street. That is why Pessoa—famous now for taking his commitment to multiple perspectives to the point where to be 'Fernando Pessoa' was also to be (and to be astonished by) the other poets within him—insisted that Soares was 'solely a mutilation of [his personality]'. Soares' life looked too much like his own as a writer and translator of business correspondence (for the agent and importing firm Casa Serras in 1934–35) in the Rua Augusta, which runs parallel to the Rua dos Douradores, for him to qualify fully as a *heteronym*, the term Pessoa invented to describe his fictive personalities. 'I grew soon to have no personality at all except an expressive one', he wrote, describing a kind of revelation he had in March 1914. 'I grew to be a mere apt machine for the expression of moods which became so intense that they grew into personalities and made my very soul the mere shell of their casual appearance.' He had found his voices even as they unmade him.

There were three principal heteronyms. Alberto Caeiro, a tranquil shepherd who wrote simple pagan poems full of nature mysticism (and the one the others acknowledged as the 'master'); Ricardo Reis, a strictly rhyming classicist with Horatian poise and manners; and Álvaro de Campos, an exuberant, hyperbolic, squabbling modernist in thrall to movement, loudness and sensation: it was he who advanced the doctrine of multiple personality that governed their relations. The three members of this 'non-existent coterie' even compelled their first reader, the medium called Pessoa, to discover how the old notion of a single, self-possessed authorial presence ('know thyself', as the oracle at Delphi instructed) might actually be an impediment to a life of writing. Bootstrapped from the *ex nihilo* paradox of creativity itself, these three personages were secure enough in their literary identities and opinions to argue with Fernando Pessoa. So much do they argue that when the semi-heteronym, Soares, chips in with a comment about his being the living stage 'where various actors act out various plays', it may well seem that the observation properly belongs to the pen of the principal player, Fernando Pessoa—whose surname is cognate with the Latin word *persona*. (Long before them, the eighteenth-century Scottish philosopher David Hume, in comparing the self to a form of theatre, had already denied the likelihood of there being only one authoritative player on stage at any time.)

The forthright and even rather overbearing Álvaro de Campos—who had purportedly studied naval engineering in Glasgow, travelled the world and wore a monocle—even intervened on the occasion of Pessoa's only known romantic liaison, with a secretary called Ofélia Queiroz (note the given name) in the employment of one of his clients, telling her in a letter to abandon any idea of marriage with her 'Fernandinho'. Even then, Pessoa (the *orthonym* Fernando Pessoa, to be technical about it) was capable of writing wildly different poems under his own name, publishing avant-garde works in the famous literary publication 'Orpheu' while reserving his more reactionary outpourings for a monarchist periodical. It is almost as if he expected his readers to be cognitively dissonant too.

When he died the day after checking into the Hospital de São Luis dos Franceses, the French hospital, in November 1935, of fulminant liver disease brought on by heavy drinking, most of the 523 fragments of what became *The Book of Disquiet* were found in an envelope marked 'L. do D.' (*Livro do Desassossego*) among the 27,543 documents (number still growing) that constitute Pessoa's considerable oeuvre. 'The saddest book in Portugal', as Pessoa called it, had no design, and it is unlikely Pessoa himself could ever have given it a definitive shape.

Compiled by a team of editors and published in 1982, *The Book of Disquiet* is now Pessoa's most frequently read volume. It is by no means all as slack or lugubrious as he suggested: some entries are droll and self-mocking. In view of Pessoa's lifetime obsession with astrology and the occult, it is amusing to read Soares complaining (like a true aesthete) about the stylistic shortcomings of the mystic masters: '[They] all write abominably. It offends my intelligence that a man can master the Devil without being able to master the Portuguese language.' And he doesn't provide excuses for the holier kind of mystic either. 'To have touched the feet of Christ is no excuse for mistakes in punctuation.'

Forestalling the phenomenon that has been prematurely called, since the 1960s, 'the death of the author', Soares's philosophical musings could even be regarded as a spoof on the entire genre of wisdom literature. 'Travel?' he writes. 'One need only exist to travel.'

*The Book of Disquiet* could even be said to be a self-help book in which the writer starts from the premise of having no very fixed self.

*

Pessoa himself had much stronger feelings for his native city than Soares, who rarely ventured even as far as the marina and port area of Cais dos Colunas. He even admitted to *The Book of Disquiet*: 'I have no social or political sentiments, and yet there is a way in which I'm highly nationalistic. My nation is the Portuguese language.' Yet Pessoa himself insisted, in a memorable phrase, 'To be Portuguese is to be European without the discourtesy of nationalism.'

Born in Lisbon in 1888, Pessoa lost his father at age five and was taken to colonial Natal (South Africa) when his mother married again, this time to the Portuguese consul in Durban. When he returned to Lisbon at the age of majority it was to settle there, and he never left the city again except to make a couple of trips to provincial towns. And while many modernist writers have had a strong link with a particular city—think of Joyce and Dublin, Kafka and Prague, Svevo and Trieste, Musil and Vienna—Pessoa did for Lisbon something that few other leading writers have done for their home cities. He wrote a tourist guide to the city that his own poems have since helped to remake in their image. Was this part of the 'infinite sightseeing cruise' Soares mentions somewhere in *The Book of Disquiet*? Or was it a commissioned work—given that Pessoa wrote it in English—from one of the commercial firms that employed him, for the use of foreign visitors to the city on the Tagus?

His guide is particular noteworthy in view of the generally critical relationship that modernism has had with 'tourism' as an economic and cultural activity, in which it is invariably and unfavourably contrasted with travelling—although it is probably true that in the eyes of indigenous people *all* visitors look like tourists. Pessoa certainly had no interest in leaving his native city once he had rediscovered it in his late teens. The city of Lisbon has all the specificity his own life lacks.

*What the Tourist Should See* is a bare eighty pages, and like nearly everything he wrote was retrieved from a manuscript found after his death. It imagines a voyager approaching the city from the sea, already smitten by the sight of the red roofs of Alfama and Mouraria and the dominating citadel of São Jorge, and only too eager to get through customs and on to the major sights.

This, of course, is Portuguese history in reverse, as I observed when I took the train from the Cais do Sodré train station, where Pessoa handled correspondence for a firm called Toscano & Cruz in 1920, past the famous squat castellated limestone Belém Tower—which marks the ancient northern district of the city from which Vasco da Gama set out for India in 1497 and Pedro Álvares Cabral for Brazil in 1499—to Cascais, the upmarket resort at the northern tip of the Bay of Lisbon. Nearly all the passengers on the train sat on the left: they wanted to look out to sea, to admire the yachts sailing on the Tagus, and measure their progress along the coast by the Bugio lighthouse that stands between Lisbon and the abyss. This was where they could commune with 'the ancient Portuguese speech of the sea', as Pessoa put it in one of his poems.

Pessoa's guide to Lisbon is therefore really a museum guide, since this splendid city on seven hills, 'which rises like a fair vision in a dream' (as he puts it in his decorous English) has always had mythical pretensions. As one of the oldest European cities it was formerly called Olissipo, in homage to Ulysses (Editora Olisipo was the name of a short-lived publishing house run by Pessoa between 1921 and 1923 in the Rua da Assunção, which among other titles published a couple of volumes of his not very convincing poems in English). Nowadays Lisbon cannot separate itself from its revenants. Every square seems to boast massive, muscular effigies of kings and explorers whose very bulk delivers a verdict on the mediocrity of the present. What convinced this city's inhabitants five centuries ago that reality doesn't flatten out at the horizon? How did a seafaring kingdom that once commanded half the world owing to its knowledge of the Atlantic gyre and the *volta do mar* ('turn of the sea')—from Brazil in the west to entire countries on both coasts of Africa as well as scattered entrepôts in Asia—retreat to this recess on the edge of Europe where the loudest debate on the quays is the price of cod?

The vast space of the Praça do Comércio, for instance, is crowned by the mounted effigy of King José I, his charger busily crushing snakes. This square, and nearly all the districts of the city close to the river, were rebuilt by his prime minister, the Marquês de Pombal, after the devastating earthquake and following tsunami of 1 November 1755, a catastrophe that swept away the seafront as well as the old doctrine of metaphysical optimism. The marquis has his own statue at the top of the imposing Avenida da Liberdade. Camões, the great epic poet of *The Lusiads*, Portugal's own *Aeneid*, stands on another baroque pedestal in the Chiado surrounded by less illustrious bards. Even Pessoa has been copperplated and placed in effigy outside the famous coffeehouse *A Brasileira* in the Rua Garrett, his left leg jauntily resting on his right. Tourists can't resist being photographed sitting next to him.

It is difficult to imagine a more inappropriate memorial to Pessoa, whose likeness in one of the few photographs of him shows a man reduced to the bare semiotics of gabardine, bowtie, specs and tache striding along the street. The artist Júlio Comar caught this visual-kit image of the poet too, in a sketch preserved in the Calouste Gulbenkian museum. This is what Tintin might have looked like, if he had progressed from being a boy-reporter to the cosmic disillusion of middle age. Álvaro de Campos, his loud-mouthed heteronym, even blurted it out on one occasion, 'Fernando Pessoa, strictly speaking, doesn't exist.'

\*

My Pessoa moment in Lisbon occurred in the famous *eléctrico* 28, one of the ramshackle but appealing narrow-gauge vintage trams manufactured between 1936 and 1947 that still serve the narrow streets of the city's hills. I got on at the Rua da Conceição stop, and found a seat at the back (seats for only twenty persons, standing room for almost twice that number) as it trundled around the Chiado and slid down the Rua da Loreto in the direction of the Estrela park. The driver had to get out once to readjust the pantograph, which had become dislodged on one of the sharp bends ascending the Chiado, stepping smartly out of his cab with a long pole in his hand. But we didn't get very far. A funeral was being held in the Santa Catarina church, with a hearse parked outside the steps to bring in the coffin. The tram had no option but to wait behind it as the bells pealed down the narrow street. Bowing to the inevitable in what appeared to be another fairly common occurrence, the driver got out of the cab again, this time to have a smoke. Half an hour later, with several other trams piled up behind us, we were able to continue the journey to Pessoa's last home.

This was the tram to Prazeres, in the neighbourhood of the cemetery in which Pessoa was interred on 2 December 1935, when it rained and rained. He lived in this district for the last fifteen years of his life, and the apartment he leased at 16, Rua Coelho da Rocha where his mother and other members of the family lived at various times has been transformed into a museum, Casa Fernando Pessoa: it holds his personal library, his bed, his personal astrological chart cast in marble on the floor and some of his school reports from his British colonial education in South Africa. He had clearly been a studious pupil.

At the Casa Pessoa, I picked up the exhibition catalogue 'Os lugares de Pessoa'. I used it to visit all of 'Pessoa's places' in a single day, from the fourth-floor apartment on the Largo de Sao Carlos were he was born in 1888 (and which is now guarded by a sculpture with its head appealingly lost in a book); the Church of the Martyrs where he was christened; the apartment of his aunt ('Tia Anica') on the Rua de São Bento, close to my own hotel, and his residence on his definitive return to Portugal in 1905. The Café Martinho de Arcada, an upmarket restaurant recessed in the arcade behind the Praça do Comércio, even has a little shrine to Pessoa from the days when it was called Café da Arcada, and he was a regular. It still does his favourite menu: Portuguese cabbage soup, cod and fried eggs with cheese.

In 1988, on the centenary of his birth, the writer's remains were transferred to the famous Mosteiro dos Jerónimos (Monastery of the Order of St Jerome or the Hieronymites) in Belém where the country's greats are buried. The monastery is the centrepiece of his *What the Tourist Should See*, where he describes it as 'the most remarkable monument which the capital contains'. Commissioned by King Manuel I five hundred years ago, its western front is a masterpiece of Renaissance stonework: made of worked limestone, it is richly ornate and incorporates maritime symbols and objects gathered during the naval expeditions of the Age of Discovery. Its vaults and pulpits are no less remarkable, and also full of memorabilia: 'The vault which rises over the cross is an admirable work, and contains the real bronze escutcheons which belonged to the caravels that went to India and to Brazil.' Once the visitor has seen the monastery, Pessoa suggests, he will never forget it.

Strange, I thought as I walked back the few miles back from Belém on those rain-slicked cobblestones, to come upon the mortal remains of such a timid and inward man in such a place—'glorious' as he said it was—alongside those of the adventurer Camões. Pessoa had always maintained that imaginary travel was superior to the actual thing—but it's true that in his early writings he had also written about dream-caravels sailing off to discover transcendent 'New Indias' and flirted with Sebastianism, the doctrine of the sleeping messianic king who was supposed to return and restore Portuguese culture to its former greatness (after leading it to disaster in North Africa in 1578). His theatrical splitting into three heteronyms, a semi-heteronym, various other ghosts and shadows, and not forgetting someone who claimed to be called Mr Person was perhaps the only way a twentieth-century poet could hope to emulate Camões's epic dispersal. A one-man band became a 'super-Camões'. Self-coherence yielded to subsidiary psyches. Instead of going to the tropics, Pessoa multiplied the 'desire to die another person beneath unknown flags'. Esoterism was made to stand in for exoticism. Pessoa had discovered that the world isn't a globe at all; it is flat, as flat as a sheet of paper. One of his dialogues is called 'The Anarchist Banker': it isn't difficult to see Pessoa as a kind of speculative investment banker himself, juggling the sundry assets, stocks, bonds and derivatives that constitute the *carteira* Pessoa.

Pessoa intensified to an almost hallucinatory pitch Calderón's supposition, already adumbrated in the title in his famous seventeenth-century Spanish drama *Life is a Dream*, that 'though no man knows it, all men dream the lives they lead'; and while his attitude may seem resigned and restful, or even have a mystical Zen quality, it has its recessed and loveless elements too. The heteronyms—of whom scholars have identified 136 variants, still counting—can even be seen as a means of concealing rather than expressing aspects of Pessoa's personality, or even as an improbably early exercise in product branding. Ivo Castro, one of the editors of the critical edition of Pessoa's work, has remarked, 'Hiding from his own editor is perhaps the most subtle form of disguise which Pessoa ever adopted'. Whether masked or muted, Pessoa evidently stands at the antipodes of Dante's orthodox strictures about the moral need for coherence in a human life.

The immobility of Pessoa's life has a haunting and even oppressive quality. You only need to chance on one of the excerpts in *The Book of Disquiet*—most certainly not a book to be read cover to cover—to be seized by a renewed sense of what the title suggests. 'I don't know how many will have contemplated, with the attention it merits, a deserted street with people in it. This way of putting the phrase already seems to want to say something else, and indeed it does. A deserted street is not a street where nobody ventures but a street on which people walk as if it were deserted.'

Scale that up, and you're contemplating a complete urban geography of Lisbon. Walk in Pessoa's footsteps, especially in the rain, and you'll discover his insomnia too. *Saudade*, that uniquely Lusitanian quality, isn't just nostalgia for the past, but for the future too.

# A Philosophy of Buttons

*Steven Connor's Everyday Objects*

*Paraphernalia*, the latest offering by the cultural phenomenologist Steven Connor, the Birkbeck scholar who gave us a dermatological vision of the cosmos in magnificently distended detail in *The Book of Skin* (2004), has eighteen chapters, each dedicated to a single object. He is deeply impressed, like Mr. Biswas in V.S. Naipaul's best novel, by 'the endurance and uncomplainingness of inanimate objects'—objects which also happen to be ubiquitous features of contemporary life. Thingamajigs, you could say. Here they are, all eighteen of them, in alphabetical order: bags, batteries, buttons, cards, combs, glasses, handkerchiefs, keys, knots, newspapers, pills, pins, pipes, plugs, rubber bands, sticky tape, sweets, wires. His brilliant extemporisations on the standard and non-standard uses of these familiar things ought to acquire for their author the reputation—if he doesn't enjoy it already—of being a kind of academic Nicholson Baker (although the person he first made me think of, with his obsessive eye for detail, was Alfred Hitchcock).

The word 'paraphernalia' itself comes from the Greek term *parapherna*, meaning those goods and chattels which a wife could keep for herself and were not the articles of Roman dowry laws that made her property her husband's. Like gear, stuff or clobber, the word now conveys the idea of a miscellany. It designates the modest little generic things we need to be ourselves. And there is a decidedly feminine, if not necessarily feminist slant to Connor's eighteen articles. We talk about 'emotional baggage' as if the emotions were an encumbrance, but the truth is we need baggage to jostle emotions into life.

And Connor is surely on to something when he suggests that bags are 'female-seeming objects', irresistibly suggesting 'wombs, bellies and breasts'. Not that the drooping is limited to the female of the species only. As we get older the more we all become like bags and sacks, 'the more we sag and dangle'. Samuel Beckett—one of Connor's earlier interests—is 'probably the great, hitherto uncelebrated dramatist of bags'.

Rubber was to the nineteenth century what plastics were to the twentieth. The British rather imperially called it India rubber and the French, although just as imperialist, introduced the native Peruvian term 'caoutchouc' into their usually not very accommodating language. The fashion industry wasn't slow to latch on to rubber's importance: clothes could be made to 'stick' to the flesh by being elasticised. Dutch caps and sheaths followed, and rubber was impregnated (preservatives notwithstanding) with sulphur, which enabled Goodyear to make its name and fortune. But ours is not an era that revels in rubber, except in select circles. 'Like the rubber band itself', writes Connor, 'rubber has started to recoil on itself': it is an ugly grotesquery in a design world that prefers brushed steel and reinforced composites.

As Connor observes, the 1960s—an era in haste to consign the past to oblivion—hated buttons, which were all too redolent of ceremony. Barbarella's space suit had zips, so that the space-angel of the swinging sixties could rip her clothes off and surrender to her impulses that bit more quickly. But buttons have a lot in common with keys, as Connor points out, being 'part of an economy of lost belongings'. Buttons have also been reconfigured by modernity into push-buttons: the possibility of 'setting in train or discontinuing a massive, complex and ramifying set of operations by a single elementary motion, one that is almost indistinguishable from pointing'. The black nuclear briefcase with its keyboard allowing an attack to be authorised while the American president is away from fixed command centres comes to mind: so little effort for so great an effect!

The history of many of these items is tied up with the development of urban civilisation and learning itself. Reading glasses were invented in the thirteenth or fourteenth century, and wearing them produced a theatre of effect all of its own: the first fool in Sebastian Brant's once famous book *The Ship of Fools* (1494) is a bibliomaniac wearing bottle-bottom spectacles so thick they look to us like goggles. Although it is often called an accessory, the handkerchief was crucial in separating manners from bodily processes, and that only comparatively recently: people eating in the days of Elizabeth I never thought twice about using a sleeve or the corner of a tablecloth as a snot rag.

Connor talks about knots being tied in handkerchiefs to alter their flatness (like those head coverings improvised at village cricket games in the English home counties when the sun finally comes out of hiding), and reminisces about his mentor, the French thinker Michel Serres, who used a handkerchief in lectures to illustrate how apparently separate events on the flat frame of time could be brought into contiguity by his folding and crumpling its square of cotton. Gilles Deleuze's book *The Fold: Leibniz and the Baroque* and Pierre Boulez's composition *Pli selon Pli* have made us familiar with the notion of endless folded structures in which the whole universe is mirrored. Even more exotically, knitting and crochery were introduced in mathematics classes at Cornell University by the Latvian mathematician Daina Taimina in 1997—a rare instance of the application of techniques from a preponderantly feminine handicraft to the austere science of geometry—so that her students could physically appropriate the intrinsic qualities of hyperbolic planes as they are manifested in lettuce leaves and sea slugs (and she has since created a beautiful installation called 'The Clouds of

White Thoughts', which consists of many of these crocheted hyperbolic planes in suspension). Knots, on the other hand, are straining to become metaphysical entities—just look at the long mystical life of the pretzel (or Bretzel, as it is called where I live now), a loop of dough pretending to be an infinity sign. Such knot forms contrast with the power of flatness as exemplified in cards and newspapers—that quintessentially Joycean 'organ', as dismembered, cut up and redeployed in *Ulysses*. Flatland, though, is a place nobody appears to want to inhabit: Thomas Mann's character Hans Castorp in *The Magic Mountain* stays up on his mountain-top sanatorium so that he won't have to come down to it, and the wildly successful self-publishing American information theorist Edward Tufte describes his life's work as an attempt to escape the same. There is certainly an irony in so many people aspiring to be 'whole' persons when we spend each and every day extending the two dimensions of paper and screen with which we conceptualise (and control) the wider world. Perhaps the French are clearer about these things: *mettre un problème à plat*, they say, which might be idiomatically (if confusingly) rendered into English as 'looking at a problem from all sides'. What the French are insisting on, however, is the flatness of pure perception: problems have to be unfolded and spread out, i.e. on grid-paper with Cartesian coordinates.

*Paraphernalia* doesn't seek to rise above the quotidian; it wants to sink into it. And play with it. Bits of it, anyway; and especially those haptic design objects that allow the child in us to discover what makes up the world, including ourselves. They are the things we love to 'fidget' with. Objects have attitudes. As the Chilean poet Pablo Neruda—a tireless collector of objects which caught his fancy—wrote in his *Memoirs* (1974): 'the man who doesn't play has lost forever the child who lived in him and he will certainly miss him'. The child is a materialist in the most direct and playful sense.

And no object, according to Connor, 'not even the elastic band, is more allied to active contemplation than the paper clip'. Indeed, that is why the French call it a 'trombone'. The philosophical trick, as in the related book *How are Things?—A Philosophical Experiment* by the philosopher Roger-Pol Droit, or *The Evolution of Useful Things* by Henry Petroski, is to fiddle with a thing until you can work out what it is you want to do with it. (Most of the time Connor seems to fondle words rather than fidget with things; and his fondling extends into extravagantly riffed etymologies that bring the most disparate things, as with Serres' handkerchief, into contiguity.)

Baudelaire has an intriguing phrase in one of his critical essays: 'The mysterious attitudes that the objects of creation adopt before the human gaze'. These days we have to remind ourselves (partly because of the object fetishism of the market) that the behaviour of inanimate objects is indeed determined by something other than themselves, i.e. human agents, and that we are not obliged to assume odd poses when confronted by objects of our own creation. When W.G. Sebald suggested in one of his books that 'things know more about us than we know about them: they carry the experience they have had with us inside them and are—in fact—the book of our history opened before us', his hypallage would have been regarded by our ancestors as frankly idolatrous. 'Stuff' offers something beyond its materiality, although it might seem that in dealing only with humble handhelds Connor has perhaps avoided confronting the intense glamour consumer objects have for us today. What makes the magic go sour? How exactly are paraphernalia exempt from the superstitious force of what Karl Jaspers called 'magic's aberrations'? (After all, the book's subtitle 'the curious lives of magical things' could justifiably have been 'the magical lives of curious things'.)

Connor cannot be accused, however, of what has derisively been called 'tchotchke criticism' ('tchotchke' is a Yiddish word for trinkets and baubles): the kind of materialist critical talk about the 'eloquence' of things that is ultimately beholden to Heidegger's notion of 'tool-analysis' in *Being and Time*. This kind of writing seems to suggest that the agency of objects is somehow inherent in their making, and scants the cultural settings that make them useful and meaningful in the first place. Connor's friendship with things when he was growing up in a typical household with appliances in 1960s' Britain is much more expansive and personal: there is, for instance, the delicious anecdote of the family's pet dachshund Ringo, who swallowed hankies, for them to emerge a day later from the orifice at the other end of its intestinal tract tightly rolled 'as though the sausage dog has been transformed into a kind of hanky dispenser'. Nobody could say Steven Connor has a thin notion of the self.

And here he is at his best, still trying to convince us that he is fidgeting and not fondling. 'In Latin, as in English, cogitation, the favoured term for thinking about the act of thinking since Descartes coined his *cogito ergo sum*, means not so much to reason, as to reflect, to ruminate, to chew or turn over in the mind. No wonder, then, that we should so habitually accompany this mental action with physical actions of turning over, reflection, reversal, revolving, rubbing things up the wrong, and right, way. The "*Internal Energie*" of thinking always seeks an external theatre of cogitable, fidgetable things in which to work itself out. Thinking on these kinds of things, we cannot help but think with them. The secret magic of such things is their capacity to give our thought to itself as we give thought to them.'

# The Pitch Drop Experiment

*On Slowness*

Bernard O'Donoghue's poem 'What's the Time, Mr Wolf?' in his collection *Gunpowder* (1995) opens with a snatch of hearsay about the amorphous inorganic material that allows natural light to cast its lustre on our lives:

> Glass, someone once told me, is a liquid
> Of such density that its sluggish
> Downward seep takes centuries to work,
> So medieval windows are thicker
> At the bottom than the top.

To imagine that old glass flows imperceptibly, much as we imagine time itself flowing, is a beautiful conceit; alas, like so many poetic ideas, it isn't true. It resembles the belief, which persisted into the twentieth century, that as pressure increased with depth the sea became more solid: our ancestors thought that in the deeps of the oceans there were floors' on which sunken objects gathered according to their weight.

O'Donoghue reflects that our flesh is subject to the same gravitational pull as cathedral windows, sagging as the years pass: 'It creeps for the earth...'. The German poet Gottfried Benn said the same thing, more laconically still, in one of his expressionist poems: 'Erde ruft' ('Earth calls'). Our lives aren't time-reversed symmetrical; and our bodies not even especially shapely. They perdure a few years, but with ever less buoyancy. And though we can't perceive time with our senses, we notice from the evidence of change around us that we must be living in it. And even living it non-prepositionally. So O'Donoghue's

ESSAYS ON THE ART OF LIVING

poem is actually a *memento mori*, an ancient and perfectly respectable theme for a poet to address.

Gravity doesn't 'relax' glass. Vitreous silica at room temperature is as mechanically unremarkable as most other solids, except for being a bit brittle. And while it is true that old windows are often thicker at the bottom than the top, the observation is based on a false assumption: the glass made by the original glassblowers was never uniform to begin with. It was made by the crown glass process, in which the molten silica is spun to form a plate; commonly the edges of the disk became thicker as the glass was spun. This was beneficial: a thick bottom edge gave added stability, and prevented rainwater collecting inside the lead cames that were applied to the wooden framework to hold the glass in place. Early mass production using cooling tables also produced unevenly thick panes of glass, so the phenomenon is by no means solely a pre-modern one.

There is one substance, however, which is obdurately solid but has liquid properties: tar pitch.

In one of the longest-running experiments in history, Thomas Parnell, professor of physics at the University of Queensland, set up a simple device in his lab in Brisbane to demonstrate to his students that pitch or bitumen— the naturally occurring petroleum extract used as mortar, according to the Greek historian Herodotus, in the walls of Babylon, and as waterproofing for medieval ships and modern roofs—is actually fluid (a viscoelastic polymer) although it looks just like a lump of coal. Blocks of solid pitch will even shatter, like glass, if subjected to a hard blow.

In 1927, Parnell heated a sample of pitch and decanted it into a glass funnel with a sealed stem. The pitch was allowed to solidify in the funnel over three years, and then the seal cut. The experiment proper was now under way: at room temperature the pitch began to seep through the funnel. It was hardly in a rush: pitch is a fluid of such sluggishness that all Parnell's students had long since left his class and graduated when the first drop fell. Parnell himself died in 1947. Eight decades later, only eight drops have collected in the beaker placed beneath the stem. The experiment still has over a century to run. The apparatus—which is the very model of a low maintenance device—is currently displayed under a bell-jar in the foyer of the Department of Physics; nobody has ever witnessed drop impact, although now that the experiment can be viewed by web camera that may well change. Actually, it might be more instructive to watch grass grow, since the interval between each drop lasts from seven to twelve years. Pitch, under normal atmospheric pressure and even at the relatively high mean annual temperature of southern Queensland, is more than a hundred billion times more viscous than water.

Had he known about it, I suspect the composer John Cage would have been greatly intrigued by the simplicity—and the audacity—of the pitch drop experiment. One of his younger colleagues, George Brecht, a member of the international Fluxus movement, wrote an 'event score' called *Drip Music*, first presented to the public in 1963, in which 'a source of dripping water and an empty vessel are arranged so that the water falls into the vessel'. In a different register, slowness supplies the organising conceit of two recent novels: Milan Kundera's *Slowness* (1993), an essay disguised as a story that ties what Walter Benjamin called our 'fear, revulsion and horror' with modern life to its press and speed, suggests that purposeful remembering is contingent upon slowness; and Sven Nadolny's best-selling German novel *Die Entdeckung der Langsamkeit* (1983), which follows that stubbornly individualistic explorer Sir John Franklin in his fatal attempt to find the North-West Passage in the remote Arctic 'where nobody would find him too slow'. Nadolny's book is now recommended reading on contemporary management courses that seek to hoop concepts such as environmental sustainability within systems thinking. And much more recently Don DeLillo dwells on slowness in his fable *Point Omega*, which has one character in a New York gallery watching Douglas Gordon's film project, *24 Hour Psycho*, a slowed-down video installation of the notorious shower scene from Hitchcock's film, and another stubbornly seeking to move beyond the super-personalised highest stage of consciousness—towards which all sentient life is striving according to Pierre Teilhard de Chardin—into something inorganic and rocklike.

All the same, neo-Dada performance pieces and speculative 'transhuman' novels seem way too tidy and efficient (the very brevity of Kundera and DeLillo's novels suggests their authors are perhaps more on the side of speed than they would allow) when compared to the metaphysical implications of allowing a lump of pitch in a laboratory in Australia to extrude a drop of itself once a decade, give or take a few years. Nothing really happens, we might think, and yet the evidence is there to see in the bottom of the beaker: all that is solid doesn't necessarily melt into air—sometimes it turns out to be in flux.

Very slow flux.

Slowness doesn't mean standstill: it is the music of what takes 'centuries to work'. Evolution hasn't equipped us with a sense organ for appreciating geological time. It is our failure to appreciate the slow flow of the pitch drop experiment that gives us an odd sense of vertigo when we encounter it for the first time. The Earth isn't solid. Our planet has been cooling ever since it started out as a molten ball over 4 billion years ago: its solid core of iron and nickel at a temperature of 5,000° C is enveloped in a molten ocean of the same metals some 2,000km thick, itself sheathed in a mantle of rock that is between 500 and 900° C, at which temperatures it behaves for moments like a solid and for longer periods as a liquid. It is this core that creates the magnetic field to protect us from the solar wind.

We are the tiny figures on the lithosphere or crust, a kind of viscoelastic planetary skin, which affords us the illusion of being on a planet where most of the time only the weather is changeable; meanwhile, far below, tectonic plates shunt to and fro, stirred by massive convection currents in the mantle's red heat. The molten rock close to this hot liquid ocean rises up and the colder rock beneath the crust sinks down to take its place, just like water heating in a pan. But ever so slowly.

Slowness, according to the German cultural historian Heiner Mühlmann, 'is a movement that lasts longer than a generation. To observe it, we need to work together with people who lived before us and people who will live after us.' Recent historical practice has turned away from the grand old narratives of universal history to imagine interior life behind the windows of ordinary houses. The sediment of these micro-histories is the *event*, pregnant with its own immanence. If every single thing connects, if one event contains the germ—molecule or monad—that might account for another, then the remembered world is bound to come to seem sluggish and compacted. As dense, perhaps, as a lump of pitch.

Our failure to grasp the true nature of slowness, Mühlmann suggests, is what we call 'transcendence'.

Then again, the British idealist philosopher R.G. Collingwood once formulated what he called the 'substantialist fallacy', which consists in mistakenly extracting from a simple chronological sequence a continuous transcending 'something'. And that doesn't just refer to the creep of days across the windowpane, but to time itself, falling away, into epochs.

# The Low Shores Where We Walk

*Postcards from Europe's Mystic River*

The figures in the principal fountain of the little village of Goldscheuer, just across the Rhine from Strasbourg, are a reminder that, for more than two millennia, gold that had been washed down with other ores from the mountains of the Aar region of Switzerland was extracted from the river, as suggested by the title of Wagner's opera cycle: *Das Rheingold*— his 'preliminary evening' to the remaining parts of his cycle, *The Ring of the Nibelung*. Unlike the already fashioned marvels being brought up in their hands from the river bottom by the coiling allergorical naiads in Henri Fantin-Latour's 1888 painting *L'Or du Rhin ou souvenir du Bayreuth*, the most noble of the noble metals had to be won by the backbreaking ancient practice of shovelling and sifting masses of sand and gravel, 'gescheuern' being the old German expression for panhandling: about 700 tons had to be worked through to yield a piddling 3.5 ounces of gold. Strabo mentions the practice in his geographical writings, and the Romans are thought to have shifted tonnes of the metal south every year. Almost two millennia later, the river was still yielding the precious metal: according to David Blackbourn in his book *The Conquest of Nature*, 'the Baden census of 1838 listed four hundred gold-washers on the right bank of the Rhine alone'.

When the Rhine was rectified and canalised in the 1840s, the profession died out, since the new hydrological conditions made it impossible for goldbeds to form and be exploited: the floodwaters came and went in the spring, and the river no longer meandered at different speeds in a way that allowed deposits of quartz and mica and gold gravel to sediment out in some of the side channels and wetlands that used to sprawl the breadth of the Rhine valley. The famous four-minute opening meander in E flat major on horns and strings of Wagner's opera, which opens the entire legendarium of *The Ring*, was presented at the National Theatre in Munich in 1869 just as the Rhine goldwashers were disappearing from European history to stake their claims in the wilds of California, Ballarat or South Africa.

This historical irony finds a parallel in the cycle itself, which in the broadest terms is about hunter-gatherers living on the margins of a more complex and organised society in which the power to rule the world has been illegitimately secured by the gold stolen by the dwarf Alberich to fashion a magical ring.

Nietzsche travelled to Bayreuth for the first full performance of *The Ring* in 1876, and observed, to his dismay, that the opera cycle was just another tacky display of what he called 'the ugly, the distorted, the overseasoned'. 'Fast habe ich's bereut' ('I almost regretted it') he wrote to his sister, making a nice pun on the city's name.

THE OTHER GERMANY

With the publication of W.G. Sebald's *A Place in the Country* (*Logis in einem Landhaus*), with its separate essays on Robert Walser, Gottfried Keller and Eduard Mörike, and given its author's known lifelong affinity for lesser known Swiss and Austrian writers, it becomes possible to see what German literature (and perhaps even German culture) might have resembled had its centre of gravity not shifted from the Rhine

Valley in the sixteenth century to Saxony, under the dramatic impact of Luther's translation of the Bible into Saxon German.

Perhaps the most interesting essay in Sebald's book is on Johann Peter Hebel (1760–1826), principally known for his poems in Alemannic—the middle high German dialect spoken around the Upper Rhine which finds contemporary expression in the dialects of Baden, the Swiss city of Basel and across the Rhine, in French-speaking Alsace. His dialogue poem 'Die Vergänglichkeit' ('Sic Transit')—in which a father (der Ätti) bringing logs on his oxen cart to Basel tells his greenhorn son (der Büb) about nothing less than the entire world going up in flames—seems terribly contemporaneous:

> Ie 's isch nit anderst, lueg mi a, wie d'witt,
> und mit der Zit verbrennt die ganzi Welt.

## GREEN AND GREY

Andreas Gursky's *Rhein II* achieved notoriety in 2011 by becoming the most expensive photograph ever sold: a large-scale, panoramic print of this image was auctioned at Christie's for 4.3 million dollars. It shows the Rhine, somewhere in its lower course, flowing across the field of vision between flat green fields and an overcast sky. The entire composition, which was digitally manipulated to remove a factory and dog walkers, is a study of grey and green horizontal bands. It has been interpreted as the quintessential Romantic landscape brought into the age of abstract expressionism. It is transcendentally dull.

It is, in fact, a minimalist abstraction of the same tamed river exactly as seen when I run along the towpath of its upper part near Strasbourg, except that here the image wouldn't need to be manipulated to suggest a sense of abstract space.

But it doesn't mean this straitened river is lacking visual fascinations. Twice now in five years I've seen a kingfisher bolt along the edge of the river, past the ecclesiastical herons and bottom-feeding swans, its mythical blue flash a reminder that the Keeper of the Winds is about to deliver two weeks of temperate weather.

## AN ETIOLATED IDYLL

German literature has many instances of a genre that hardly seems to exist at all in English literature: the idyll. The presupposition of the idyll (which derives from the Greek *image*) is Arcadian: man exists in harmony with the nature around him and desire is never more than reason will allow. Goethe's experimental fiction in *Wilhelm Meister's Journeyman Years* and *Conversations of German Refugees* provides, I believe, the deep model for W.G. Sebald's stories, an impression which becomes stronger when it is remembered that Goethe's loose collections of stories and adages are themselves parodies and travesties in the manner of Laurence Sterne. These miniatures established the novella as a reputable literary form in German.

The debt is perhaps most obvious in Sebald's *The Emigrants*, which, in its four intertwined stories of individuals displaced by the Second World War, echoes the tales of those noble families which 'abandoned their property in the region and fled across the Rhine in order to escape the afflictions threatening persons of any distinction'. This bickering, aggravated, mutually inconsiderate world on wheels shuts out the threat of revolution yet seems on the point of disintegration itself, and its members have to learn to repudiate their personal interests if they want to survive. Good manners are the basis for a potential new society. But even in the early nineteenth century these novellas must have evoked a strong sense of nostalgia for a social order that was being eradicated by the new industrial order. It is not for nothing that Goethe's subtitle to *Wilhelm Meister's Journeyman Years* is *The Renunciants*: part of what is being renounced is the big idea.

The displaced persons of Sebald's stories, on the other hand, have already renounced too much of the world to leave them with anything more than a vestigial attachment to their own lives.


MIGRATORY INSTINCTS

I was doing the washing up in the kitchen when I realised that the bird on the lawn was a striking one I hadn't seen before. It was a solitary hoopoe, with its long, curved bill, distinctive crest and dramatic black-and-white-striped wing markings. It strutted around the lawn hunting for grubs for half an hour while I tried to photograph it stealthily from the back door. My ornithology guide tells me it is seen on rare occasions in the Rhine Valley. It has certainly not been seen on our lawn since.

This was the bird that Solomon sent to the Queen of Sheba, and which the great Sufi poet Farid al-Din 'Attar made the wisest of the pilgrim birds in his masterpiece *The Conference of the Birds* (*Mantiq al-Tayr*): the hoopoe leads the other birds, each of which represents a human fault that baulks enlightenment, in search of the legendary Simurgh (a Persian pun on 'thirty birds'). When they get to its dwelling place, after many physical and spiritual exactions, what they find is a lake in which they themselves are reflected. They are the shadows cast by the story's unveiling.

## THE ONE AND THE MANY

I was reminded that the first thinker I sought out when I finally acquired my student-reader's card to the university library at Glasgow (gaining access to an expansive library was why one went to university after all) was Nicholas of Cusa, the philosophical originator of 'learned ignorance'. A Rhineland Mystic, of whom there have been many.

The movement started in 1248 with the learned German Dominican friar Albert of Lauingen ('Albertus Magnus') whose mystical theology developed out of Graeco-Arabian thinking about the metaphysics of flow (*fluxus*) in which beings emanated 'from the First Source that is the font and origin of all forms'. His writings inspired the iconography of the tympanum and archivolts of the portal of Strasbourg cathedral.

Martin Heidegger, the last and most notorious of all these mystics, followed the same pattern as the fourteenth-century Dominican speculator, Meister Eckhart, also an innovator of the German tongue—thinking his way not to a first cause ('Grund'), as advanced by Aristotle and all succeeding rationalist philosophers, but to the abyss ('Abgrund') between Being and beings.

## THE HYDROLOGICAL BUDGET

'The River of Lethe', Bacon remarks in *Of Vicissitude of Things*, 'runneth as well above ground as below'. That notorious river is bound to take its major course underground, where it will be sludgy and slow, and yet even as the upper river sinks into the fluvial bed, hidden groundwater percolates up to the surface through rock and sand, as crystalline as spring water.

Or 'boils up', to use the neo-Platonic phrase (*ebullitio*)

preferred by Albertus Magnus, whose metaphysics of flow conceived God, as the First Principle that, unable to hold back its abundance of Being, multiplies as the Word in corporeal and intelligent beings: what emanates from God ultimately returns, by divine hydrodynamics, to the source.

We can observe this percolating phenomenon right next to us, in the various pools and tarns that are the residues of the meandering old Rhine prior to its rectification in the 1840s: in one spot you can watch the currents laughing up from below to disturb the surface. ('Lachen', the German word for laughter, is also the term for puddles.) And I like too the phrase 'das Wasser quillt'.

HIDDEN LIFE

On a balmy Sunday evening in August, my wife and I sat outdoors in the shadow of Strasbourg's famous St Thomas church with about forty other people to watch an open-air projection of films and documentaries of local interest. The second film on the bill—*L'Homme qui aimait les images*—was a fifty-minute documentary made in 2002 for Ana Films by Jean-Marie Fawer; it featured a local actor Michel Rapin, who had made a name for himself, at least in audiovisual circles, by playing bit parts in over seventy mainstream French and German films, musicals and TV series in a career lasting thirty years. Michel Rapin was a cook by trade, but he had made a more lucrative and interesting career out of being an *extra*, or, as the French say, *figurant*, without whom, as he remarked in the documentary, it would be impossible to make very many convincing films at all.

Here was Rapin turning up to eat *choucroute* in a scene shot in a tavern with Gerard Depardieu in the foreground. Here was Rapin marching out as a recruit with the French Second

Army Corps in one sequence, and returning to barracks with the Prussian Third Army in another. Here was Rapin turning up as a nineteenth-century cleric or major in SS uniform or detective in leather raincoat; what these films had in common was that he almost never said anything very much at all—at best a command, a greeting, a request. He showed Fawer the contents of his archive, which went back to Fernandel and other wartime stars of French cinema. It contained signed photographs from almost everybody he had met on set: André Bourvil was his favourite actor—'un vrai gentilhomme'.

Now in his seventies and still living in the Krutenau, Rapin was in the audience, and fielded questions once the film had ended. As soon as he began to speak, it was clear why he had never been allowed to mumble more than a few words in all those films in which he had been an extra: his voice was high-pitched and nasal. He remarked on it himself. Then he quoted Truffaut in *La Nuit Américaine*: 'Je suis amoureux des images, mais pas de la réalité.'

But it was his reality that suggested to me that this was really a film about Alsace itself: the region as the eternal bit-player in history, the region with ideas above its station, the region self-conscious about its accent, the region called upon to show its mettle and colours when events bigger than itself were going on around it—*l'acteur de complément*. And what was the outcome? It could only be the passive aggression and pronounced depressive tendencies observed by Frédéric Hoffet in his now classic text *Psychanalyse de l'Alsace* (1951).

In fact, this film reminded me of one of my early experiences here, just after arriving in Strasbourg, when I paid a visit to the old-fashioned barber's shop—long gone now—in the rue Boecklin. As I waited my turn, I heard the barber, Alsatian born and bred, say to his client, 'Pour vivre heureux, vivons cachés'. A good life is a quiet one. The barber was improvising on Descartes' watchword, which he in turn had adapted from

Ovid's *Tristia*: 'bene qui latuit, bene vixit…' Strictly speaking, the perfect tense of the Latin can only be applied to a life that is through with living: Descartes had it engraved on his tombstone.

RIVER VOICES

Today it was so still while I was walking on the raised path along the French bank of the Rhine, the ground dusted with snow, the atmosphere sub-zero and cloudless and a weak sun oozing over the silhouette of the distant city, that I realised I was listening to a couple of men talking to each other half a kilometre away on the other—German—side of the river.

Then I recalled the old Chinese story about the man who could hear the noise of the fish swimming in the river.

# Doing the Locomotion

*Paolo Sorrentino's La Grande Bellezza*

Half a century ago, in *La Dolce Vita*, Federico Fellini caught a mood of change as Italy entered the 1960s: Marcello Mastroianni played Marcello Rubini, a handsome, youngish, enervated gossip columnist who lives out a week's succession of nights and dawns in the most spectacular of cities: Rome. Fellini's masterpiece was a film of echoes, many of them ironic—like the famous opening scene of the sunbathing women looking up at the plaster statue of Christ the Labourer being transported overhead by helicopter and the disquieting final scene of the monstrous stingray dragged up dead on the beach while an angelic young girl, met earlier in a seaside restaurant, tries to shout across the sound of the waves at the insouciant Marcello: all were allegorical images in which a not entirely submerged past was constantly threatening to rear up unexpectedly in what is soon to be everybody's future. This was already dominated by the glamour of celebrity and its hangers-on, not least Signore Paparazzo, the camera-toting associate attached to Marcello whose family name gave us the plural noun *paparazzi*.

Paolo Sorrentino's *La Grande Bellezza*, which won the Oscar for Best Foreign Film of 2103, is, so to speak, the footfall of an echo, the similarities with *La Dolce Vita* being at times so manifest as to suggest the film is a remake rather than a reimagining. That, I suppose, is partly Sorrentino's point: the band plays on. Jep Gambardella, played by the expressive Toni Servillo, is an ageing patrician roué with the melancholic jowls of a basset-hound: he wrote a promising novel called *The Human Apparatus* in his twenties, and appears to have lived out on it ever since. Indeed, Gambardella could almost be the young Marcello gone to seed. Still smitten by the desirability of the high life, sporting a permanent mask of irony, he isn't a jot surer about what to do with his talent—which he tells himself early in the film is a kind of 'sensitivity'—now that the partying is a permanent fixture. His hollow ambition, he recalls, was 'not just to be part of Rome's high life but to be its King, not just to make parties but to have the power to spoil them'.

And here we are, gatecrashing his sixty-fifth birthday, no less. 'Look at these people, this wildlife', he exclaims. 'This is my life and it's nothing. Flaubert wanted to write a book about nothing: he didn't succeed. So how could I do it?'

Jep doesn't have sharpened incisors, but he is in other respects a vampire. Like the rest of his kind he has successfully drained from the young the vitality lacking in his own vision of the world, and it now pleases him to torment the less fortunate (and perhaps himself) with a hint of aristocratic impertinence, of days when the pleasure principle attached to a single class only. The middle-aged, as this film suggests, have a flair for hedonism: they have the money (earned at jobs that might have gone to the young) and consequently the leisure time to throng the absurd discos and art happenings that provide Sorrentino with so much rich material for satire: one woman called Talia Concept (who lives on 'vibrations' as she tells an unimpressed Jed in an interview, and is surely modelled on the performance artist Marina Abramovic) bloodies her forehead by sprinting naked (except for a veil) into the stone pillar of an aqueduct, another young man hosts an exhibition in which every day in his life is represented by a photo (perhaps modelled on Roman Opalka, the obsessive painter who every day took a photo of himself, thereby literally numbering his days on canvas from 1968 until his death in 2011), and the prepubertal girl whose father—'the most important art collector in this miserable country'—encourages her to have expressionist tantrums with tins of paint: we are told that the canvases sell for a fortune. (The French writer Philippe Muray was on to this kind of happening years before Sorrentini— and called it 'enfantillart'—as was W.H. Auden who, in his poem *For the Time Being,* foresaw 'the daubs of schoolchildren ranked above the greatest masterpieces'.)

The satire extends beyond the art world. In a hilarious scene in a botox clinic 'patients' wait in opulent surroundings to have their number called so that they can enter the inner sanctum (the treatment room) and receive a jab from the master's syringe (at 700 euros a squirt): even a nun is spied sitting demurely in the queue in the consulting room. About to go to bed in another scene with Orietta, an elegant forty-year-old met at a dinner party, Jep asks her what she does for a living. 'I'm rich', she replies. 'Nice job', is his rejoinder. But when she decides to retrieve her laptop in order to show him some nude photos of herself on her Facebook site, he slips out the back door: self-absorption has its limits, unless the ego being admired is his.

Indeed, other characters in the film are paper-thin, not least the forty-two-year-old stripper who has a relationship with Jep and then disappears from the narrative (a very brief scene informs us that she has succumbed to the complications of an operation). The French actress Fanny Ardant, who once starred in an Antonioni film, enjoys a tiny cameo too, of no particular relevance to the film's development except perhaps to remind us of a glamorous actress who has aged well (unlike Anita Ekberg, the blonde star of Fellini's film, who in her old age has apparently fallen on hard times).

*La Dolce Vita* was in black and white; *La Grande Bellezza* is shot in sumptuously ripe cinematic colours, the camera making saccadic swoops among the fountains and statues as the film opens on the city at dawn. A Japanese tourist faints (or worse) at the splendour of it all, a victim of the hyperaesthetic appreciation syndrome first described by Stendhal on his visit to the same country.

Then we see Gambardella sauntering down a street in his elegant blazer and brogues for another sybaritic evening event where he will disenchant the not yet fully disabused: he gives one 'Marxist' female novelist a lesson in Schopenhauer for being unaware that her life is in tatters 'like the rest of us... You should look on us with affection and not contempt.' Given that he is only an occasional writer with no other visible source of income, Gambardella seems to enjoy a very high-maintenance lifestyle in his penthouse apartment looking over to the Colosseum and a giant Martini ad blinking into the night sky. Such luxury apartments are certainly not the Rome of most people, who live in cramped and ugly apartments on the edge of the ancient city, in *borgate* miles away from anything that might resemble the 'Fontanone' built by Pope Paul V on the Janiculum Hill, as seen to maximum effect at the film's opening. (In fact, these apartments can be seen all over the place in *La Dolce Vita*—as not yet finished construction sites.)

Gambardella's observations as he walks along the Tiber are, we dimly gather, fragments of the difficult second novel he has never had the courage to tackle. How could he? He is too immersed in the presence of the eternal city, so sucked into the vortex of that mysterious urban quality of *Romanità* once thought crucial for papal understanding of the fleeting vanity and glory of human ambition, to construct anything resembling a coherent narrative. He is happy to give advice to others on their literary creations, such as his friend Romano, who is trying to adapt D'Annunzio for the stage and maintain an expensive mistress: after all, he has a high degree of tolerance for human weaknesses, his own included. Especially his own. Pleasures are so much more enjoyable when they come unpredictably, even if their randomness carries the risk of allowing something more dangerous—aimlessness and despair—to seep into a life. But Gambardella is just the kind of person to tell you decadence is actually a word to describe a highly advanced and complex state of civilisation, and its loss of spontaneity and unselfconsciousness. But if salvation is out of the question, at least a man can make himself comfortable: life doesn't have to be a *via dolorosa*.

Even though he has the keys to the city—one character even offers to take him on a tour of its hidden treasures—Jep doesn't possess its soul. Where should he find it? It's not as if he hasn't been looking all these years.

One day Gambardella has an unexpected visit from the husband of a woman called Elisa, who had been his girlfriend when they were young. Elisa has just died. Having calmed the agony of his bereavement by reading his wife's diary, the widower tells Jep that she had confessed in it to only ever truly loving one person, and that person is him. (We are never told why exactly.) The memory of this girl who loved him when they were both young and callow and never stopped loving him inspires him to ponder—a little more deeply, a little more nostalgically—the beauty of passing things.

Our access to the 'purity' of this rather trite recollection comes through the film's sublime score (those scenes not given over to the frenetic bass-beat of the nightclubs): much of it is sad, sensual and strange. Haunting compositions by David Lang and John Tavener are upstaged by Arvo Pärt's marvellous adaptation of Robert Burns' romantic ballad 'My heart's in the Highlands, my heart is not here...'—Else Torp's clear voice peals out like a sudden burst of rain over sere ground. This surely is the great beauty, the grace that initially blinds us in its unexpectedness and then helps us to see, anew, the last ritual element of the great tradition still embodied in the Church that so fascinates Jep Gambardella. But it casts a neo-baroque mood over *La Grande Bellezza*, making it seem more operetta than film.

Sorrentino has saddled his film with literary ambitions. The attentive viewer will notice that it opens with nothing less than the epigraph from Céline's famous first novel *Voyage au bout de la nuit*. Sorrentino obviously wishes us to draw parallels between his film and that merciless novel about trying to come to terms with the world under the terrible circumstances of the Great War (and that in spite of Céline's dismissive comparison of going to the cinema in the 1920s to paying for an hour with a prostitute—'le nouveau petit salarié de nos rêves'). Jep is, we infer, a kind of hardened cynic like Bardamu in Céline's novel, who refuses to compromise his autonomy or pretend to feelings he does not have, especially concerning the opposite sex (again like Marcello in *La Dolce Vita*). It is a literary character reference that seems strained, not least because Jep's circumstances are so much more fortunate than those of any of Céline's characters. His life lacks any real conflict: all Jep has to deal with is ordinary *Weltschmerz*.

At the end of the film, he sums up his experience in Céline's terms: 'I was looking for the great beauty and I didn't find it… This is how it always ends, with death. But first there was life, hidden beneath the blah-blah-blah.'

Even Maria, the saintly and cachexic Mother Teresa-lookalike, reputedly aged 104, who gets trundled on in the closing scenes as a kind of living relic, seems to be an allusion to the Abbé with the frighteningly bad teeth in *Voyage*. Maria's role in the film—and that of the mildly sinister Cardinal Bellucci, one of the top exorcists in Europe and a character who fascinates Gambardella (especially since his passion is not for the things of the spirit but for food and its rites of preparation)—is actually an ironic comment on how cinema recoups what is lost to the novel, and indeed on how cinema stands in relation to the millennial history of the Church's experience of staging things. It takes the presence of the withered and frankly ugly Maria—who has devoted her life to the poor in Mali—to cause a group of pink flamingos to scatter into the evening sky above the Eternal City. 'It's just a trick', Jep adds, after his comment about 'the blah-blah-blah'. It may have been another sighting of the great beauty; Jep has surely registered the implication of the flamingos taking flight.

In one dislocated sequence Sorrentino can't hold himself back from turning his portrait of Jep into a condition-of-Italy movie, when he teletransports his hero to the Tuscan island of Giglio (miles away from Rome) so that he can gaze like a disconsolate janitor at the wreck of the Costa Concordia cruise ship. What Jep really needs to do is stay at home for a couple of nights and get out his battered old copy of Pascal's *Pensées*. 'If our condition were truly happy we shouldn't need to divert ourselves from thinking about it.'

But as Pascal also wrote, nothing is harder for us than to stay quietly and contemplatively in our rooms. So it's down to the disco again, where the bodies writhe in a fantastically contorted scene that could have come from Bosch, making Rome resemble its archaeological anti-city, Berlin, where people party all night long every night.

Italian parties like to close on a ritual. Tired of the latest swing-house version of *We No Speak Americano* or *Far l'Amore*, the guests line up in a long farandole to do the congo. Jep knows this number as *il trenino*, the little train. 'They have the most beautiful *trenini* here in Rome. They are beautiful because they go nowhere.'

# Where Are We Now?

*Necrology for a Starman*

The earthling dies; then his body is taken away to be buried
in secret, as used to be the custom on the death of an actor.
This old ploy to get around what canon law used to decry as
the offence of contumacy came to mind, when I read about
the death and disappearance of the talented David Bowie...
except that his mortal remains weren't buried but cremated,
and the ashes reportedly scattered somewhere on the island
of Bali.

But what was he doing dying anyway—who dies these
days? Especially not a rock star who made alternative lives
his speciality. In fact, Bowie had already lived several lives:
as the polymorphous astral hippie Ziggy Stardust ('Nijinsky
meets Woolworths', *ipse dixit*) whom he had the creative
instinct to kill off in 1973, Major Tom, Aladdin Sane, the
Jean Genie, Halloween Jack ('a real cool cat'), the Thin White
Duke, 'the cracked actor', 'Mr X'. Ziggy hadn't been satisfied
with celebrity and thought himself a 'leper messiah': he was
seduced by his own erotic beatitude. It was time to murder his
darlings—to stage a rock 'n' roll suicide before he became the
first rock martyr. Bowie had so many identities he had none.
As soon as he got rid of one, another would rise up from his
imagination. That is why he insisted there was no definitive
Bowie. He knew long before he became famous that the fame
he craved was hollow. But still he craved it.

Critics tell us that the seven songs of *Blackstar*, launched on
his sixty-ninth birthday, constitute his best album for three or
four decades. Two days after its release, a press release revealed
that he had died of liver cancer, eighteen months after initial

diagnosis. 'Something happened on the day he died', he sings in 'Blackstar'. 'His spirit rose a metre then stepped aside / Somebody else took his place.' And in 'Lazarus' he tells us: 'Look up here I'm in heaven… Everybody knows me now.' This was a singer preparing to die and not just theatrically or conceptually, as in the English version of the Jacques Brel song 'La Mort', which he used to cover as a cabaret piece in the 1970s.

Almost half a century has lapsed since that decade, and its grot and glitter. Nine days before Apollo 11 touched down in the Sea of Tranquillity in July 1969, Bowie released his single 'Space Oddity', the first title in a roughly eleven-year period of wild living and creative experiment. Bowie thought he was an artist-alien poised to lead youth into the future, where everybody would be wearing platform soles, at a time when the caul of the youth generation was still moist with promise. Things were not so *pre-determined* in the 1970s. Popular culture was still open-ended, not packaged for global consumption: home video, MTV and the Walkman had yet to emerge. But the moon landing in 1969 turned out to be the culmination of the space age, not its dawn. Three years later Apollo 17 closed the programme and the moon was left to cultivate its dark side. Bowie's persona Major Tom seemed to realise this too.

The alienated (most young people in general) seemed to recognise themselves in Bowie. He fashioned a personal mythology out of a schoolyard scuffle (when he was Davy Jones at Bromley Technical High School) that deprived his left eye of its pupillary reflex. A blue right eye and a brown left one with a fixed pupil were the sign of his chosenness. Later he would discover the myth of the Egyptian god Horus who injured one of his eyes and after its healing became a symbol of perfection. His alien avatars talked about the future but largely in terms of his own hermaphroditic person, who was bordering on anorexia. What might seem an era of anything goes ('let all the children boogie'), of rebellion and revolt, of future fixation, was the start of a massive investment in the self, rather than society: a kind of androgynous archangel called Starman played 'Tops of the Pops' in 1972, at a time when my parents, wiser than they knew, refused to have a television in the house. I must have seen it elsewhere. The boys in my class at school, some of whom confused Bowie's music with the 'ultra-violence' of the Kubrick film *A Clockwork Orange* (a confusion encouraged by Bowie himself, since the costumes for the Stardust band in 1972 had been modelled on the shiny space-suits worn by Kubrick's droogs), were actually witnessing the birth of the kind of individualism that these days is dear to those on the right. He was living the Lord Byron experience, discovering that in the music business fame could be had at the minimal cost of a listener's attention. And in the early 1970s, although we didn't do pop music at home, there was no escaping the figure of Aladdin Sane, with the zigzag across his face, red feathered haircut and dramatic Yamamoto tour costumes. I even went through my own glam phase at school, mercifully short-lived. Bowie was some kind of intimation that I was going to grow up into a person uncomfortable with his origins.

Bowie seemed clear-headed enough, in spite of the drugs he was doing. As he said in 1974, 'A society which allows people like Lou (Reed) and me to become endemic is really more or less lost'. By then he was a funky young American, and yet two years later was obsessed with ideas of fleeing Los Angeles, where he was reportedly surviving on a diet of 'red peppers, cocaine and milk'. Cocaine and amphetamines were doing his head in—LA was 'the most repulsive wart on the backside of humanity'. His album *Station to Station* is full of references to gnosis and kabbalah: he was reading Aleister Crowley rather than Joan Didion. He had his house and swimming pool exorcised. And he played himself as an extraterrestrial in Nicolas Roeg's film *The Man Who Fell to Earth*. A pop-Zarathustra, he called Hitler 'the first rock star' and saw something of his own talent at manipulating the media in Goebbels: like that amused creative guru Marcel Duchamp he was at risk of despising his admirers simply because they followed him. He thought Britain, then at its post-war economic and productive nadir, might profit from a dictator. At which point a love affair with the once famous Dutch transsexual Romy Haag brought him back to Europe: he became an anonymous Berliner in 1977. He stopped tinting his hair orange. He wrote some of his best music in his Schöneberg apartment with his friend Iggy Pop, abandoning the conventional AABA structure of most pop songs for the pulsing rhythms and sharp attacks of minimalist music. He had stepped out of the blinding sunlight of celebrity into the dank mists of Cold War Berlin, the grey city divided by a wall: it was the making of him. He was a queer straight uncle thriving in the shade.

The album *Ashes to Ashes*, in 1980, tried to bury this past ('we know Major Tom's a junkie, strung out on heaven's high') and according to the critics initiated the post-punk 'New Romantic' movement. A couple of years later, with the song 'Let's Dance', co-written with Nile Rodgers, he had a planetary success that allayed his anxieties about money, but also marked the end of his experimentalism. Even the song's title was an invitation to sociability. This was the MTV decade, the show-biz years. At its end, he had his teeth redone, capped in a perfect, whitened, incongruously American way. He speculated on future rights to his music on Wall Street and raised a capital of no less than 55 million dollars. He married an unusually beautiful supermodel from Somalia, and had a child with her. He had calmed down, and if he was happier in his ordinary social life, his later albums all seemed to be commentaries on the kaleidoscopic multiverse he had established in the seventies, though it is difficult to imagine him sitting at home in his New York apartment and taking pleasure in listening to his own 'Bowie-osity'.

He certainly had insights into the peculiar paradoxes of our age of mirage, where we all seem to be mesmerised by our apparent ability to transcend our own situations and be 'anyone'. Modernity seems to offer a sealed autonomy in which the need for mediation has been magically erased. We are rather caught, like creatures in a painting by Hieronymus Bosch, in a bubble of mass vanity. And Bowie was so familiar with the Western Mystery Tradition he could believe he was Parsifal, on a quest for redemption. 'In retrospect', he told an interviewer, he was sure that 'so much of what I thought was adventurism was searching for my tenuous connection with God. I was always investigating, always looking into why religions worked and what it was people found in them. And I was always fluctuating from one set of beliefs to another until a very low point in the mid-Seventies where I developed a fascination with black magic. And although I'm sure there was a satanic lead pulling me towards it, it wasn't a search for evil. It was in the hope that the signs might lead me somewhere.'

Yet it seems occultism claimed him again, stocktaking at the end of his life. The poignant video for 'Lazarus', sung with the same unashamedly fragile voice as in his 2013 song 'Where Are We Now?' revisits the central Christian story of resurrection even as its namesake steps backwards into a dresser, trembling, eyes blindfolded and buttoned, and closes the cabinet doors on the viewer. Pieties never die; they simply become displaced on to other objects. It takes no instruction in the mysteries of the Egyptian Book of the Dead to choke in the necromantic atmosphere of the ten-minute video to 'Blackstar' and all its baleful, waxy gloom. The skeletal corpse of an astronaut is found in a stylised landscape dominated by a collapsed star, the 'black star' that provides a kind of event horizon for an entire galaxy. Near his corpse is the mysterious 'villa of Ormen'. Women with tails retrieve the bejewelled skull of the astronaut, and use it ritualistically to invoke dark powers. This is the primal scene of some kind of feminist religion: 'On the day of execution, on the day of execution / Only women kneel and smile'. The female actors in the video twitch spasmodically. A parody of the crucifixion is seen against an ominous backlight, each of the three figures blindfolded, straw peeking from pockets, again sockets with button-eyes. The songtrack proclaims him the 'Great I Am'. In the centre of it are 'your eyes'—that is, *our* eyes watching what must be one of the most sinister music videos ever made.

Someone wrote that Bowie was a 'major liberator', always poised to lead young people into the future. I can't see that at all. This funerary spectacle is no hymn to modernity; we are back in the Aeon of Horus, talking to the dead.

# Pictural Propositions

*Wittgenstein and Photography*

In the train of the acclaimed exhibition 'Wittgenstein and Photography', on display at the LSE to much acclaim in the summer of 2012, Michael Nedo, director of the Wittgenstein Archive in Cambridge and editor of Wittgenstein's writings in the definitive *Wiener Ausgabe* has produced a sumptuously illustrated biography of the philosopher under the imprint of the Munich publisher C. H. Beck. Like his earlier co-edited volume *Ludwig Wittgenstein: Sein Leben in Bildern und Texten* (1983), it combines the visual and the textual in an original and compelling way: this book is an album of over 500 images—family snaps, letters, postcards, patent depositions, walking routes, manuscripts with handwritten annotations by Wittgenstein—accompanied by over 2,000 excerpts and citations from the work and letters (in both of the philosopher's languages) many of which engage with his insistence on the ostensive—the form of communication which takes for granted the presence of objects, whose meaning is tightly 'case-based'.

Wittgenstein himself would appear to concur prospectively, observing in the introduction to *Philosophical Investigations* that his work was 'really only an album'.

Though he was always keen in later life to play down his privileged background, Ludwig Wittgenstein, who ended his life a British citizen and is buried in St Giles' cemetery in Cambridge, started it as the youngest of eight surviving children in the second richest family in the Habsburg Empire, and grew up in the most cultivated and elegant surroundings: his industrialist father Karl—a fascinating, driven and energetic figure in his own right—was a major patron of the arts, and funded much of Vienna's musical and artistic life (of which the shimmering Klimt wedding portrait of Wittgenstein's sister Gretl in 1905 is one of the most widely known relics), including the Secession movement and its later offshoot, the Wiener Werkstätte. Like that other great dynastic contribution to modern British culture, the Freud family, the Wittgensteins seemed to know everybody who was anybody: their palatial home in Vienna's Alleegasse, according to the conductor Bruno Walter, exuded an 'all-pervading atmosphere of humanity and culture'. It is striking to see a photograph of the young Brahms—with whom music came to a 'full stop', as Wittgenstein told his friend Maurice O'Connor Drury in 1930 (and even there he could begin 'to hear the noise of machinery')—dedicated to the philosopher's grandparents, followed by an image of the composer as a bearded old man ('Jehovah' Brahms), in the company of the budding philosopher's aunts.

Music permeated the lives of the Wittgensteins; his brother Paul, who lost his right arm in the war and became famous for his association with Ravel's brilliant Concerto for the Left Hand (to which he enjoyed lifetime performing rights after commissioning it) used to tell his younger brother that he couldn't practice 'because I feel your scepticism seeping under the door'. (In many ways, Paul was all too like Ludwig: he refused to play some of the other left-handed works he commissioned for himself, including large-scale pieces by Prokofiev and Hindemith, claiming to be unable to understand their 'logic'.)

It was at Neuwaldegg, one of the family's magnificent summer houses around the capital, that Wittgenstein worked on the *Tractatus* while on leave from the eastern front in the last months of the Great War, finally completing the manuscript in his uncle Paul's house in Salzburg. Many of the group pictures were evidently taken in or around the hunting lodge at Hochreith, their favoured summer residence, in the company of nannies and retainers; Wittgenstein's sisters evidently liked to indulge that old aristocratic penchant for dressing up in folk costume. Image after image in these years attests to the fact that the philosopher who seems the archetypal outsider actually came from the heart of cultural events in central Europe. There were far fewer than six degrees of separation between Wittgenstein and some of the most prominent central European names of the early twentieth century: Rilke, Trakl, Kraus, Loos, Musil (whose apartment looked on to the famous gleaming white Platonic house which Ludwig built in a pared-down, starkly delineated, ornament-hostile manner for his sister Gretl) and Friedrich Hayek, who was a second cousin. Each is present, and many more besides, in this monument to the transplantation of high European culture to the island of tea-drinkers and phoney manners which, to Wittgenstein's considerable disarray—and in the face of his puzzlement, as related by his former student J.P. Stern in the introduction to his posthumous collection of essays *The Dear Purchase*—proved to be a solid moral and physical redoubt against the ignominious catastrophe of continental history.

An early photograph shows a surly-shy young Ludwig with his pony Monokel, a present from his brother Kurt (one of three brothers to commit suicide); a year or so later, the eleven-year-old can be seen seated at his lathe—first evidence of the interest in technical objects that would be one of the constants of his life. At that tender age, he had already assembled a working model of a sewing machine out of wooden rods and wires: his sister Hermine writes in her family memoir that it was actually able to make a few stitches. In a few years kite experiments in Glossop and the design of a motorless 'aero-engine' (British Patent No. 27.087, 1910: 'Improvements in Propellers applicable for Aerial Machines') were to emerge out of his interest in anything that could be cranked and levered; and a keen appreciation of the mechanics of photography was not slow to follow.

One of the more curious exhibits in the book is a composite image Wittgenstein made by superimposing individual facial portraits of himself and his three sisters with the idea of drawing out 'Familienähnlichkeiten', the incarnated resemblances in a family that he presumed would transcend its individual members. The attentive reader will immediately be reminded of Wittgenstein's insistence that language itself has no essence but is united in a relationship based on family resemblances.

This slightly eerie superimposed image of the philosopher and his three sisters is rendered all the stranger when we remember that the criminologists of the nineteenth century were experimenting with exactly this kind of anthropometric mug shot in order to identify recidivistic 'traits' in criminals. Indeed, Wittgenstein had read about the technique of composite portraiture in the work of Francis Galton, who spent many years perfecting his technique in the hope of being able to identify deviations from the normal in the infirm and criminal—he was looking, in a word, for *types*. These flattening assumptions didn't bother Wittgenstein. He took a blithe, ingenuously naïve, even somewhat mystical view of the perceptual apparatus: he offered it, in his famous lecture to the Heretics Society at Cambridge in 1929, as an analogy for his notion of ethics, progressing through the relative aspects of ethical dilemmas so as to glimpse something of a schematic and overarching nature emerging from them.

These multiple relational instances of a single concept—the individual as a composite whole—was the model Wittgenstein offered later in life to replace what he (and Nietzsche before him) considered the pernicious influence of Plato's theory of stable essences and their immutable definitions. When we say Ludwig and Paul are 'alike', what is at issue is not an instantiation of a pure essence. It is more a question of overlapping traits, similarities rather than identities. It is because of such related differences that we recognise families as unities.

This 'polythetic' approach—as opposed to the classic 'monothetic' definition, in which a taxon is defined by the presence of a set of attributes—avoids what Wittgenstein himself called 'the contemptuous attitude towards the individual case': as J.P. Stern comments, 'it gives the particular case its meaning as an element in a coherent and perspicuous, surveyable (*übersichtlich*) picture. In other words: the method offers a remedy against avoidable abstraction.'

If photography has trained us in the almost two centuries since its invention to recognise subtle facial likenesses between people whom we expect to share a certain 'look', the originality of its methodological training can be found in other spheres. Ever since Darwin, biological taxonomists have realised that the concept of evolution can only be given its proper place in biology if phylogenetic relationships are granted primacy over a list of traits 'possessed' by a named organism as necessary and sufficient properties for an understanding of how taxa are defined. Order is not inferred after the fact by conceptual explanations but recognised to be a central tenet from which taxonomies can be deduced.

And if 'diagnosis' is applied as a synonym for 'definition', the cultural scope of Wittgenstein's 'family resemblances' approach becomes very clear indeed. In *Philosophical Investigations* (§71), Wittgenstein writes: 'Is it even always an advantage to replace an indistinct picture by a sharp one? Isn't the indistinct one often exactly what we need.'

Given that Wittgenstein so frequently leans on the analogy between pictures and propositions in his writings, with their insistence that everything lies open to view, a visual biography seems twice over a clever strategy to catalogue his life. The photograph is an index, as the American polymath C.S. Peirce first observed: it presents an object immortalized in its natural 'projective relations' without any need for a formal aesthetics other than its scenic framing (Wittgenstein liked to crop his photos too). A photograph can't be called 'fictional', since that flat surface going nowhere in particular is a trace of something immanent and actual—although a photo can of course be 'doctored', airbrushed and enhanced, especially now in the digital era, and even have its context 'fictionalised', as in some of W.G. Sebald's novels, where some of the images are deliberately blurred or darkened. 'Despite the presumption of veracity that gives all photographs authority, interest, seductiveness', as Susan Sontag observed in her essay *On Photography*, 'the work that photographers do is no generic exception to the usually shady commerce between art and truth'. Nonetheless, in its first hundred years the analogue photo, like so many Victorian technical advances, must have startled our ancestors with the fresh insights it offered into the intricacies of social and individual life. The camera was a technical artifice that provided a hitherto unsuspected and startling degree of verisimilitude through textural differences to the visual nature of experiential reality—photographs offered 'the feel of the real'.

The ethics and aesthetics of the photo are therefore hardly unproblematic issues, and complicate the long-standing debate in our cultural history about the nature and worth of images generally. It is perhaps strange that some of these doubts did not lead Wittgenstein to ponder whether 'showing', being to his mind more persuasive than 'saying', might also be a method that more readily leads us astray. A photograph is less a composition, than a reproduction: it reproduces a moment in time without telling us anything specific about its circumstances. However dramatic its impact or emotional its appeal, it is historically folded in on itself, so to speak.

This means that its interpretation is largely the viewer's prerogative: the 'meaning' of a photograph—what Roland Barthes termed the 'punctum'—isn't entirely or even necessarily inherent in the photographer's intention, with its deference to circumstance and expediency, and the half-coordinated, half-impulsive moment of the 'snap'. And the effect may be all the more potent when the compulsion behind the snap is obscure—images say little about the person behind the lens. They may even create an experiential reality all their own. The influential American street photographer Garry Winogrand confessed, tautologically but revealingly, that he photographed 'in order to see what things looked like in photographs'. And the viewer's prerogative (or picture editor's power) may be anything but benign: the famous Magnum co-founder George Rodger, the first photographer to enter the concentration camp at Belsen, was distressed to discover that the editors of *Life* magazine had knowingly 'recontextualised' a photo of a small boy looking away from a row of corpses as he walks past them in order to make it seem as if he were German (and coldly indifferent), whereas in fact he was Dutch (and merely separated from his parents). The ease with which an image could be skewed and manipulated between exposure and replication shook Rodger's sense of mission, and he never again took a photograph of suffering individuals in a war zone.

After his initial attempt to continue his studies in aeronautical engineering at Manchester in 1908, Wittgenstein moved to study philosophy with Bertrand Russell at Cambridge in 1911, who referred to him in a letter to Ottoline Morrell as 'my ferocious German'. The outbreak of the Great War a few years later found Wittgenstein in Vienna: he promptly enlisted in the Austrian Army even though he had distinct forebodings about the outcome of the war, not least for Austria. He served with courage and even valour in heavy fighting on the Galician front, where he was known as 'the man with the gospels', owing to his constant reading of Tolstoy's *The Gospels in Brief*, and later in the Tyrol where he ended up as an Italian prisoner of war in a camp at Cassino, an episode that many years later provided the title for a remarkable 'machine-part' sculpture by Eduardo Paolozzi. Wittgenstein, who had always been attracted to monkish and even puritanical ways of life, especially after being exposed to the 'intellectual superficiality' of Cambridge—as the several photographs of Norway, where he built his own wooden cabin at Skjolden near Bergen, and Connemara attest—took it into his head after the war that he ought to be a simple schoolteacher in various villages in the Semmering area of Lower Austria, and wound up in the isolated village of Puchberg am Schneeberg: a double page spread taken outside an Alpine hut with snow on the tiles shows him with his charges, girls lined up in front, boys behind, all more obviously used to life on the farm than in the classroom. If a philosophical problem has the form 'I don't know my way about', Wittgenstein had clearly strayed into the valleys of stupidity (where 'a philosopher always finds more grass to feed upon', as he remarked elsewhere) rather than taken up Nietzsche's example of exposing himself on the crystalline summits. Both are self-consciously 'authentic' poses, and both look pretty silly. Wittgenstein's attempt to shed his patrician identity and go 'among the people' ended badly, by most accounts, although there is no documentary evidence in this book of what has become known as the 'Haidbauer incident', when he himself petitioned a court to judge him after he was accused of physically ill-treating one of his slower pupils: he was acquitted.

Perfectly out of place in rural Austria, he subsequently put in two years' penance as architect and fittings designer to his sister Gretl, the outcome being the aforementioned house whose 'lines, planes and volumes' were so pure his other sister Hermine felt unable to live in it. The early twentieth-century tendency—a trait held in common by the philosophers of the Viennese Circle and the theorists of the Bauhaus movement—to reduce complex things to their simplest formal expression (a movement sometimes dubbed 'simplexity'), had found an avid if independent adherent in Wittgenstein. What he had built was the general proposition of a house plus fixtures, or, as he wrote elsewhere: 'I am not interested in erecting a building so much as in having the foundations of possible buildings transparently in front of me'. This was Wittgenstein's unofficial contribution to Carnap's 'logical construction of the world'. Haus Wittgenstein is now the cultural institute of the Bulgarian Embassy, having been saved from destruction in the wreckers' decade of the 1970s by the concerted efforts of an organisation devoted to preserving landmark buildings in Vienna.

By 1929, stung by the criticisms of his close friend and translator Frank Ramsey about the incompleteness of his early philosophical certainties Wittgenstein was back in Cambridge—for good, this time—where he was generally contemptuous about the insider knowledge required to 'be' a Trinity don—a status he had acquired by the expedient of having his now famous (at least in philosophical circles) *Tractatus Logico-Philosophicus* submitted as his doctoral thesis. The British accepted such eccentricities. They knew this exigent intellectual type from their literature. Wittgenstein fits the image of Sherlock Holmes, especially as played by the gangly and severe-looking Basil Rathbone, to a T. And some famous people were prepared to range his eccentricities on an even higher level, even if the suggestion was made tongue in cheek. Keynes wrote to his wife: 'Well, God has arrived. I met him on the 5.15 train.' It is certainly an interesting reflection on our very correct—and, I would venture, less creative—times that the author of a work even of the order of *Tractatus* would today be most unlikely to secure a doctorate, no further scrutiny required. Without the proper paperwork 'God' wouldn't get a sniff at a chair in Cambridge.

Over the rest of his life Wittgenstein was to turn away from the inert, unhistorical summation of facts that seem to constitute the world in the *Tractatus*—a boxed-in Brownie camera vision of reality—to a realm in which many kinds of conceptualisation are possible, and indeed welcome. In his writings on the nature of language itself Wittgenstein found what he had been denied in the Austrian Alps. As the later photographs seem to suggest in their altogether more modest scenery and even bleakness (cottages in Ireland and deserted British beaches), even though Wittgenstein in his philosophy turned towards the notion of language as providing communal and cultural legitimacy for thought, personally he showed no interest at all in politics and scarcely more in social issues. It seems fitting enough that a search engine like Google should cope with the problem of the enveloping polysemy of natural languages by applying some of Wittgenstein's rules about syntax, the famous algorithm for keyword searches now being linked to the context in which keywords occur. 'Hot dog' and 'wet blanket' are now perfectly transparent expressions for the search engines.

'Don't look for the meaning, but for the use': it could almost be a new Mosaic pronouncement for the age that owes so much to Wittgenstein's quondam colleague Alan Turing, who designed a discrete-state logic machine based on propositional language that he expected to inherit the future, guilelessly, in man's image. A product, it might seem, along with photography, of modernity's obsession with *flatness*.

# Fiddleheads and Horsetails

## On the Sex Life of Ferns

*À défaut de la contemplation du géologue,*
*j'avais du moins celle du botaniste...*
Marcel Proust

When I was in practice in Strasbourg in the late 1990s, my landlord Philippe Stoll-Litschgy, an elderly artist and restorer, would sometimes come down first thing in the morning from the top-floor studio workshop in the building he had inherited from his adoptive parents (I rented the ground floor) and pass through the surgery before patients turned up. He was there to water the bracken ferns in the small courtyard directly across from my desk through the louvred window at the back of the practice. This was his fern nursery. I was fond of Monsieur Stoll with his beehive haircut and his limp, which made him appear to be an even more theatrical personage than he actually was; and I liked him too for his appreciation of ferns—*'Faut bien que je m'occupe de mes fougères!'*, he would exclaim when I interrupted him during their tending. There was never any question of his not doing so; it was his apartment after all.

I've always been a fern-fancier myself, owing to their antiquity and their simplicity, and the fact that their method of reproduction for so long remained a mystery: Linnaeus himself, in his *Species plantarum* coined the term 'cryptogamia' to express what seemed to be the hiddenness of the sexual cycle of algae, lichens, mosses and ferns, as opposed to that of phanerogams—plants whose reproductive organs are readily visible as flowers.

It is all done by spores. While flowering plants rely on their seeds, protective capsules with a double or diploid set of chromosomes, sporing plants—like the ferns (or filicinophyta to give them their technical name)—disperse single or haploid copies of the plant's chromosomes from the underside of their fronds. These dispersed haploid spores develop into a separate plant unit called the gametophyte, which looks nothing like the diploid plant or sporophyte: fern gametophytes are relatively undifferentiated structures and resemble tiny weed tangles, which is why Linnaeus overlooked them. Sporophyte and gametocyte thus run separate households: the fern sporophyte is overwhelmingly the dominant structure (although the opposite is true of the more primitive mosses and liverworts, in which the gametocyte is dominant). Being vascular plants, ferns need humidity to survive: there must have been a lot of water around when they developed as a phylum since the sperm produced by the gametocyte also needs moisture to swim to the egg and fertilise it.

This complicated two-step contrasts with animal reproduction, in which haploid gametes or germ nuclei—and the haploid state pertains solely to the gametes—are produced by specially dedicated diploid cell lines as a terminal process, and are thus directly present in every generation. Reproduction in nearly all plants, with diploid sporophytes and haploid gametophytes, is known as 'alternation of generations': the stable and relatively static process of asexual reproduction is kept at a distance from the unpredictable and volatile act of sexual reproduction. At any rate, what we take to be the prospect of the elegantly simple fern is only ever half of its life-story—indeed, only half a self, so to speak.

Although I'd grown up in the wet midlands of Scotland among gardens that sometimes seemed to contain nothing but ferns and rhododendrons, I came to associate the former (rather than the latter) with exotic places on the globe. I knew Les Murray's companionable definition of humans as a coherent presence in the natural world in his striking early poem 'The Noon-day Axeman', written in honour of his father Cecil (whom I met at Les's place in Bunyah in 1990) and in which the line 'walking knee-deep in ferns...' stands as his vision of intimate freedom in nature; it would be some more years before I read Oliver Sacks's *Oaxaca Journal*, dedicated to the 'foray' he made to the Mexican province on the cusp of the new millennium with a bunch of North American fern-seekers; and more years still (2006) before I would be able to visit with my family the little stretch of Gondwana east of Mackay in Queensland, where the tree ferns with their crowns of fronds, all members of two predominant families, *Cyatheaceae* and *Dicksoniaceae*, towered over us—as close to ancient megaflora as anything that exists in the modern world. Sacks says that he saw growths like these in Kew Gardens when he was young—'simulacra of the fern gorges of Hawaii and Australia'—and because of this imagined that these two sites had to be the most beautiful places on earth.

Charles Darwin was astounded by a similar spectacle when he visited Hobart, capital of Van Diemen's Land, during his round-the-world voyage in HMS *Beagle* in February 1836, and walked to the summit of Mt. Wellington. He conveyed his amazement at the size of the Tasmanian ferns to his journal: 'In some of the dampest ravines, tree-ferns flourished in an extraordinary manner; I saw one which must have been at least twenty feet high to the base of the fronds, and was in girth exactly six feet. The fronds forming the most elegant parasols, produced a gloomy shade, like that of the first hour of the night.'

Pteridomania (the fancy term for passionate fern-fancying) was a Victorian craze, with ferns being cultivated as indoor plants as well as appearing as motifs on pottery, glass, cast iron and pottery—Mauchline Fernware boxes (which are now prized collectables) were made by a factory in Ayrshire not far from where I grew up using a process in which fern fronds were applied to sycamore, the wood stippled and the ferns then removed before varnishing. Fern adoration was a singular form of eroticism permitted our celebrated world-exploring and knowledge-cataloguing ancestors, who liked to vaunt their morals but were never candid or overt about their sexual longings. The way Monsieur Stoll stroked his sporelings reminded me that there was indeed something pertly erotic about the morphology of ferns, those Jurassic whorls in abruptly startled self-presentation. They nod their heads out a sense of inner delicacy, and stay pure in their pleasures.

Darwin called some of the biological forms that he observed on his journey 'living fossils'. Perhaps for that reason I've always been moved by the relic tucked away in the larger story of the disaster which befell Robert Scott's Terra Nova expedition to Antarctica (1910–1913), which was still known by schoolchildren in the United Kingdom before such accounts of imperial enterprise became deeply suspect. Scott and his team reached the South Pole in January 1912, a full month after the better organised, rival Norwegian team of Roald Amundsen and his men (who made use of survival techniques acquired from the Inuit dwellers at the other pole); they famously died in severe weather conditions on the ice shelf on the way back to Ross Island. Remarkably, thirty-five pounds of fossil rock, which Scott's men had kept in their baggage despite having had to discard much of their gear in their effort to return to the supply stage at One Ton Depot, was found beside their bodies: this rock bore the imprint of a tongue-shaped fossil fern now known as *Glossopteris*, a Permian period relic also found in India, Latin America, southern Africa, Madagascar and Australia. It provided some of the first testimony as to the existence of an original supercontinent. In fact, *Glossopteris* had been extinguished, along with 95 percent of all species on Earth, in the great end-Permian mass extinction circa 250 million years ago.

Ferns—living ones—were also the star exhibit in Karl Blossfeldt's *Urformen der Kunst*, a book of photographs that became an international bestseller during the Weimar era and made its compiler famous overnight. Blossfeldt (1865–1932) was a professor of applied art at the Berliner Kunsthochschule who amassed a series of photographs taken with a homemade camera fitted with a thirty-times magnifying lens that allowed him to reveal the detailed and often dynamic structure of buds, flowers and seed capsules. These photographs were initially circulated among his students as examples of primal design elements in nature: 'The plant never lapses into mere arid functionalism; it fashions and shapes according to logic and suitability, and with its primeval force compels everything to attain the highest artistic form.' In Blossfeldt's book the furled fronds of ferns stand out as crosier staffs, scrolls for a string symphony in which Nature subtly gives form to its own creative forces. It doesn't take much to see ferns as poems themselves: furled so that they can unfurl for the person who cares for them.

A Japanese friend of the poet Seamus Heaney called Toraiwa surprised him during a meal in which they appear to have been eating steamed fern greens by asking him about the erotic. 'He said it belonged in poetry and he wanted more of it.' So Heaney presented him (in his short prose-poem 'Fiddleheads') with a little basket of them—'frilled, infolded, tenderized'.

In some circumstances, the simplicity of ferns would seem to be the ultimate kind of luxury.

# Saxony's Other City

*Books, Bombs and Bach*

This must have been how Leipzig saw its future in the 1910s, I told myself as I took in the dimensions of Leipzig's massive *Hauptbahnhof*, and the long row of six ironwork train sheds distantly modelled, like those of most important railway termini, on the arches of Europe's cathedrals (that's why 'sheds' doesn't seem quite the right word). A hundred years after its construction, this railway station—Europe's largest in terms of floor space—still dominates the city. Most of the city's tram and bus lines draw up outside, on the platforms of the Willy-Brandt-Platz; on the other side is the Brühl, an important street in the old town; it used to be the city's Jewish quarter and at one time was the centre of the global fur trade. Richard Wagner was born there, in 1813.

I hadn't spared a thought for Leipzig since 1989. I'd just got married and was living with my wife's family near Munich: smoggy Leipzig was on the news every day in that fateful week of October. The city had drawn attention to itself—in what was supposed to be a celebration of the fortieth anniversary of the GDR—with a mass demonstration of 70,000 people outside the St Nicholas Church made famous by Bach, all of them chanting 'Wir sind das Volk'. It was a bold step to take, since many expected state forces to intervene and suppress the protests bloodily, much as the Chinese had done in Beijing only months before. But only days later, the Berlin Wall proved permeable, not to say friable, and a government committed to liberalising the country was soon sitting in East Berlin. That December, after the 'Wende', the turning point when the process of change to democracy had become irreversible, East German television screened a documentary with the ominous title 'Ist Leipzig noch zu retten?' (Can Leipzig still be saved?) Aside from some high-visibility modernising projects in the GDR years such as a new home for the city's famous Gewandhaus orchestra and a thirty-six-storey skyscraper in the shape of an open book, the tenement blocks and warehouses all the way to Gohlis in the north and Connewitz in the south had been neglected; much of Leipzig was crumbling away.

This same documentary was showing as one of the exhibits in the museum dedicated to Leipzig's history on the second floor of its *Altes Rathaus* (Old Town Hall), built in 1556 in the Saxon Renaissance style: it has been a museum since 1909. Noticing my interest, one of the helpful assistants offered me an illustrated catalogue of the museum's history that had been printed for the occasion of its centenary in 2009: there I learned that Leipzig's 'Geschichtsverein' (historical association) had been founded in 1867, and, as the forty-ninth of its kind in Germany, was 'a late-comer'. Extraordinary, I thought, since the concept of the 'city museum' became a common notion in the English-speaking world only in the 1990s. But perhaps I shouldn't have been so surprised: the oldest museum of book culture in the world (Deutsches Buchgewerbemuseum) had been set up in the city in 1884, and is now the Museum of Books and Writing, part of the Deutsche Nationalbibliothek campus in the south-eastern suburbs. Perhaps this historicising impulse was why Nietzsche—who had studied classical philology at the University of Leipzig and whose last publisher was based in the city—once argued that the Germans were becoming overwhelmed with the sheer volume of antiquarian knowledge, most of which he considered paralysingly trivial if not downright life-negating.

Leipzig manifestly *has* been saved, although it had taken all the time I wasn't thinking about it to restore many of its solid *Gründerzeit* villas and apartments. Adventurers and speculators had come and gone (bust). The city's dilapidated heavy industry had been dismantled, and livelihoods lost. But the *Hauptbahnhof* had reopened after being revamped in 1997 (with the obligatory shopping concourse on two levels beneath), and the S-Bahn commuter train network extended to link up with the network in Halle, over thirty kilometres away, and a shared international airport. Leipzig has recently even been voted the most liveable city in Germany.

But there are still barrens, some not far from the city centre. I had a view of them from my hotel close to the central station in the north, and others cropped up around me as I walked through the eastern districts of what used to be the Graphisches Viertel to the house where Robert and Clara Schumann enjoyed their first few untroubled years of marriage. Until the end of the Second World War, this was the centre of the German book industry: it housed more than 2,000 publishers and printers including large companies such as Brockhaus, publisher of the famous encyclopaedia; Tauchnitz, which published English-language editions for continental distribution; and Reclam (which long before Allen Lane's Penguin editions popularised paperbacks through its Universal Bibliothek series and inspired the dismissive term 'Wegwerfliteratur' or 'throwaway books') as well as smaller avant-garde presses like Kafka's publisher Kurt Wolff. The city's reputation as the most important centre for music between Vienna and Paris was further consolidated by its piano manufacturers and music publishers: Breitkopf & Härtel, the world's oldest, was established in Leipzig in 1719. The German Publishers and Booksellers' Association (Börsenverein der deutschen Buchhändler) was founded in 1825, to regulate the book trade, and played an important role in establishing copyright, fixed book prices and combatting censorship. Between 1875 and 1920 the number of printers, bookbinders, sellers and publishers in the city tripled, just like the city's population: by 1905, Leipzig had a population of over half a million, a little under today's count. Thousands were employed in the various artisanal branches of the book industry, and the technical innovations that made it possible for them to produce 20,000 titles a year in 1900 can be seen (some of them in use) on the four storeys of the present-day Printing Arts (Druckkunst) Museum. Leipzig had always been a merchants' city; now it was hosting the largest trade fairs in the German-speaking lands: the first International Book Industry and Graphic Arts Exhibition (BUGRA) took place on a hundred-acre site in the summer of 1914 and was considered by the correspondent of the *New York Times* to be a marvel of organisation and sophistication. It was cut short by the outbreak of hostilities in Belgium: the print presses had gone to war.

The lawyer and industrial pioneer Karl Heine was one of the major figures responsible for unleashing the energies of industrialisation; his name now adorns the long straight avenue that cuts through the western district of Plagwitz. He organised the construction of a canal between the White Elster and Saale rivers, and reclaimed the marshy land—just like Faust in the second part of Goethe's classic drama. (The first part was Reclam's first-ever paperback.) It was on his land that entrepreneurs built one of the most modern and extensive cotton factories in Europe: the cobblestoned streets of the *Spinnerei* are now an artists' community and exhibition centre, the disused workshops being occupied by some of the famous names of the New Leipzig School, including Neo Rauch and Rosa Loy. Their figurative paintings—German Expressionism meets Pop Art—resemble the work being produced in my home city of Glasgow in the 1980s by artists like Peter Howson and Stephen Campbell. A kind of socialist surrealism, in which serious themes are given 'the exuberant, floating, dancing, mocking, childish and blissful' treatment Nietzsche thought would be required of modern art. Central Europe as exotic? Glasgow as exotic? They certainly were for a while in the New York art-buying scene. (Another thing the cities of Leipzig and Glasgow have in common is an impenetrable accent in their respective languages: the Saxons have the remarkable habit of coughing their sentences back into their throats. And the parallel can be extended: the rivalry between Saxony's two main cities of Leipzig and Dresden isn't at all dissimilar to that between Glasgow and Edinburgh: one an energetic, industrial, socially engaged city, the other a somewhat superior capital and royal residence...)

It was the heavy industry and arms manufacturers in this part of the city that the 400 bombers of the Royal Air Force intended to strike in the massive air raid that took place on 4 December 1943. Most of the bombs missed their primary target. Instead, about 1,800 people died, a relatively small number for the large tonnage of explosives dropped, but 50 million books in the Graphisches Viertel went up in flames. The city museum had a small but effective replica of the raid—which I almost missed—under the draughty rafters of the town hall: a chilling experience in both senses, since downstairs I had just seen photographs of the roof as a skeleton of beams after the raid. This conflagration was, in essence, the end of Leipzig's reign as book city. It had already been seriously compromised by the Nazis, who had torched books in Leipzig in 1933, and whose laws against Jewish businesses led to an exodus of publishers; after the war, the last private companies shifted to the Federal Republic in 1953, and the few remaining publishers in the east were never going to stage an even modest revival when paper supplies weren't regular. Although the incunabula and valuable books in the university library had been prudentially deposited in smaller collections in the villages around Leipzig and returned to the city at war's end, some were seized as war booty: a priceless copy of Gutenberg's original forty-two-line Bible is still in the Russian State Library in Moscow. It is estimated that 40 percent of all books in public collections in Germany were destroyed during the war, and the ones that hadn't been destroyed underwent the indignity of being read in the Communist years only if they had first been 'gesäubert' ('purged'). And this was a country which—officially—had no censorship.

Walking around the old city, which boasts several of those opulent arcades or 'Passagen' dear to Walter Benjamin (including in one the famous Auerbach's cellar mentioned in the first part of Goethe's *Faust*), enclosed inner spaces for consumption and modest precursors to the multilevel shopping mall at the central station, I realised that it wasn't the events of 1989—scenes of which are on public display in the bunker of what used to be the old Stasi headquarters (Museum in der 'Runden Ecke')—or even of the last war which had most marked the city: it was a much earlier battle, in October 1813. At the battle of Leipzig or, as it is sometimes more grandly called, the Battle of the Nations, a coalition of Russians, Prussians, Swedes and Austrians faced up to Napoleon's own multinational Grande Armée. Armies from different German states were fighting on both sides because Germany was still in the making (and this battle was one of the events leading to it). For Napoleon, it was the beginning of the end of his Empire dream of dominating the continent, in particular Prussia, and it was truly the end for as many as 110,000 soldiers, more than died in any battle in Europe until the Great War. It was, in short, one of world history's many terrible moments. Cholera and typhus broke out in the city, and local people were still burying corpses a year later. There must have been an awful lot of dead horses too.

The biggest battle in Europe had to have the biggest monument. It wasn't enough to have fifty human-sized memorial stelae—called *Apelsteine* after their initiator, the Leipzig writer Theodor Apel—planted in the mid-nineteenth century at various sites around the city to record the exact position and sizes of the different armies and names of their commanders on the three days of the battle—and the fact that I saw the same disposition of forces etched onto a glass beaker displayed in the Museum für angewandte Kunst (Applied Arts), one of the three museums in the Grassi museum complex, suggests that the battle must have cut a furrow through the ordinary people of Leipzig too. By 1900, lotteries and donations had raised the sum of 6 million goldmarks for the construction of the Völkerschlachtdenkmal, to give it its full title ('Völki' to the Leipzigers): it took fifteen years to build and was one of the first granite-clad concrete constructions. Everything about this pile of twenty-five thousand blocks is larger than life, starting with the gargantuan Statue of St Michael who guards the entrance ('Gott mit uns' is written in Jugendstil script above his impassive helmet) and continuing with the constellated warriors keeping watch a hundred metres up in the sky. It has Wagner's influence written all over it, but also conveys something Mesopotamian and body-trampling: it is the kind of power-pose exterior furniture that would have appealed to Marduk of Babylon. When the building was finally complete and the memorial unveiled, the fields of Flanders were only a year away. Its bombastic supersize seems exactly the kind of monument that a society poised to worship military valour and ultimately the cult of itself might design. Hitler, of course, made it his venue of choice for massed meetings in the city. It was only spared in the Communist era because the Russian forces had been present at the original Battle of the Nations.

Coming afterwards, we don't have the same susceptibility to ceremony and grandeur. Life doesn't have to be applauded for being larger than it thinks it ought to be. I beat my own retreat to the city's other great church, St Thomas, where the man to whom God owes everything (to quote E.M. Cioran) used to preside over the choir. His purported remains now repose in the nave. I picked up a brochure at the entrance which reminded me: this was no museum, but a working church. There are indeed a lot of museums in Leipzig, I thought to myself. It was oddly uplifting to know that it has a couple of working churches too.

# IV

# Vagaries

# Zest

*Tobias Smollett in the South of France*


'This cannot be the south of France, (said I to myself) it must be the Highlands of Scotland!' In Letter XII of his occasionally grumpy but frequently entertaining *Travels through France and Italy*, written in Nice on 6 December 1763, Tobias Smollett, MD, surgeon, translator of *Don Quixote* and author of various picaresque adventures dedicated to the doings of Roderick Random, Peregrine Pickle and Ferdinand Count Fathom (among others), recounts the time spent in the port city of Fréjus, 'the *Forum Julianum* of the antients'. He also goes into detail about the day he climbed on the back of a mule and hiked up to the mountains behind the city in order to inspect the famous aqueducts left by the Roman water engineers. Smollett and his Jamaican wife Anne ('Nancy') had left London a couple of months beforehand. They were fleeing two calamities: the death of their only child Elizabeth and the failure of the newspaper *The Briton*. Smollett had edited this weekly in support of the government of the Earl of Bute, negotiator of terms with the French after British victory in what was essentially the first global conflict, the Seven Years' War (1756–63), when the latter expanded their territorial claims in India, Canada and west of the Appalachians to the Mississippi. Smollet and his wife hoped to find a climate that might restore them to health.

A few years ago, I climbed these mountains to see the aqueduct for myself. Part of it runs close to the fortified village of Mons, high up in the hills behind the towns of Fayence and Grasse—respectively famous for pottery and perfumes—and offers a panoramic view of the distant Bay of Cannes as well as, weather conditions permitting (as they did), the island of Corsica crouched against the horizon. The aqueduct lunges out of a rocky spur of the gorge cut by the Siagnole river, a little below the village, which still uses part of the old waterway for its own supply, and is at least forty kilometres from the former Roman city and its harbour on the Mediterranean. Quarry pick and chisel strokes gouged and rasped by the workmen on the limestone cliffs two thousand years ago are plainly visible on the dry walls of the rock ('roche taillée'): this was probably an interception channel, to gather and hold water from the surrounding hills before it was channelled south. It is one thing to read about Roman accomplishments, but here was actual evidence of their prowess in civil engineering. I was viewing the works of an advanced civilisation, made before it had suspected it might be mortal.

In the neighbouring hills of the Estérel ('Esterelles') which, owing to its extinct volcano stumps, was a source of porphyry (giving the hills their red tinge) for the Romans, and after passing through stippled arbours of parasol pines, cypresses, cork oaks and olives, Smollett made halt in the post-house, and dined in a room in the shade of the mountains that was so cold he began to shiver. Even to remember it, he told his readers, caused his teeth to chatter. He was travelling in his postilion in December, and a fierce north-westerly Mistral had been blowing, so cold and biting that even flannels could not keep him 'tolerably warm'. But after dinner he went into another, south-facing room of the house and, on throwing open the window, was astounded to find himself facing— 'within a yard of my hand'—a citrus tree loaded with oranges, many of them ripe. 'You may judge what my astonishment was to find Winter in all his rigour reigning on one side of the house, and Summer in all her glory on the other.'

The weather ran through the mountain. The post-house stood on the boundary, not just of winter and summer but also

France and Scotland. Smollett, who delighted in the vistas of the Mediterranean framed by the window of his coach and was generally an attentive observer (in consequence of his medical training) of natural matters, had just anticipated another boundary—that of the *handedness* of nature.

His delight about the orange tree stayed with him, as the coach rolled down towards the sea through a natural plantation 'of the most agreeable ever-greens, pines, firs, laurel, cypress, sweet myrtle, tamarisc, box, and juniper, interspersed with sweet marjoram, lavender, thyme, wild thyme, and sage'. For a man from the North these shrubs and herbs were the natural evidence of the South as a different way of life.

It was during his trip to France and Italy that Smollett acquired the soubriquet 'Smelfungus' from Laurence Sterne, who was also travelling around Europe at the same time, publishing his *A Sentimental Journey* a couple of years after Smollett's book, and to considerably greater success. Although Smollett gave as good as he got (famously referring to Dr Johnson as 'that great Cham of literature', which archaic term suggested the Good Doctor ruled over letters like an oriental despot), his reputation never entirely recovered from Sterne's byname. (He had also been dubbed 'Smallwit' in *The Briton*'s rival publication.) It is true that Smollett can be a grouch with a tendency to expatiate about lavatorial conditions (the fastidious John Ruskin called his books 'open filth'), although it can be safely assumed that some of the inns he had to stay in were indeed as dirty and bug-ridden as he says they were and the *aubergistes* little better than thieves. Provence was still the lair of brigands and cutthroats in the eighteenth century, the roads unsafe for any kind of *petite diligence*, especially after dark. And while there is a decided element of hyperbole and theatricality about his complaining ('One finds nothing but dirt and imposition'), Smollett could never be accused of wanting to ingratiate himself with his readers, which the much more genteel Sterne does all the time. He 'had an invincible dislike and opposition in his nature to gravity;—not to gravity as such;—for where gravity was wanted, he would be the most grave or serious of mortal men for days or weeks together;—but he was an enemy to affectation of it... only as it appeared a cloak for ignorance, or folly'. That was Sterne explaining in *Tristram Shandy* why his jester Yorick hated men who were all pomp and no substance, and suggests that, in terms of literary sensibility, Smollett and Sterne shared more than ever separated them.

Like George Orwell, the American cultural historian and eighteenth-century specialist George Rousseau considers Smollett the Scottish writer with the greatest sense of style: it certainly shapes his attacks on other writers (his contemporary Henry Fielding was ridiculed as 'Habbakkuk Hilding'), and his inimitable blend of sesquipedalianism and slang. He could be critical of medical colleagues too. He certainly wasn't much taken with the celebrated Dr Fizès whom he consulted about his phthitic lungs in that distinguished southern city, Montpellier. His own medical knowledge must have told him he knew as much as this distinguished old medicus whose eyes 'sparkled at the sight of the fee'. Dr Fizès prescribed bouillons, opiates and goats' milk; but no exercise. Smollett was indignant. Already a sceptic concerning the fashionable virtues of taking the waters in Bath, Smollett made the empirical discovery that a brisk swim in seawater might be remedial for some kinds of medical conditions, his skin problems included. He certainly felt the better for half-an-hour's disporting in the Mediterranean in sight of Nice.

Smollett had a good eye: he recognised the appeal of the little village of Cannes, and the corniche road to Nice, which was then a possession of the House of Savoy and outside the Kingdom of France. He informs even as he inveighs.

In his 2003 biography, Jeremy Lewis draws out the parallel

between Smollett's time and ours: 'we live in a time of luxury and ostentatious expenditure, when, more than ever, people are judged by what they own and wear and look like; and those of us who look on, with a mixture of envy and disdain, are torn between a Smollettian loathing for the vulgarity and crassness of a materialistic age, and a Johnsonian suspicion that this is, in part, how society renews itself, and keeps atrophy at bay'. It was those loathed qualities, Smollett thought, that had done for the Roman Empire. And they might well be the ruin of London, the 'overgrown monster; which, like a dropsical head, will in time leave the body and extremities without nourishment and support'. Lewis considers Smollett 'the quintessential 18th-century man of letters', a harried wordsmith who wore himself out writing sheaves of now forgotten historical works, plays, translations and reviews: his tasks in the 1750s included compiling *A Compendium of Authentic and Entertaining Voyages*, editing *A Treatise on the Theory and Practice of Midwifery*, an influential textbook assembled by his Glasgow 'man-midwife' colleague William Smellie, and contributing entries to *An Universal History, from the Earliest Account of Time* (published in sixty-five volumes over that decade and the next). As one of his enemies quipped, 'he undertakes to fit up books by the yard on all subjects'.

And he could be clairvoyant too, which perhaps came from being a Scot in eighteenth-century London when, as André Parreaux notes in *Smollett's London*, no other nation was more resented for its foreignness (other than France). In 'Dying Prediction', a letter addressed to a correspondent in Northumberland a few months before his death, he foresaw the breaking away of the American colonies (which he thought might be beneficial for both parties) and the coming revolution in France, and suggested that the history of slavery in the West Indies would return to haunt the colonisers: 'It has ever excited my astonishment that nobody, either in England or those islands, should entertain... the smallest compunction for the enormous wickedness of the act, exaggerated as it is, a thousand degrees, by being perpetrated by men whose nation sets so high a value upon their own liberty, and who pretend to such an aversion from deeds of cruelty.'

But that unexpected anecdote about the sharp initiation of the orange tree goes a long way to redeem Smollett from the dank backshop of literary history.

Rasp or grate an unpeeled orange and the outermost skin—the flavedo or epicarp—gives off the sharp volatile aromatic smell of its essential oils. One of them, d-limonene, a chemical of the terpene family, is the isomer—the same molecule but its mirror-opposite—of l-limonene, which can be extracted from pine needles. It suggests another dimension to the literary concept of doubleness that has long been associated with Scotland, and which Karl Miller explored in depth in his book of essays *Doubles* (in which he gave only the most glancing of mentions to Smollett). Even the sense of smell is up for stereo effects.

Nature is in two minds. Handedness is its tendency to produce everything in mirror image, and to compel its creatures to prefer one side of an image to the other: it was thought until recently that only humans displayed handedness (90 percent of us have the right-handedness that goes with a dominant left brain), but this partiality has been discovered in many living animal species, and palaeontologists have also begun to find traces of 'preferential laterality' in extinct animals. Handedness was around long before hands, as it were. And whether it bears any relation to this phenotypical handedness, asymmetry is found at the molecular level too, as in the smell of orange/pine. It has even been a key part of the discovery of strangeness in particle physics.

A kind of bistability animates Smollett's writings (in a

sentimental age he took a mordant pleasure in being blunt and sometimes Juvenalian), and although he would have known plenty, at least at an unspoken level, about cultural handedness, he and his contemporaries could hardly have suspected that nature came rigged in what are called 'chiral' forms as well: a little too much emphasis on the 'Winter rigour' (Scotland and the north and conifers) moves him over the mountains to the secondary stable position of 'Summer glory' (France and the sun and citruses), and back again. That was what it took to be a *homo duplex*.

I like to think of Smollett trundling through what was not quite modern France on his way back to his hackwork in the mud and rain of jaded literary London. Somewhere in his bags there must have been a dried orange wrapped in manuscript paper from the Ardèche firm of Montgolfier, and smelling of a place called Esterelles.

# Ultimate Islands

*Island-hopping with Peter Conrad*

Islands are philosophically odd things: they were central to John Locke's bold moves against feudal tenure rights in the seventeenth century, which made property something that could be abstracted from the physical effort put into finding, cultivating and ultimately consuming the produce of the land which delimited it on paper. Islands as emergent land (and on our watery planet all land starts out that way) are more easily circumscribed by such activities: that is why Shakespeare sets Prospero on an isle, and Defoe has Robinson Crusoe take possession of his, a tiny dot of rationality (an 'I-land') in an ocean of contingency. Islands are rafts of righteousness that provided a new standard of independence in laying claim to the biggest parcel of land of all, the United States, which is manifestly not an island. The land title of the continent's first peoples had been extinguished by the ancient Papal doctrine of discovery (adopted by the United States Supreme Court in 1823), supplemented by various treaties, executive orders and federal statutes. In turn, the 1856 Guano Act laid out the US claim to possession over the phosphate-rich patches (and their 'appurtenant' resources) of the world's oceans without ever having to incorporate them within the federal jurisprudence, an act of legal fudging upheld by the US Supreme Court rulings of 1905 known as the Insular Cases: the constitution doesn't necessarily follow the flag.

Legal and fiscal ambiguity has also characterised the more recent appearance of 'treasure islands' prepared to service money of any colour or heat in return for a modest rate of corporate tax, no questions asked, from 'shell companies';

these islands' speciality is to circumvent—in all legality—the rules and regulations of mainland politics while remaining networked to the major commercial capitals. Companies have often been regarded as 'little republics'—Venices in the sea of the market economy. It is hardly coincidental that most of the world's successful tax havens are former bits of the British Empire, allowing the British Virgin Islands (population: 22,000) to be listed in 2010 as the biggest investor in the Chinese economy after the special administrative region of Hong Kong. The City of London itself, as some people have suggested, enjoys an island jurisdiction in relation to Europe and even within the British state itself. Dodging taxes has a long tradition: back in the 1620s, Thomas Hobbes identified taxation as the nodal point at which what the crown claimed were fiducial duties collided what its subjects asserted were traditional rights. Spiritual jurisdictions work in an offshore manner too: in 1929, Mussolini made it possible for the forty-four hectares of the Vatican City to acquire a legal personality. *Offshore* is therefore a word with a special freight: it suggests how identity becomes a congealing property that attaches to more solid structures in the liquid flux of exchange even as these structures themselves retain the option of moving on. What counts is the flux.

Islands have always had unbargained-for 'subtleties', as Prospero called them: the power of generating noises, apparitions and events of their own account. Their very names—Trobriand, St Kilda, Ceylon, the Dry Tortugas—are imaginatively potent: these could be the names of Wallace Stevens' 'islands at the end of the mind'. But however mythic islands might sound, the people who live on them tend to be tight-knit, gruff and reserved: they are people with a strong sense of things in their proper place. They know where land ends and limits start. The islanders I know would be the last to entertain the notion of *islomania*, an affliction of the spirit which affects some people, according to Lawrence Durrell, for whom 'the mere knowledge that they are on an island, a little world surrounded by the sea, fills them with an indescribable intoxication'. He claimed that these people were descendants of the survivors of Atlantis, and their yearning was a subconscious desire to reacquaint themselves with the contours of their drowned realm.

One reason for preferring islands may be more prosaic, and yet more compelling than a lost-city mythology. Many natural history researchers like to work there: it balances the mind. Islands are good to ponder on, resident island species being finite and therefore manageable. 'As long as there have been biologists they have sought out islands to keep profusion from making them crazy', writes the entomologist Fredrik Sjöberg, who became a world expert on hoverflies after moving to an island near Stockholm. (Which is a reminder that 'insulate' isn't just a term for heating specialists and electrical engineers—it means 'to make into an island', from the Late Latin *insulatus*.)

The biogeographies of islands may even serve as models or laboratories of the earth's own history: Charles Darwin and Alfred Russel Wallace inferred the basic principles of evolution through encounters with islands; Darwin—famously—by observing changes in beak shapes of related finch subspecies on neighbouring islands of the Galápagos chain; Wallace—who even wrote a book called *Island Life* (1880)—by noting the radical discontinuities between Bali and Lombok, which are separated by a strait no wider than fifteen miles. Inbreeding has made islands natural experiments, not just in evolution but in epidemiology.

After a visit to Napoleon's grave on St Helena on the way back home on HMS *Beagle* in 1836, Darwin called the isolated volcanic island 'a little centre of creation'.

Peter Conrad was born on an island and, like any writer worth his mettle, hardly intends to sell his birthright, even though he has been a don at Christ Church, Oxford, for the best part of forty years now. The island in question is Tasmania, which is a rather large island even if it does lies at the end of things. He writes: '[it] immediately determined the way I would see the world. I see that world from a distance, as if I do not belong to it—or has it perhaps expelled and ostracized me?' As with most of its penal inhabitants, who were banished rather than born there, Tasmania—'that small, morbid island'—fostered dreams of escape.

For sure, islands are peripheral, but in these days of negotiable, imagined centres, it might be thought that growing up as a castaway offers the skewed advantage of perspective. In their atmosphere of exclusivity and self-sufficiency, especially to infant eyes, islands and families have much in common. Sometimes Conrad writes as if he grew up an orphan: quite a bit of this short book is taken up with a discussion of how Daniel Defoe seized on the story of the Scottish sailor Alexander Selkirk—who was abandoned for four years on Juan Fernandez Island and eventually lost the ability to speak, taciturnity being another characteristic of islanders— and turned it into the modern gospel story of Cartesian man with no option other than to use his wits and conquer the self-shaped land he could call his own. Napoleon measured out his life in islands, from Corsica to Saint Helena, and even considered Paris an island in the middle of France. But aren't some islands too big or historically important to be thought of as such? 'The British Isles, for Defoe, were an extension of Crusoe's little kingdom', asserts Conrad—what of Japan, Greenland, Madagascar, even Australia itself?

Tasmania made Peter Conrad an introvert, although it would implausibly seem the entire grounds for his intellectual and stylistic restlessness. Indeed, once the infant recollections are put to bed again, Conrad embarks not on the hugely ambitious journey offered by his subtitle but on a rather whimsical round of island-hopping. The island as imaginative construct is his thing. Aside from the day trip to Crusoe's private island, we pay fleeting visits to Marguerite Yourcenar on Mount Desert Island off the coast of Maine, Anton Chekhov taking the hard route across Siberia to Sakhalin and then sailing back via Hong Kong and Ceylon, Auden in Iceland revolted by fish-soup served with a dollop of brilliantine, Marlon Brando purchasing the atoll of Tetiaroa near Tahiti where he could pretend to be Fletcher Christian off-screen too, and Robert Louis Stevenson's brave and principled attempt to stand up to the German colonisers on behalf on the natives of his adopted, final island of Samoa.

Conrad transports us from the island as paradise—Calypso, Cythera, the Greek Islands, Tyre, Goethe's Sicily—via the fabled Atlantis and even Utopia (Bougainville, in his famous log from Tahiti in 1768 which had such an effect on the *philosophes* of the Enlightenment, couldn't decide whether the fortunate isles he had stumbled on were a 'Nouvelle Cythère' or 'Europie') to rather more purgatorial, not to say sinister instances: Böcklin's 'Isle of the Dead', the volcanic Stromboli, inaccessible Pitcairn and Napoleon's decline and death on St Helena. Islands can be places of incarceration and banishment, a penal tradition that goes back to classical times: Trotsky started his years of exile on the island of Prinkipo in the Sea of Marmara. Conrad being Conrad, we are apprised of the fascinating snippet that Ingmar Bergman chanced upon Fårö in 1959 while looking for a location to shoot *Through a Glass Darkly*, and that he had originally intended filming it on Orkney. And Defoe's Crusoe provides him with an opportunity to fast-forward not just to Michel Tournier's novel *Friday*, in which the main character emerges as an existentialist, but to J.G. Ballard's memorably bizarre *Concrete Island*, a parodic tale of a man stranded for days on a traffic island in the middle of the Westway in London.

Hopping between islands without really knowing which one you're going to next (or even why you're headed there) can be an exhausting and ultimately futile exercise. What Conrad offers in archipelagic erudition is drained from his analysis of his own need for detached territorial expression. I read his book on a health mission to St Lucia shortly after visiting an old friend from school who settled twenty years ago on Shetland; both places are islands, but there most of the similarities end. The one has all problems of being a micronation in the Caribbean chain with a neighbour, Martinique, that enjoys a standard of living almost on a par with Europe (and is actually considered an 'ultraperipheral' part of the EU); the other of preserving through judicial use of North Sea oil revenue its semi-Norse identity within a Scotland newly asserting its own within the United Kingdom. Before that, I had the luck to get to know over three years parts of Indonesia, a multi-ethnic archipelago of 17,000 islands, some of which, from year to year, even vanish into or emerge from the ocean. It is thought that roughly the same number of islands across the world (between 15,000 and 20 000) could disappear, submerged by the raising ocean level, during the twenty-first century.

Conrad himself must have visited many islands in his life, although there is no evidence that he has actually visited all those mentioned in his book, and no shipping route that might have governed his often surprisingly wistful and drifting prose. Given his allegiances, it is surprising he doesn't mention René Daumal's cult-novel *Mount Analogue*, especially since it, like one of Gulliver's half-imagined islands, is set close to where Van Diemen's Land (Tasmania) turned out to exist: it manages to fuse the appeal of the island with that of the mountain, a no less mythic construct. Daumal, it has been suggested, wanted to do for metaphysics what Jules Verne had done for physics.

(One variety of writerly consciousness, it seems, is irresistibly attracted to rafts with summits.) And if you want to read a brilliant book about the difficulty of living on an island with no population and nothing much to offer except 'a bit of dry land in the middle of a lot of water', then James Hamilton-Paterson's *Playing with Water* (1987), a fascinating account of his life on 'Tiwarik', in the Philippines, is the book to read. As Hamilton-Paterson, a trained marine biologist, avers in one of his musings on the seven-tenths of the planet that is water, 'the whole concept of the island, which until recently was implicit with all manner of promise, is now redolent of loss'.

If you weren't born on an island, Conrad suggests, you will in the course of your life 'have adopted or acquired one'. Some people wealthy enough actually do so, of course: there is even an internet realtor agency catering solely for clients 'of significant solvency' who wish to become 'isolatoes' (as Herman Melville called them) on the sea-lapped strand of their personal erotic fief; others want to rid their island of the imported rats and give it a second chance, all pristine and green (Scilly Isles). Islands are places where you won't be defiled by the contemporary world, even if you've profited greatly from its money or star system. After September 11, there was a rush of Hollywood stars buying up islands where they could sit out the next terrorist attack: Johnny Depp acquired Little Hall's Pond Cay in the Bahamas, Leonardo DiCaprio a hundred-acre island with an airstrip in Belize, and Mel Gibson Mago in Fiji. The bankrupt Greek government is even now being advised to sell some of its 3,000 outcrops, only eighty-seven of which are properly inhabited. As the realtor guys like to say: 'the next best thing to being king is ruling over your own private island'.

When Conrad points out that some islands started out as blessed, but became a synonym for perdition because they chose separation—'like devils', that being Milton's view of Tenerife in *Paradise Lost*, and in *The Tempest* the Bermudas are confused with the Bermoothes, a dangerous former district of London—you begin to suspect *fallenness* is truly what he is talking about: 'Remorse makes us value what we have destroyed or discarded: geopolitically, islands are once again an attractive proposition'. But remorse can't change the fact that Donne was wrong to say that no man is an island—'every man inhabits one'. That would seem to be true at least for most of the inhabitants of big modern cities. We aren't just isolatoes, we are co-isolated: we exist as an interdependency of loosely adjacent insularities which, in Conrad's analogical world, might call to mind those claustrophobic modular pods— capsule hotels—offered to Japanese businessmen for a couple of thousand yen a night as a refuge from (and preparation for) the corporate team-game.

An island doesn't get smaller than that in terms of habitable space. 'Wohnung für das Existenzminimum' as the German modernists used to say: minimum-existence housing.

# Room for Fetishes

*Redmond O'Hanlon's Travel Philosophy*

With his mutton-chop whiskers and snowy-white hair, Redmond O'Hanlon is every inch everybody's idea of the eccentric nineteenth-century naturalist, a kind of Indiana Jones in recessed retirement. In thirty years, he has written some of the most colourful, funny and archly mischievous travel books around: his *Congo Journey* (1996), an account of a six-month trip through the northern Congo basin rainforest is now a Penguin Classic, although equally of note are *Into the Heart of Borneo* (1984), an expedition up the Rajang river in Sarawak with the poet James Fenton (who told O'Hanlon when he tried to entice him to join a later expedition to the Amazon, 'I wouldn't come with you to High Wycombe') and a sleep-deprived, 'unhinged' (O'Hanlon's word), few wild days in North Atlantic fishing grounds in *Trawler* (2003).

In fact, Redmond O'Hanlon resembles the British zoologist Apsley Cherry-Garrard, who began his famous account of Scott's Terra Nova expedition to the Antarctic in 1911 by observing that 'polar exploration is at once the cleanest and most isolated way of having a bad time which has been devised': his book was titled *The Worst Journey in the World* (1922). Cherry-Garrard was after Emperor penguin eggs; O'Hanlon is usually 'after something' too—the rare Sumatran rhinoceros in his Borneo book—but the prize often slips away unnoticed in the heat of the writing, never having been what it was about in the first place. Even the locals in his Congo book tell him they don't believe in the existence of Africa's version of the Loch Ness monster, the legendary Mokèlé-mbèmbé, a sauropod from the age of dinosaurs that, he tells us, is rumoured to haunt the Congo basin. (Whose, then, is the magical thinking?) O'Hanlon also gets to keep his clothes on, at times for as long as a polar explorer, although his smalls don't end up freeze-dried and blanched by the prevailing weather: he doesn't shy away from revealing a glimpse of himself in Congo Journey sitting in his diarrhoea-stained breeks among the livestock in the hold of the boat.

In the Netherlands, O'Hanlon has long enjoyed cult status: Rudi Rotthier, a younger Flemish travel writer, was dispatched by a couple of enterprising Dutch publishers to spend two weeks with him; and *The Fetish Room* (Dutch title: *Over God, Darwin en natuur*) is the result, a journey into the heart of a writer (though one might feel that this hypostatic shorthand for a directly personal if troubling revelation has, ever since Conrad's novel made it famous, been rather overdone). Sixty hours of recordings have been condensed into what reads like an extended interview, with scope for explanations and interjections from the admiring—but certainly not uncritical—younger writer. He ought to take full credit for editing the looping dialogue which O'Hanlon, it appears, merely fact-checked. As a foreign visitor, Rotthier can walk all over the class lines that immediately lead your average Brit, as O'Hanlon claims, to pigeonhole him as a member of the upper middle-class and treat him accordingly.

One of O'Hanlon's specialties is to terrify his readers (and presumably himself first) with lists of dire local diseases while hinting at the untold natural perils lying in wait for the unwary: these include parasitic worms, pit vipers, wild-boar ticks, thread leeches and assassin bugs—although the common *Anopheles* mosquito is probably the greatest menace of all. It is a discomfiting thought that Nature in all its amazing diversity is going to try at some point to exploit even the gentle author as a primary resource. The genre is sometimes called 'horror travel', and suggests why O'Hanlon has been compared to Hunter S.

Thompson, another writer willing to go to extremes for the sake of writing about them—and how he survived them. Sometimes the sheer variety of nastinesses he lists distracts from the fact that there is a nugatory quality to contemporary travel writing: the Victorians (as well as working in the service of the British Empire) faced real dangers and privations that, in some cases, brought them very close to death. Often the most fuss they made about their imminent demise was to sing hymns to drown out the shriek of the storm around them while yearning (as they later confessed to their diaries) for a tin of peaches.

At the beginning of the twentieth century, Charles Hose had explored and exposed as its colonial administrator the fetidly lush interior of Borneo (*The Field-Book of a Jungle-Wallah*, 1929), leaving his name on several species of mammals and amphibians as well as the mountain range in the island's centre. Joseph Conrad (subject of O'Hanlon's doctoral thesis and his first book) kept a copy of Alfred Russel Wallace's *Travels in the Malay Archipelago* beside his bed: now there was a truly intrepid man. Wallace, like many of Conrad's heroes, never thought about using his entrepreneurial talents to his own advantage: he also quite happily deferred to Darwin as the elder and more eminent naturalist, even though he too had a solid claim to be the originator of evolutionary theory. O'Hanlon for his part has never pretended to be especially intrepid: he is always being saved by more clued-in or competent companions—or by sheer luck. He likes to play the fool in the most improbable situations. And he certainly has the gift of the gab: Rotthier even has a Boswell moment when a *New Yorker* journalist drops in for a brief interview with O'Hanlon and he finds himself unexpectedly becoming jealous, only to make the mordant discovery, as the afternoon wears on, that everyone gets to hear the same stories. Timing is everything in the performance art of self-presentation.

The most striking feature of Rotthier's trip to O'Hanlon at home—Pelican House in Oxfordshire—is its comically humdrum pace. The odd couple visit the wilds of Wiltshire, Dorset and Kent. They stop in Calne, where O'Hanlon spent a largely unhappy childhood, and at Marlborough College, the school from which he claims he was expelled for riding a motorbike on the campus. Much time is spent at the local pub, downing pints of Old Tripp and talking about his early life and gifted friends—Julian Barnes, Ian McEwan, Martin Amis and the old *New Statesman* gang. A new genus of clerid beetle has been named after him by an American entomologist: *Ohanlonella esperanzae.* His wife Belinda, who has just come out of hospital, and his children Puffin and Galen, have cameo roles, mostly to rescue O'Hanlon from unwashed dishes and other pile-ups. It was Belinda's dressmaking business that had kept the family afloat in the early days. O'Hanlon's academic career petered out when it was discovered that he was teaching his students the works of the wrong century (although he was natural history editor at the *Times Literary Supplement* for many years). Other shortcomings include being unable to read a road map. He is also undergoing analysis (recurring nightmares arrive like bad weather in his travel books), which seems to have much to do with the casual cruelties of his histrionic mother and narrow-minded Anglican clergyman father when he was young: on one occasion while his father took him out to lecture him over lunch on his wayward ways his mother sneaked into his apartment and made a bonfire outside of all his books ('vile, indecent, an absurd waste of time') except for Wordsworth, whose works he has naturally been unable to read since.

O'Hanlon is determined to be in holiday spirits, but it's clear his own life is a bit of a mess. He can only marvel at the productive regularity of Charles Darwin's when their trail takes them to his property, Down House, near Bromley in Kent, which Darwin had chosen because it was sufficiently removed from the nearest railway station to deter casual visitors: never trained formally as a biologist, Darwin's vast orders of evidence were gathered at a tortoise pace and in an impressively expansive way, in constant discussion with both learned authorities and practical people whose knowledge of nature did not originate from books. O'Hanlon, by comparison, is like a Jack in the box.

Darwin had his dark days too, and recorded the symptoms for years after his *Beagle* voyage of what O'Hanlon thinks was a psychosomatic illness. Cherry-Garrard also suffered from depression after returning from Antarctica, where many of his friends had perished; his therapy was to write *The Worst Journey in the World*.

Rotthier catches the scent of something compulsive in O'Hanlon's own nature when he discovers his trophy den— the fetish room of the title. Since childhood, O'Hanlon has been collecting relics and objects of interest for what American Indians would recognise as a 'sweat lodge': a place he goes to recoup his forces in preparation for writing. Many people enjoy the passion of collecting, and nobody would be surprised to find that O'Hanlon's personal museum contains some odd items. Along with his childhood bird-shells and the paraphernalia of stuffed animals and preserved insects—shards and relics of the *bellum omnium contre omnes* that Darwin's work inadvertently helped to fetishise—are the remains of his university friend Douglas Winchester who burned himself to death aged twenty-four when they were students together at Oxford: a few tatters of his foot now reside in a Maxwell House coffee jar. After encountering this gruesome mojo it seems logical enough that, having carried a protective fetish on his person throughout the expedition recounted in *Congo Journey*, O'Hanlon was eventually taken by the native bearers to be a kind of sorcerer himself.

O'Hanlon is clearly exercised by, while being at loggerheads with, the basic attitudes and assumptions his piously unfeeling parents left on his doorstep—one of which was clearly a Puritan anxiety about idolatrous habits and the true nature of the logos. *The Fetish Room* recognises on the other hand that the category of what is called 'performative utterances' (most spectacularly, Joshua commanding the sun to stand still for a day until his army had quashed the Emorites, surely more than anything else a tribute to the power of speech) has become ever more crucial to our supposedly rational world, even in science. The whole of the Western world—with its confusion about the boundaries between reality and fantasy, faith in the image, and devotion to accumulating digital money tokens—is a kind of fetish room, and seems to have wholeheartedly embraced the kind of thinking former colonialists once thought was disappearing for good. We rarely recognise our own idolisation of cars, computers and other prestigious goods as fetishism, and overlook the fact that older animistic practices were at least informed by a fiercely protective feeling for the materials at hand, whether stone, wood or bronze. When it comes down to it, writers are just as busy as anyone trying to manipulate hidden agencies in order to feel 'invincible' (O'Hanlon's word) in the marketplace. In a commodified society, all kinds of things acquire anthropomorphic attributes, not least rationality.

This muddle of idealism and materialism was even anticipated at the outset of his career when he referred, in the gloriously incongruous setting of the Sarawak jungle, to the 'universal fetish-philosophy of the events of life'. That phrase came from a scholarly text by the Victorian anthropologist and cultural evolutionist Edward Burnett Tylor—who believed that 'research into the history and prehistory of man [...] could be used as a basis for the reform of British society'—and it is gone before you can properly register its telltale presence, like the brightest blue-banded kingfisher (*Alcedo euryzona*) in the mighty hanging gardens of the Rajang.

# Polish Projections

*Ryszard Kapuściński Comes over All Ethical*

LITERATURE ON FOOT

Posthumously published, *The Other* will come as a surprise to admirers of Ryszard Kapuściński's taut and vivid accounts of some of the globe's major wars, coups and revolutions of the last forty years in *The Soccer War*, *The Shadow of the Sun* and *Shah of Shahs*. A collection of three lectures delivered in 2005 at the Institute for Human Sciences (IWM) in Vienna accompanied by three addresses, all on what is rebarbatively known in academic circles as 'alterity', it could be described as a catalogue of pieties. Except for the shortest piece, 'My Other' (1990), the book dates from the time when he was working on his last major work, *Travels with Herodotus*, itself a rather mellow and reflective look back at his life as a conscientious reporter. Herodotus, it will be remembered, although the 'father of history' was also accused in his day of being a terrible fibber.

As Neal Ascherson remarks in his introduction, as journalists get older they tend to reflect more on the perspective they have acquired. This may be a mixed blessing. Some people spend their entire adult life in the dim light of their bedrooms and are acclaimed great novelists; Kapuściński went to some of the sunlit dark places of the earth (mostly in Africa) before he became famous. Authenticity was the thing: the flat mirage of heat and hardship were his Alps, arduous ascension of which had first marked out those Romantic poets who made a scene about being in thrall to their visions.

Kapuściński slogged it out on the level. 'Being there' was his trademark and perspective: a white man in Africa in the years of decolonisation, a sober journalistic master of *neue Sachlichkeit* whose base was in the Soviet bloc, and last—but by no means least—a Pole treading self-consciously in the footprints of Józef Korzeniowski, better known as Joseph Conrad: 'I seemed at one bound to have been transported into some lightless region of subtle horrors, where pure, uncomplicated savagery was a positive relief, being something that had a right to exist—obviously—in the sunshine'. That was from *Heart of Darkness*, but it could have been filed by Kapuściński.

Perpetually short of funds and resources unlike his more generously sponsored colleagues at Agence France Presse and Associated Press, Kapuściński ('Kapu') practised a journalism of reduced means: staying in third-class hotels, sharing 'le taxi-brousse' with entire families (and their livestock), suffering the indignities of intestinal amoebiasis far from anything resembling a toilet, being threatened with the barrels and butts of Kalashnikovs, even going hungry at times.

It was the making of him. In an interview in 1987 he defined his style of writing as follows: 'I feel sometimes that I am working in a completely new field of literature, in an area that is both unoccupied and unexplored... I sometimes call it literature by foot.' Except that it wasn't quite so unoccupied and unexplored, and it was rarely as pedestrian as he pretended. Ascherson astutely puts him in the line of the central European tradition of the 'roving reporter' first developed by the German-speaking Prague writer Egon Erwin Kisch, although Joseph Roth is a more obvious example of a writer who sent in copy that was hard-nosed, exotic and entertainingly written. It is not without interest that both these central European writers managed to keep their novels quite distinct from their reportage, though journalistic deadlines and formatting techniques greatly influenced their approach to the former.

## HATS AND LIGHTING MANUALS

Kapuściński was a brilliant raconteur, but he was no anthropologist and certainly no ethicist. Indeed, it is telling that the propriety of his self-presentation has recently been challenged by various parties, including members of the British school of anthropology which, ironically indeed, was founded by a Pole, Bronisław Malinowski (1888–1942): what distinguished Malinowski's anthropology was the anti-speculative tendency that complemented (and complicated) its solid commitment to fieldwork.

Kapuściński, for his part, seems to think fieldwork is the sole commandment—'an indispensable condition of getting to know Others'. Fieldwork, arduous and taxing though it may be, is often the intellectually straightforward part of ethnography: it is dominated by the clamour of the present. Although Kapuściński scolds foreign correspondents for their breezy ignorance, he has himself been charged with getting quite basic ethnographic facts wrong (John Ryle), of lacking journalistic probity (Jack Shafer), and even of drifting into 'the liberal version of neo-colonial racialist discourse' (Aleksandar Hemon)—in other words, of being an ecumenical relativist who out of respect for other traditions is unable to entertain the idea of human behaviour as shaped by anything other than the culture into which people are born. For the preceding generation, that same behaviour-shaping category had been called *race*.

*The Other* will not reassure these critics. It would have been instructive, on all accounts, to have read more about Kapuściński's literary motivations and strategies: why, for instance, in *The Emperor: Downfall of an Autocrat*—his much-praised 'eye-witness' account of the last days of the Ethiopian monarchy—which ends with an obit from *The Ethiopian Herald*, does he attribute honorifics to Haile Selassie—'His

Most Puissant Majesty', 'His Most Singular Highness', and so on—that derive not from Amharic, as he admitted in an interview with a German newspaper, but an old history book on the kings of Poland?

This, his most famous book, is actually a study of a *type*. Its structure derives from a series of interviews with initialled courtiers who, for all their tragicomic comments on the fall of the despot, are stylised heraldic personages. Which political structure are they really commenting upon? While a European might read the novel as both modern and baroque, and perhaps even concede that Kapuściński had found a cunning cipher with which to evade the domestic Communist censors (Ismail Kadare adopted just this approach in his memorable political fable *The Pyramid*, setting his story of life under the communist dictator Hoxha in the monumental death culture of ancient Egypt), an Ethiopian could only read the novel as a travesty— as if his country had been textually colonised, although in point of fact Ethiopia was the only African country never to be subjugated to a European power other than during its brief occupation by Mussolini's troops in the late 1930s.

Kapuściński sometimes even forgot which hat he was wearing. Sometimes he was wearing both at once, as *The Emperor* suggests. And he lent hostages to fortune by telling a British newspaper in 2001 that 'we have too many fables, too much make-believe. Journalists must deepen their anthropological and cultural knowledge and explain the context of events. They must read.' On his actual travels, he was filing agency reports from Ougadougou and Addis Ababa for the PAP [Polish National News Service]; it was only when he got back to Warsaw that, with the help of his diaries, he was able to write the surrealistic stories that aspired to be more than journalism, news that stayed 'news', even while continuing to feature himself in the starring role with full journalistic credentials.

He was writing stories truer than the truth, as his friend the film maker Werner Herzog has insisted. But the truth can be vengeful, especially with those who try to best it. Richard Leacock, one of the pioneers of Direct Cinema, liked to quote an early Hollywood lighting manual: 'When shooting Westerns, use real Indians if possible; but if Indians are not available, use Hungarians.' Kapuściński might have become famous for writing a lot about 'Africans', but for projection purposes he was always using Poles—although, as Ascherson can't help pointing out, 'he never wrote a book about the racial and national prejudices that were endemic in Poland'.

Kapuściński's 'confession' isn't so much a book that cuts to the heart of things as a book missing one: ever since Rousseau, it has been a mark of ethical superiority to place oneself, so to speak, on the margins. Kapuściński says nothing about how Malinowski spoke directly to his compatriots in the grim years when world history (as represented by the baleful weight of Soviet dictatorship) seemed to have marooned Poland's national aspirations in a backwater. Kapuściński himself could well be the model for the European writer setting out to 'embrace' the continent in Binyavanga Wainaina's sardonic essay *How to Write about Africa*—'in your text, treat Africa as if it were one country'.

Perhaps anthropology, like charity, ought to begin more often at home.

STUFFED SHIRTS

Kapuściński's Polish reference points in *The Other* include Father Józef Tischner, a Kraków theologian and confidant of the late pope, and Emmanuel Levinas, the French philosopher born to a Jewish family in Lithuania: dialogists to a man. Perhaps because he had settled in the land of

Descartes, and certainly as a reaction to the events on Polish soil during the war (in which his family perished), Levinas insisted that what really counted in philosophy was not cognition, but *re*cognition: 'the self is only possible through the recognition of the Other'. Not acknowledging others is an ethical dereliction. In a genuine commitment to universal justice, the other (possibly vulnerable) person has to be confronted face to face (*panim el panim*), an old observance out of the Book of Deuteronomy which did its best to get us to see, long before Kant, the encounter with other people as something ethically meaningful in its own terms and not just as an occasion for one's own selfish and possibly reprehensible intentions.

Kapuściński's glosses these teachings in his most sustained lyrical passage: 'Stop, he seems to be saying to the man hurrying along in the rushing crowd. There beside you is another person. Meet him. This sort of encounter is the greatest event, the most vital experience of all. Look at the Other's face as he offers it to you... The Other has a face, and it is a sacred book in which good is recorded.' Instead of self-deification, deification of the Other—'he brings you closer to God'. The mystery of the Incarnation would invite us to seek the face of God in *every* face we encounter.

Levinas called this 'the wisdom of love', although they are words from a sermon so often acknowledged in the breach: the ethics of the face-to-face is routinely subverted by the logic of global economics, which subordinates social issues to the abstract workings of the market. Kapuściński, like a waif who has just heard about America, calls the latter 'the Planet of Great Opportunity'. But the real problem is that the Other doesn't have a face, not a face we would recognise as that of somebody we know or care for: it is a generalised, totalised, indefinable other, and can only be imagined by projecting our own subjectivity upon it.

After 1945, all cultures were proclaimed equal: being Eurocentric was the deadliest intellectual sin. Revulsion against social exclusion was accompanied by a need to expiate European colonial guilt: the universal community of discourse was predicated on amends being made by oppressor to oppressed. Anthropology—the science that Octavio Paz called 'the remorse of the Occident'—prospered. Soon the myth of the Noble Savage was reborn in the guise of *tiers-mondisme* (the famous 1955 Bandung Conference was held a year before Kapuściński got his first foreign posting, as he recounts in *Travels with Herodotus*), a hermeneutic turn that generated a lot more heat than light—as it was bound to do: the ideals of moral refinement always come with a haze of specious rhetoric and bad faith. But the guilt about the colonial adventures of the past had consequences. Anthropologists would have to prove that their models of alien societies were not simply tools for their ultimate domination. 'Respect' became the universal password. And *bien pensant* European intellectuals began to bemoan the world-historical trend towards urbanisation.

Here is what Kapuściński says: 'establishing identity, which is achieved *inter alia* by defining our relations to Others, has been complicated in the past few decades for many reasons, and sometimes proves quite impossible. This is the result of a weakening of traditional cultural ties, caused by the migration of rural populations to cities, where a new type of identity is starting to be formed—a hybrid one, previously unprecedented on such a scale... today only half the world's citizens are peasants, and this class is gradually disappearing. The peasant class used to be the most faithful depository of tradition and identity.'

Alas, the unwelcome and possibly even slightly embarrassing truth is that quite a few of the Others want to be like Us. Hans Magnus Enzensberger observed some time ago, in his essay 'Reluctant Eurocentrism' (1980), that symmetry in cultural relations is just as difficult to achieve as it is in personal ones; and in any case the idea of otherness, now that borders have become porous, has long been a platitude—'The true Eurocentrics are the others'. The others, not having read Levinas, are still eager for the culture-transcending truth of what it takes to produce cognitive and productive growth— the conditions that gave us the word 'Eurocentric' in the first place. Now 'alter'-traditions and identities contribute to the internal patchwork of industrial societies. And they don't have to wrangle with a bad conscience.

Kapuściński shows no sign of appreciating the difficulty of calling on the services of this anonymous, pulseless, hypostasised 'Other'. If alterity is a philosophy dedicated to the second person, then it's odd that the second person has been so objectified as to resemble the third.

*The Other* commends curiosity, but shows no real inquisitiveness about this state of affairs. Kapuściński has forgotten that he is first and foremost a *writer*. Like any writer, his own creative efforts are *post hoc* stylisations requiring ruthless editing, heightening of effect, structural reworkings— lots of cutting and curtailing. Style is an expulsion, a pruning, a condensation; just as being an effective member of a culture requires a sense of discrimination. Even if he thinks, he's praying out loud or atoning for years of self-centredness—like Kafka, with his '"You", I said…', or even Beckett in his urgent addresses to the imaginary auditor in his novel *Company*—the writer ends up banishing the Other from the page. Well, that *is* what an author does: writing takes its directions from the self. It is never 'life', however much the writer would like it to be. (Outside his humdrum days as a writer, he is of course at liberty to pop down to the pub for a dram of conviviality in the evening just like anybody else.)

Ryszard Kapuściński's real business was dream-work not documentary. Why he tricked out his writings with so many extraneous supports, chief among them his press-card, is something he never gets round to explaining, and perhaps never fully explained to himself either. It is bewildering that a writer who could produce stories that read so naturally and compellingly (and which show others getting his name comically wrong, *vide* the courtier 'E.' who addresses him as 'Mr Kapuchitsky' in *The Emperor*, surely a hint that *he* was the Other) felt he had to write a rulebook in his declining years in favour of 'a positive atmosphere for dialogue'. Only bureaucrats talk like that. His dream-work resembles the classic, slightly old-fashioned European projection—one inflected by self-censure, doubt and negativity, but certainly not unwilling to enter the maze of ambiguities. That is where he ought to have left it.

# Music and Metabolism

*The Composer Slamet Abdul Sjukur*

'What's that you're listening to?' asked my wife the other day. 'It sounds like Darmstadt music.'

Darmstadt is the German city that was famous for its International Summer Schools for new music in the 1960s, a regular fixture in the creative calendar for names such as Stockhausen, Xenakis and Nono. To go to Darmstadt you had to be a twelve-tone serialist, and (according to Hans Werner Henze) submit your manuscripts to Pierre Boulez for prior approval. 'Anyone who has not felt—I do not say understand—but felt the necessity of the dodecaphonic language is *USELESS*.' Condemnations of that kind were one reason why the school, to which my wife's family in Munich had some loose connections, eventually folded.

I was listening to some pieces of music played by German musicians from the Musikhochschule Lübeck which were manifestly post-1945, post-Viennese School, perhaps even post-historical. They were otherwise absolutely unidentifiable on the musical map of the nations, although I knew their composer came from the other side of the world. The CD had been graciously sent to me in my Jakarta hotel by the composer Slamet Abdul Sjukur, born in Surabaya when Indonesia was still the Dutch East Indies, after an entertaining exchange of missives—in French—on my mobile phone.

This, to my ear, was more psychoacoustics than music. Anxiously metaphysical sewing machines were being speeded up and slowed down in taped sequence before being dramatically cut short by a succession of boisterous clacks, whistles and honks. One of these pieces, 'Uwek-Uwek', was listed as being for two 'mouth explorers'. It all gave way in one piece to the aerial ejaculations of what might have been a cosmic telephone—of the new-fangled kind Nietzsche accused Wagner of being (and not just of using)—or the drone of a Zen master's negation of a negation. The closest analogue I could think of was the zany prose of Gertrude Stein, which wants to tell us that most of life is repetition: even our most exalted moments occur against a background noise of sirens, ticks and hoots, as well as the aural by-products of car engines and vacuum cleaners. It's not so much that we are mechanical beings, running on molecular clockwork (as some like to think); it's that so much of what we experience is rhythm and recombination.

But two pieces on the CD seemed to me to be true Darmstadt music, 'Darm' being the German word for the intestine. (A millennium ago the city's recorded name was Darmundestat, so the contraction to 'intestine city' is entirely fortuitous. But nothing is fortuitous, the Zen master would say…)

Both were written for a bamboo ensemble. The first, 'Orak-Arik', translates as 'scrambled egg with beans': it is a shivering, clackety contraption for a bamboo instrument ensemble, as if the music were being produced by a fantastically busy set of cutlery and skillets. The other piece, Rondo Malam or nocturnal rondo—a self-standing part of Sjukur's perhaps best-known work 'Angklung', which won the Académie Charles Cros 'Disque d'Or' award in 1975—uses the same ensemble to good effect, and with a touch of asperity. I had the impression that the composer had actually enjoyed himself pioneering this new Indonesian musical idiom. Here was all the percussive strangeness of the gamelan tradition cheekily sabotaging the formal cadences of Western music. Here were those fiendishly complex Asian polyrhythms, as one percussionist slipped out of sync with another, which allowed musicians like Steve Reich to create his 'phase shifting' techniques in the 1970s and convinced Conlon Nancarrow to write almost exclusively for the player-piano. But what made these pieces attractive to me was the disreputable appeal of the national, the quality in music that was so suspect after the end of the war—hadn't the Nazis conscripted Richard Strauss as their court composer? Nationalism in music was the scandal that had allowed Boulez to cast himself as autocrat of the universal avant-garde, and bully others with his own rage for order. What I wanted to hear were the proceeding of the Indonesian Association for the Appreciation of Grasshopper Threnodies.

An Indonesian friend who knows Skujur well sighed when he heard that I was listening to his music: 'his silences are so tremendous'. I like his sound-colour conjurations too. In fact, I don't think he would be at all upset at my finding his music 'intestinal'. Where else does music find its intentional or unintentional satire but in imitating our only partly conscious bodily rhythms and the strange urge that humans have to extol the Highest Being? Modernism might be extolled as the rationality of the Machine Age, but its hidden side was its reorganisation of the human digestive tract through environmental design and new civic structures (concepts of hygiene and cuisine expressed in the bathroom and kitchen).

Having studied for a good part of the 1960s in Paris with Olivier Messiaen (the doyen of the Darmstadt School) and Henri Dutilleux (best known for his concerto for orchestra *Métaboles*), Sjukur is a self-confessed admirer of 'French music'—a music of gadfly individualists in opposition to the brassy conformity of German music: it had been first defended by Debussy as a riposte to the vulgar chromatic Wagnerian swoons that were sweeping the boards across Europe at the close of the nineteenth century. Debussy had been so smitten by the traditional music played by a Vietnamese theatre troupe and Javanese gamelan orchestra with gongs and metallophones in their respective pavilions in the Paris Universal Exposition of 1889 that he incorporated their sonorities into what he advanced as the *other* European tradition, his anti-German one of finesse, delicacy and understatement—lepidoptery in sound. 'Let us at all costs preserve this magic peculiar to music, since of all the arts it is most susceptible to magic', he wrote later in life; profundity had nothing to do with weightiness. Ernst Guiraud, Debussy's conservative composition teacher, once played a sequence of simple parallel chords and asked him how he would 'get out of this', meaning how he intended to place the harmonies in such a way as to move towards a resolution: he found his pupil's ideas 'theoretically absurd'. 'There is no theory', retorted Debussy: 'you merely have to listen. Pleasure is the law.' His parallel and bitonal chords and sudden modulations offered a kind of texture, a modal melody that rendered harmony subordinate, perhaps best heard in the piece 'Et la lune descend sur le temple qui fut' in *Images, deuxième livre.* No composer was more important in delivering the Western tradition from its exclusive concern with the line of the note to non-European music's relish for sound—sound as a sphere, with depth and pitch and volume. (It was at this same exhibition that Paul Gauguin, similarly infatuated by the exotic, first thought of leaving Europe and settling in the Marquesas.)

With its five-note scale, Gamelan music, according to Debussy, 'contained all gradations, even some that we no longer know how to name, so that tonic and dominant were nothing more than empty phantoms of use to clever little children'. Debussy became a sonic adventurer into the pentatonic, using wholetones, antique modes and his 'floating chords' as a new way of building towers of sound—and an alternative modernism. Debussy's orchestration was brilliantly fresh and novel, especially in terms of the geography of the orchestra and dealings between instruments, as well as being full of figurations and motifs that were quite unknown to the symphonic tradition. Even scrambled eggs and beans are poetry for a hungry person! (Later, I discovered that Slamet had actually studied Debussy's affinity for the gamelan on a grant from the French government.)

Asian composers have repaid the compliment to Debussy many times over. The history book *Rhapsody in Red: How Western Classical Music Became Chinese* tells an anecdote about an American visitor to China telling everyone around him, on first hearing some Chinese music, how much it sounded like Debussy. The composer replied testily. 'No, this piece doesn't resemble Debussy! Not at all! Debussy resembles me! Debussy resembles China!'

That's how you discover what the World-Spirit resembles when your intestines are rumbling. You have a musician in your belly and you have to get him on your tongue.

# Other Varieties

*A Compacted History of Decomposition*

If any condiment can claim universal status, it's that sweet-and-sour sauce produced in industrial quantities in sachets and bottles to liven up everything from pommes frites to omelettes. Tomato ketchup, that is; though it might seem as if the modifier is redundant. Isn't ketchup *always* a tomato-based relish?

In fact, no: ketchup has an entry in Samuel Johnson's *A Dictionary of the English Language* (1755) where it is spelled 'catsup': he defines it as 'a kind of pickle, made from mushrooms'. Tomato ketchup is a modern version of a much older sauce. In the eighteenth century, catsup was indeed made from mushrooms, and sometimes even walnuts, which would be fermented with vinegar and sugar and then bottled with spices and ginger to produce the savouriness that our palates crave. This savouriness is what is now hyped as *umami* or the fifth basic taste; it is owed to the presence of free glutamate, an amino acid.

Condiments, dips, pickles, achars differ from stocks or fonds; they are elements added after cooking as taste enhancers rather than constituents of the cooking process itself. In Chapter Twenty-six of his *D'Amboinsche Rariteitkamer* (published in Amsterdam in 1705 and translated into English without 'us[ing] any locutions that were not current prior to 1700' almost three hundred years later by E.M. Beekman as *The Ambonese Curiosity Cabinet*), the great German-born naturalist and ethnographer Rumphius (Jörg Eberhardt Rumph), who lived most of his adult life on Ambon, one of the Spice Islands in the Netherlands Indies, wrote about condiments.

Freshwater crabs and shrimps would be washed downriver to the deltas after the rainy seasons and caught in cloths in huge numbers, 'whereafter they are crushed and pickled, which turns them into a thick, brown paste which is thinned with Lemon-juice and then used for dipping; this is called with a Chinese word *Kitsjap*'. This is now the Malay word *kecap* (pronounced 'kechap'), used to indicate any kind of flavouring sauce at all in contemporary Indonesia and Malaysia.

Fermentation of foods using the naturally occurring bacterium *Lactobacillus* has been a method applied for centuries in central Asia to preserve foods and improve their taste: the process gives rise to lactic acid which, along with salt, keeps foodstuffs in an edible condition by inhibiting the growth of other microbes, especially those responsible for putrefaction, thereby allowing the foods to be stored for winter consumption. In northern China, beans were fermented, specifically soy beans. The Japanese refined the process, inoculating them with sporulating *Aspergillus*, a fungal species, before exposing the mixture to salt and *Lactobacillus*: the outcome is that other universally popular cooking aid, soya sauce (*shoyu*).

Fish sauce is also a fermentation product: the action of salt (which draws water out of the tissues by osmosis) and the proteolytic enzymes or proteases occurring naturally in the viscera of the fish break down organic substances into simpler compounds even as they prevent rotting. It has been around for millennia: the Greeks and Romans used it as an unguent medicine for burns and bites (according to Pliny the Elder, who calls it a 'choice liquor' in his *Natural History*) as well as in cooking, and the words 'garum' or 'muria' are still occasionally seen on brand labels. Fish sauce was traded all over China in the Han dynasty but then declined drastically in popularity in the north, remaining common only in the southern provinces of Fujian and Canton, where the local sea traders traditionally did business with everybody in the South

China Sea region, from Thailand and the Mekong delta to Sulawesi and the Philippines, all confirmed fish sauce-using areas. James Murray, editor of the OED, correctly surmised that the word had come into English from the first colonial attempts to break into the Chinese domination of world trade in the seventeenth and eighteenth centuries (and perhaps even via the British garrison Fort Marlborough on the west coast of Sumatra), and figured that catsup or ketchup was a corruption of *kôe-chiap*, a dialect term in Amoy and Hokkien, two related dialects of the Southern Min region of China.

It wasn't just this brine of pickled fish that attracted the attention of long European noses. Rumphius in the same chapter of his book mentions floes of small decapods 'scarcely bigger than lice' (what we would call krill) being fished out of the Java Sea, salted and left to dry for several months in the sun. Instead of being turned into a sauce, the mash made from these dried crustaceans was allowed to harden into purple-grey cylinders or blocks of the notorious *terasi* or *belacan*, slices or pellets of which are heated before cooking and used like stock cubes. Henry Ogg Forbes, a Scottish explorer who visited the Malay archipelago just a few years after the more famous Alfred Russel Wallace, reported in *A Naturalist's Wanderings in the Eastern Archipelago* (1885) his discomposure on waking up late one Sunday morning in his house in Genteng to smell 'the terrific and unwonted odour of decomposition'. Having searched through the midden and his entire collection of exotic hornbills, lorikeets and warblers (personally shot or trapped in the previous weeks), thereby irritating his eyes for a week because of the arsenical soap used to preserve them, he finally discovered from his cook that the source of the smell was the very same 'trassi'. On the point of banning it from the house, he was nonplussed to discover that every meal he had eaten since arriving in Java had been prepared with these malodorous pellets. If, as is often said, the way to a multiculturalist's heart is through his stomach, it seems that colonial tastebuds had to make concessions too to native practices.

These days *terasi* can be bought in shrink-wrapped blocks in Asian stores almost anywhere on the globe. H.O. Forbes might have been right about its enveloping smell—even wrapped in cellophane and boxed in plastic, 'Extract of Decomposition' will come to inhabit your fridge—but a good sambal just can't be made without it.

# Archipelago and Submarine

*Field-Notes from Indonesia*

Mistaking the capital *I* in my given name for a lower-case *l*, the receptionist in the Kristal Hotel in Kupang entered my name in the register—every letter a block capital—as PAK LAIN. This made one more to add to the scores of official documents and hotel booking forms which recorded my existence, in Indonesia, as Mr Foreigner—'Pak' being the honorific extended to all adult males in Indonesia, 'lain' the bisyllabic Malay adjective indicating difference or otherness.

It is true that I have been addressed in France as 'Yann', 'Alain' and even 'Brian', sometimes even on official documents, but 'Pak La-in' was a more interesting distortion. It could even be said to be a nominal instance of Rimbaud's famous motto 'Je est un autre' ('I is somebody else') in the very archipelago that he fled, only a few weeks after landing there in 1876—a deserter of the Koninklijk Nederlandsch-Indisch Leger (Royal Dutch East Indies Army).

'Lain' made me ANDERS. This was the pseudonym chosen in 1932 by the unorthodox cultural critic Günther Anders— Hannah Arendt's first husband—in the Weimar years when a Berlin editor complained that he had too many writers on his staff called Stern. 'Give me something different', barked the editor. 'Then call me "Different"', riposted Günther Stern. And that was how he acquired his pen name: Günther Anders. Both of his parents were famous pioneering psychologists, and when he was a child his mother had confided to her diary: 'Günther is struggling with the unmistakable desire to be "different". […] He is downright afraid of disappearing in the crowd.' He remained a philosophising outsider all his life.

'Anders' is the given name Andrew in the Nordic languages, but in German and Dutch 'anders' is an adverb that signals a difference of opinion, nature or quality—'Hier stehe ich, ich kann nicht anders' was Luther's famous retort at the Diet of Worms. Here I stand; I can do no other. 'Anders' is everything that is *otherwise* or *contrary*. 'Baldanders' ('Soon-something-else') is the protean character who turns up in the last book of Hans von Grimmelhausen's picaresque novel *The Adventuresome Simplicissimus*, which first appeared in 1669. 'Anders' also was the name first adopted by Robert Musil for the personage who would ultimately become Ulrich, hero of his great unfinished novel *The Man Without Qualities*—'the man of precision who is aware that precision does not lead to happiness'. 'Der andere Zustand'—the 'other' condition—was Musil's own shorthand term for what he considered the ethical instinct as opposed to the social bedrock of morality.

A man without qualities or, better said, a man without *easily discernible* qualities is, in some senses, how I am regarded in remoter parts of the archipelago: interesting and even intriguing, but a foreigner and therefore an unknown, unreadable and unpredictable element, and best kept politely at arm's length. Hotel receptionists and interlocutors are merely trying to adopt the neutral, universal, non-committal attitude: 'How should I relate to Mr. Foreigner?' One of the lessons that any traveller learns is that his or her personhood is always questionable. We know this from the *Odyssey*, when Odysseus uses his cunning to save his skin, telling the Cyclops his name is *Outis*, which is understood by the giant's neighbours as 'oú tis' (no one) when he calls out for their assistance after being blinded in drunken slumber by his wily guest. 'Mé tis?' they ask: is there someone there? They are themselves caught up in an extended pun, since *metis* is the word for 'cunning'.

On a similar occasion Franz Kafka asked a witty question of his diary: 'Although I wrote my name clearly at the hotel, and although they themselves have written it correctly twice already, they still have Josef K. written in the register. Should I explain the situation to them, or should I have them explain it to me?'

So tonight, I'm going to retire to my room and ponder the fact that if what is alien about me has become so manifestly visible as to be conferred upon me as a temporary identity, then the other must already have the upper hand over the ego. As they say, you only have to steal a look in the mirror and a stranger's ready to swear blind he's you.

## LITTLE HOLES JOINED UP

The coastal towns in the southern provinces of Sumatra are simple elevated houses of wood hung with nets, and the spectacle is exactly the same as the one described by Herodotus in ancient Egypt two and a half thousand years ago: by day the nets serve to land fish; by night they ward off the mosquitoes. The forms of the nets and the heft of their mesh depend on foresight and planning, on the kinds of fish the local people expect to catch; on whether they intend to fish from boats or in shallow water along the estuaries; on whether they will be casting by day or night. Then the nets are brought back to the houses for removal of debris and encrustations and possible repair, because nets are made by the same people who do the sewing: with a needle made of wood, a bobbin to space the holes, and a knife to cut the thread. The lightweight nets used for fishing along the coast have to be untangled; then they are used to protect the house in the last light of the day and the first light of the next. Only the careless succumb to malaria, and mothers shiver under the bedcovers while the sun blisters the plasterwork, and their children play in the street.

You get to dream a lot when you live perched above the liquid medium and are surrounded by gossamer drapes, and the constant threat of airborne disease is kept at bay by the sheerest of filaments. Paul Strand has a photograph from one of his journeys in Mexico where nets can be seen, hung up to dry alongside the houses. Nets are the most precious tool and possession of poor families. Nets don't need the solidity of ground; they only require a medium. They are a metaphor at one remove for photographs themselves.

In the long history of trickery, the invention of nets—a spider's awnings but also the means to catch the subtle salmon—is always a central accomplishment: the trickster has to still his own hunger and bend appetites other than his own to his peculiar purposes. This world is full of dark devouring forces. In Aeschylus' *Choephori*, the second play in his trilogy about the House of Agamemnon, the dramatist even compares children to the corks that bear up a net, 'keeping safe the spun flax that stretches up from the depths'.

Language is an iridescent net that, depending on the size of the mesh and where and how it is thrown into the water, snags some fish and lets others slip through its weave. But it doesn't create fish, or exhaust their stocks. And sometimes the net gets snarled up, knotted or broken, the net being an object in the world, like the creatures it is supposed to entrap.

CLOUD NINE

Observed from the plane as it descends over the Java Sea and the Thousand Islands scattered across the bay to land at Soekarno-Hatta airport west of the city, Jakarta appears to generate its own microclimate. A towering, threatening hammerhead of cumulus congestus, alarmingly reminiscent of those startling photographs of the Horsehead Galaxy in Orion, piles up rills and protuberances that rapidly form into tower-like clouds with cauliflower tops louring over the forty square kilometres of Jabotabek, the vast urban area around and including Jakarta. This itself expands and contracts by day and night, like an enormous lung: two million people come into the mansarded modern city to work, and then all attempt to leave it at the same time in the evening.

And it is only on holidays, such as the running together of the Prophet's birthday and Good Friday on successive days (with a weekend to follow), that I have been able to observe the two volcanoes—Gunung Gede (last active in 1957) and Gunung Salak—which form the southern backdrop to the flat and formerly malarial plain on which this city is built. Only then does the smog of exhaust fumes dissipate. The vast fractus clouds of waste gases produced by thousands of motorbikes and cars on the streets yield for a few days to the weather coming in, as it were, from the exterior, and moods lift at the simple possibility of a horizon: 'The volcanoes came out today', is what people say. The current population of the Greater Jakarta conurbation (30 million) is greater than that of the entire Australian landmass (24 million).

A YEAR OF ISLANDS

'I have been on my journey of discovery, or on my pursuit, since I saw you last, and have chanced upon extremely promising coastlines—which perhaps circumscribe a new scientific continent.—This ocean is teeming with fledgling islands.'

That was how, in 1798, Novalis described the philosophy of his 'encyclopaedistics' to the members of the Romantic Circle in Jena, and although he aspired to sound like Georg Forster, assistant naturalist to Captain Cook on his second voyage around the world, Novalis was at the time a twenty-six-year-old student at the Freiberg Mining Academy in Saxony with very little experience of the sea and nautical matters.

Novalis wrote that entry when most of the known world had been explored and catalogued. Novalis wanted to go further than Diderot, who, a generation before, had hoped that the *Encyclopédie* would bring all of knowledge within the covers of a set of books: Novalis wanted to study the dynamic effects of each science on the others in order to create 'a scientific Bible'. As first suggested by Francis Bacon, this book would induct the reader into the Golden Age, whereby man would return to his prelapsarian state in a world 'rearranged' by the totality of knowledge.

Indonesia's archipelago is the real geographical equivalent of Novalis' new scientific continent in the imaginary world called 'Encyclopaedia'. Nobody knows exactly how many islands there are in the archipelago: about 17,500 is the figure generally put forward. But some of those islands—coral-fringed atolls, sandy cays or bituminous volcano slags thrust up from the ocean bed—are vanishing and surfacing every year, and global warming could remove hundreds of the lower-lying ones from the map. It's not the humans who do the wandering towards fabled islands, but the islands which appear out of nowhere, like the strange clumps of volcanic tufa seen near the Galapagos by Herman Melville and called the Encantadas. Alexander Selkirk, the model for Robinson Crusoe, was shipwrecked for four years on one of them. These were islands on the move, and nobody was sure where to position them exactly on the naval charts. The whole of the Pacific was a kind of board on which islands might roam, like the sandy islands Robert Louis Stevenson caught sight of when he sailed out of San Francisco for Samoa.

In 2010, the National Coordinating Agency for Survey and Mapping suggested that Indonesia had only 13,466 islands.

According to a survey carried out a decade earlier, there were 18,307 islands in the archipelago, but that included some of the tidal outliers on its fringes: sandbanks sitting over gas reserves near Singapore, coral reefs with remarkable avifauna in the South China Sea, upheavals of the earth's crust on the Halmahera Plate. Under the UN Convention of the Law of the Sea, islands have to be identified by name. Using a handheld geo-navigational device, the members of the survey team verified the coordinates of the island, spoke to the locals and determined its name, or names. Less than half of Indonesia's immense array of islands is inhabited. Many are indeed nameless. And yet, according to the UN rules, an island name can be recognised if it is known separately to as few as two local people.

But the Land of the Encyclopaedia is not ruled by the weathers of optimism, like those grand schemes dreamed up by Novalis and his contemporaries. The conviction that knowledge can be organised, catalogued, standardised and, perhaps most importantly, contained, has yielded to the hysteria of the flim-flam. Knowledge is exploding, so admire its ravishingly passing displays, its random swarms of insects and fish, its captivating patterns, its 'strange facts'. Islands lie at the periphery of a world we think we know, far from Jerusalem's golden navel.

The bottom line is: if you're going to write in an archipelagic manner, you have to expect your readers to know how to swim. Ernst Jünger speaks of the German philosopher J.G. Hamann as somebody who thought 'in archipelagos with submarine connections'.

WHEN THE QUAKE COMES

I watched some schoolchildren in a school near Padang practise their drill in the event of an alert from the tocsin of the fabled West Sumatran tsunami warning. First, they scampered down under their desks, and then they put their schoolbags over their heads and giggled quite a lot. The instructress addressed them sharply, and the giggling stopped: she was evidently telling them that Tsunami Preparedness was no laughing matter, though it must have seemed rather unlikely, even to a child, that hunkering down under a desk with a schoolbag on your head would ever protect you from a tsunami. In fact, it turned out that they were instead following the instructions for responding to an earthquake, which, it must be said, was an even more likely event in this part of the world—astride a major strike-slip fault that runs the length of the island—than a tsunami.

Then, once the all-clear siren had hooted, they assembled outside in the courtyard of the school. The children were chanting and it didn't sound like a nursery rhyme or patriotic ditty. 'What are they reciting?' I asked the instructress, who was fiddling with her headscarf. 'The ninety-nine names of the Great God', she replied.

THE CONVALESCENT PHILOSOPHER

There were three debts the philosopher R.G. Collingwood wished to absolve in relation to the writing of *An Essay on Metaphysics*, the first draft of which was completed on the one-month's voyage to Java which he undertook in October 1938. Firstly, to the University of Oxford, which had granted him leave of absence. Secondly, to 'a wise man of Harley Street', who had shrewdly sanctioned his leave of absence as a 'cure' for the stroke which had laid him low in 1938—other treatments were not available to alleviate the symptoms of overwork and 'stress'. And thirdly, to 'Mijnheer C. Koningstein of the Blue Funnel Line, master of the motor vessel *Alcinous*, who rigged me up an open-air study on his own Captain's Bridge where I could work all day without interruption, and thus made it possible for me to write the first draft of this book during a voyage from England to Java under perfect conditions'.

The grizzled captain of this Dutch-registered boat sailing out of Birkenhead was solicitous enough of his distinguished guest to erect an awning on the bridge so that Collingwood could sit outside and explain in sixteen days of work what metaphysics is, and why metaphysical questions are historical questions. He wanted to show positivists that they too rely on absolute presuppositions, such as the notion of verifiability; and that it is impossible, as his biographer puts it, to 'get around the back of an absolute presupposition'. Being historical, they are mutable. He had books with him including a Malay primer, but no reference material. As Stefan Collini has observed, 'it was characteristic of Collingwood's mixture of confidence and intellectual isolation that his idea of "perfect conditions" included neither library nor interlocutors.'

On 17 November, M.V. *Alcinous* docked at Padang, on Sumatra, and Collingwood was able to see a film in English and enjoy drinks in the Dutch club. Then the captain sailed further south, past Fort Marlborough, the British fortification on the southern aspect of Sumatra which had once been a stopping post on the way to Australia, and through the Sunda Strait, where the great volcano Krakatoa had erupted half a century before. In those days, Batavia, the capital of the Dutch East Indies, was a city of two parts: a large shanty town where the natives lived, and a miniature European capital, with cathedral, embassies and hotels. On Bali, he attended several of the famous cockfights which would receive their definitive anthropological treatment a decade later at the hands of Clifford Geertz, and met Walter Spies, the German artist who thought he had found a natural environment on the island that would transform him into a naïve painter (Spies told him that there was no word for 'artist' or 'art' on Bali). On Bali the terror of absolute presuppositions had been quieted by elaborate Hindu rituals and gamelan music.

Collingwood spent over three months in the Dutch East Indies, before returning to Europe just before the outbreak of war, when he was to write his last works. Germany, he observed to his dismay, was arming in order to subject Europe to a lesson in practical nihilism, its absolute presupposition being a doctrine that sought to abolish the very notion of morality, which one of its homegrown philosophers had considered the vanity of a creature whose true nature was constituted by the will to power. Overpowering was the thing. But authority, as Collingwood knew, is not acquired by being authoritarian. One of his more lasting contributions to philosophy was methodological dualism, the conviction that the humanistic sciences (history, economics) should not adopt the practices of natural science. For him the essential difference between history and natural science is that the former has an 'outside' and an 'inside'—a visible train of events observable to the chronicler as well as an inner life, the internal workings of an individual for whom external events were actions in which he had participated. The historian therefore has to remember that the event is an act, and think himself into this act, in order to discern the thought of its agent.

And yet, in truth, we swim for better or worse in a continuum in which it is very difficult to isolate anything like a raft of truth or even a person who can discern our thoughts so well as to throw us a lifebelt. Life itself is invariably a shipwreck, a thought which occurred to Joseph Conrad too, if not all at once.

A RESETTLEMENT

We were being driven with our Indonesian counterparts on our health mission through Arso, the enormous Stalinist grid-type settlement constructed around a palm-oil plantation south of Abepura in northern Papua for the *transmigrasi* (transmigration) populations ordered or enticed there from overpopulated parts of Java and Sulawesi in the 1970s, when we entered a village. Sitting in the back of the Kijang, my colleague, as was her anticlerical wont, suggested—on noticing that we had just passed a Protestant meeting hall followed by a Catholic church followed by a mosque followed by a Hindu temple—that there really ought to be a 'plague-on-all-their-houses building'.

There is, I retorted, and the locals call it *puskesmas*, and vote with their feet not to use its services unless in dire extremity. And that's why we were headed there to ponder how to improve its basic services. ['Puskesmas' is a contraction of the Bahasa terms 'Pusat kesehatan masyarakat'—community health centre.]

THIS BREATHING WORLD

Friedrich Nietzsche warned against raising anthropomorphism to the planetary level: 'Let us beware of thinking that the world is a living being. Where should it expand? On what should it feed? How could it grow and multiply?' Yet it was Nietzsche's hero Goethe who, in his famous conversations with Eckermann, talked, in rather beautiful language, of the Earth as a living, breathing being. 'I imagine the earth with its circle of vapours like a great living being which inhales and exhales eternally. If the earth inhales, it draws to it the circle of vapours which approaches its surface and thickens into clouds and rain. I call this state the aqueous affirmation; if it lasted beyond the prescribed time, it would drown the earth. But the earth does not permit that; it exhales again and sends back up the vapours of water which spread into all the spaces of the high atmosphere and thin out to such an extent that not only does the brilliance of the sun cross through them, but that the eternal night of infinite space, seen through them, is coloured with a brilliant blue tint. I call this second state of the atmosphere the aqueous negation…. If this state were prolonged beyond the prescribed time, even without sunlight, the earth would run the risk of drying up and becoming completely hard.'

In Indonesia, the world dreamer is allowed to lie back and watch the cycle of affirmation and negation, all in one morning. The intimate forests of Sumatra are lungs, the lakes are pupils seized by fright, and height is a kind of destiny that rises from the slowly coiling ravines of the Mata Hari river. Then I discovered an early work by the myopic Nietzsche where he notices: 'the dawn ventures to confront the sky decorated with many colours… My eyes have an entirely different brilliance. I'm afraid they will make holes in the sky.'

BLUE SOUP

In the endless flat scrubby plains of southern Papua, with their sandy unsealed roads, my Indonesian doctor companion and I made a wayside stop after a day's trip in the jeep to visit the health centre at Kurik. The stop was a tar paper shack run by a grandmother preparing soup over a small kerosene stove. There were no windows, but air blew in the front door from the hot expanses of scrubland out back. Two or three children popped up, as they always pop up in Indonesia, and watched us while giggling. She threw in a fresh handful of coriander and the aroma began to be appealing. I realised I was going to be given a bowl of *soto ayam*, the classic Indonesian soup, with rice and vermicelli noodles, hard-boiled egg segments and sliced cabbage, with some sambal to enliven the broth. Honest food, except that it was blue.

As I picked through its constituents it made me think of the sculptor Fuxier in Raymond Roussel's *Impressions of Africa* who throws blue pastilles into a river to produce an entrancing spectacle for his audience. In reality, this was soup which had been made with eutrophic water, probably from one of the irrigation schemes we had noticed in the neighbourhood, in which excess nitrates and other nutrients from fertilisers had caused an overgrowth of algae.

## THE FIRST GLOBAL DISASTER

It is strange that such an extraordinary feat of civil engineering as the laying of the Overland Telegraph Line between the centre of Empire and its farthest colony should have slipped into oblivion. In fact, the Australian territories were among the first to realise how much they could benefit from the new communications technology, especially if the cables were laid not just overland but across the ocean floor (it was discovered that gutta-percha extracted from the rubber trees of Borneo, Sumatra and Java was the ideal waterproofing for the miles and miles of thick-weave twisted copper wire). It was with the backing of Charles Todd, the South Australian Superintendent of Telegraphs, who encouraged South Australia to lay its overland network independently of the other colonies, that a submarine line was laid across the stretch of ocean between Darwin and Java. The line was completed in August 1872 and, although the speed at which Morse signals could be sent was sometimes frustratingly slow, it was now possible for the great imperial centre to remain in daily contact with hither and yon. The transmission time between London and the antipodes was three hours. So began what might be called the 'tubulation' of the Earth: the whole globe began to be covered in a fantastically complex cat's cradle of tubes, the latest of which are glass fibres transmitting light. And what the light transmits is information.

The significance of the event did not escape Kipling, who wrote: 'They have killed their Father Time... And a new Word runs between, whispering, "Let us be one".' Telecommunications were already global well over a century ago and already performative.

One of those first 'performances' had its origins in the Malay archipelago. A message about the initial rumblings and eruptions at Krakatoa was intercepted (on its way to Lloyds) by the duty editor and duly published in *The Times* (London) the day after the event in May 1883, while news about the final paroxysm of planetary doom and the subsequent immense loss of life on the morning of 27 August, 1883, reached newspaper readers all over the world, thanks to Reuters, before the month was out.

It is an irony worth dwelling on: the planet had reached what might be called the age of informational stability: the veracity of an item of news from a distant part of the globe could, for the first time, be verified. And what was the first major event to be reported worldwide? Sensational reports about that same planet's instability.

## COCKROACHES AND MOSQUITOES

Some kind of blattopterans—six legs, two folding wings, indiscreet optics, long olfactory antennae, chitin skeleton and obligatorily omnivorous—was crawling over the giant hibiscus flowers that had been brought in to decorate the otherwise bare wooden room of what I was told had formerly been the missionary's house. The insect could have been the last remaining terrestrial lifeform in a Philip K. Dick novel. I was still there too, of course, observing its progress across the linoleum. Cockroaches I would have to put up with. The malaria-bearing mosquitoes of Kimaam Island—off the south-west coast of Papua and one of the marshiest places on the planet—were a different proposition, and I checked every fold in the net curtain before blowing out the candle. The darkness was total and had an auditory quality; its velvet static gave me a sudden sense of the distance between me and any kind of civilisation. I was spending the night in the Stone Age. Now and then I could hear a faint scuttling noise, and the churning sound of an insect mandible dissecting what I hoped was merely a leaf or petal.

## GALACTIC OVERTONES

Were I a musician, one of my projects would be to recreate in the concert hall the astonishing acoustics of dusk in the tropics which I heard my very first evening in the garden of the Park Lane hotel in southern Jakarta in 2005. I heard it every time I visited the city in the following three or four years in which a development project brought me to Indonesia, and it became a habit of mine on every visit to go down to sit outside beside the illuminated swimming pool at the end of the day simply to listen to the threnody.

In Jakarta, the light fades towards 6 o'clock every day of the year with at most a half-hour variation between January and July. As it fades, a tremendous raucous hubbub starts up here and there in the city and then gathers strength, a hubbub with uplift and overtones over a deep bass growl: it is the Maghreb prayer being intoned simultaneously in different mosques, with the amplified sound echoing and dispersing in all directions from the neighbouring tall apartment blocks. This wailing drone to Allah amasses and is borne aloft on the roar of traffic produced by the thousands of workers returning home on their motorbikes from the high-rise office blocks of Sudirman and Rasuna Said to the suburbs and shanties further out on the periphery of the city. Every motorbike has its pitch cluster. It is a tremendous parliamentary din, this shrieking, howling, keening circulation of a city—and all the while and seemingly indifferent to it, religious men intoning a chorale for the end of time.

Then the sounds of the prayers drains away, and it is suddenly and conclusively dusk beneath the banyan trees. I had heard this eerie, unsettling, unearthly kind of music before, in the orchestral compositions of Giacinto Scelsi, whose *Quattro Pezzi su una nota sola* is a work in which, in all four movements, a single chromatic spectrum is sounded with microtonal waverings, octave transformations and innumerable subtle changes in timbre and dynamics, with the twenty-six musicians remaining faithful throughout to the true God of pitch. It is as if Scelsi had written music with an astrolabe.

Scelsi (1905–1988), last of the line of an old Italian noble family and something of a playboy in his salad days, started his composing career at Luigi Russolo's futurist noise concerts, became interested in serialism, drifted into mysticism ('I was born in Mesopotamia 2,800 years ago', he once told an interviewer), and suffered a breakdown at the end of the

Second World War which called for years of hospitalisation.
While in convalescence, he devised his own cure: it consisted
of spending hours at the keyboard, playing the same note and
listening intently to the sound decaying. This was what the
monks did in the monasteries Scelsi had reputedly visited
in India and Nepal before the war. He started composing
again in 1952, concentrating at least a decade before Ligeti
on the inner world of sound. Scelsi went back to music as
a monodist, fascinated by microtonal fluctuations and slurs
around a chosen pitch. 'Sound', he said, 'is a cosmic power that
is the foundation of everything.' He scored his pieces heavily
for low-pitched brass and percussion, achieving a density
of sound and shimmering higher overtones not heard since
Anton Bruckner. A musical mystic whose preferred symbol
was a circle floating Zen-like above a line became a specialist in
making sounds materialise, mostly out of nowhere. Scelsi used
every technique he knew to make his held notes compelling.
Indeed his music is anything but monotonous; it teems and
gasps and churns and seethes. It creates an electrifying sense
of expectation that verges on the explosive. Sometimes the
sounds are so intense as to seem mineralogical. Scelsi was
doing almost unnoticed and with a driving sense of purpose
what all those crossover musicians like Brian Eno and Moby
on the one side, and Arvo Pärt on the other, would attempt
to do a generation later: discovering a memorably expressive
style in which renunciation manifests itself as strength.

It wasn't music but words which first drew me to Scelsi's
music. These are the titles of some of his compositions: *Aion:
Four Episodes in One Day of the Life of Brahma*, which the
composer mercifully foreshortens from its 90,000 human
years-equivalent, *Anahit: Lyrical Poem dedicated to Venus* (one
of Scelsi's finest creations in which the concertante violin is
played *scordatura*), *Konx-Om-Pax* (it looks like a place-name
but all three words of the title mean 'peace'), and *Uaxuctum:*

*The Legend of the Maya City which Destroyed Itself for Religious Reasons*. The latter is grandiose galactic music created by an orchestra including a chorus and four soloists as well as an ondes Martenot, sistrum, vibraphone and percussionists playing on a two-hundred litre can, a large aluminium hemisphere and a two-metre-high sheet of metal. Scelsi's apocalyptic sounds shunt into each other, then dwindle away into silence: thus they disconcert the natural rhythm of the breathing listener, who begins to wonder if this music was actually intended for merely human consumption.

Uaxuctum is the city of Uaxactún, the ancient sacred place of the Maya civilization: it is situated on the lowland plain of what is present-day Guatemala and disappeared abruptly from the record in the middle of the ninth century, for reasons unknown. It is a reminder that in the very short history of civilisation cities have been destroyed by those who built them, and it seems there have been times in history when the reasons for undoing them were so persuasive they needed no explaining to the future at all.

CUTTING HIS LOSSES

Captain James Cook lost only one man from disease on his famous second voyage around the world, when he circumnavigated the mythical *terra australis*; his first voyage around the coast of New Holland—as Australia was then called—went reasonably well apart from his having run aground on the Barrier Reef, which determined Cook to sail the *Endeavour* along the south coast of Java and into the dry docks at Batavia for the major overhaul it needed to get home. Within a short space of time, fever and flux (malaria and dysentery) had broken out among the ship's company, and no less than a third died of disease. The unruffled Dutch skippers

he met told him that having docked in the Roads of Batavia
in the rainy season he was lucky not to have lost *half* his crew.


## WHAT ARE MUSEUMS FOR?

Friedrich Martin Schnitger, the self-styled Conservator of the
first museum in Sumatra, the Algemeen Museum Palembang
when he founded it in the 1930s, now known as the Museum
Sultan Mahmud Badaruddin (I had visited unannounced,
pushing open its creaking, unoiled door and startling the
curator) writes about the disappointment he felt when first
viewing some of the objects he had discovered with native
helpers in difficult conditions in the island's interior: stone
elephants, dancing figures, demonic images of the Buddha.
Seeing them on display did not lift his mood or make him feel
triumphant; quite the contrary. They had lost their original
aura and acquired another nimbus, one far more sinister in
its implications—and it would seem related to the way a
museum effaces the distinction between objects, acts and
events. 'A museum, however tastefully it may be arranged',
he writes in *Forgotten Kingdoms in Sumatra* (1939), 'is much
like a charnel-house.' He was contradicting his contemporary,
André Malraux, who insisted a museum is the only place in
the world that is *not* a necropolis—'le seul lieu du monde qui
échappe à la mort'.

Schnitger would therefore be startled at the vast
museography of our contemporary culture where not only 'the
metamorphosis of the Gods', but every form and artefact of
human activity has been catalogued, commented and archived
prior to its vitrification. And he would be expected, like us, to
talk there in a low voice in order to hear the 'voices of silence'.
Further disabused, it might even seem to him that some
museums have been set up to legislate against the participation

of art in the general life of the polis: they are there to protect us from art.


## WICKER WIVES

In some of the better hotels in Indonesia I often found a long sack-like pillow occupying the middle of the bed. This, I was informed, was a 'Dutch wife', a name which derived from the tough rattan bolsters originally designed to help people to sleep in humid equatorial countries by allowing them to lift their limbs off the damp sheets. Dutch wives had earlier been hand-fashioned by sailors on the long voyages to the Indies from a motley of old fabric and canvas, and wedged into their bunks to prevent them rolling about in rough weather.

Almost inevitably, there are other kinds of 'Dutch wives': some of these bolsters were made of bamboo cane and also known as 'wicker wives'. The Japanese learned about them from their trade with the Dutch—for two centuries the only European commercial partner allowed to trade with the country—and in time the word became current in Japan to describe sex dolls: the term 'datchi waifu' is still used in Japan to refer to the currently far more lifelike and sophisticated masturbatory aids for which the industry of that country has a rather perverse penchant.


## THE TALE OF THE CROCODILE SON

Over dinner in our Jakarta hotel, Albert, one of my melancholic German colleagues who had worked as a pathologist in Germany and then as an aid worker in the jungles of Latin America where he had learned Spanish (a language he was audibly more at ease with than English), told me an amazing story about his last visit to the eastern district of Jambi province, Tanjung Jabung Timur.

As a distinguished visitor he had been taken to a house about twenty miles out of Jambi where the family looked after a crocodile. The story was this. When she was pregnant, the mother had dreamt that she would have twins, but gave birth to only one son. A few days after her confinement she went for her first walk along the nearby Batang riverbank when a baby crocodile followed her home. She identified this creature as the second son who had failed to show up for his more conventional human birth, and brought the animal home. The crocodile was cradled alongside her human son, and, fifteen years later, they were both still sleeping together in the same room. My colleague called this the *Himmelbett*. The family had created a tiled tub for the crocodile to bathe in when it was smaller; now it was about two metres long, and lay impassive on the sofa most of the day. Everyone in the village knew about it, and nobody feared it: it had never attacked anyone. Its carapace was as smooth as leather, and it left a great imprint in the sofa, as if a tree had been felled in the sitting room.

My colleague showed me a couple of photographs. From its long slender snout, we determined that it was actually a false gharial, *Tomistoma schlegelii*, and not the now extremely rare Sumatran estuarine crocodile, *Crocodylus porosus*, which can grow up to nine metres in length and is perfectly capable of making off with a human. This pet gharial received a chicken twice a week, which seemed to satisfy it metabolically: gharials are generally far less predatory than their cousin crocodiles. Nonetheless, I found documented stories of very large false gharials which had attacked and sometimes swallowed humans along the littoral.

Albert said this crocodile story reminded him of his years in Mexico, where the nahuals are born and die at the same time as humans. I told him about the town of Crocodilopolis

(Egyptian 'Shedyet') which I once visited with an Egyptologist friend, when the two of us travelled out to the Fayyum Oasis, south-west of Cairo. This town received its ancient Greek name from the fact that the whole region preserved a cult to the crocodile god Sobek: a tame sacred crocodile was kept in splendour in a lake in Crocodilopolis and fed titbits by the priests to the great amusement of tourists. So wrote the Greek geographer Strabo.

When all the world was water, the crocodile must have seemed an awesome spectacle: a block of primal matter that might glide through the Nile and attack a bather on its banks. Though the deity was unpredictable and aggressive, a crocodile-god was also mighty protective magic: its fierceness could ward off all kind of evils. As a non-mammal that cares for its young, the crocodile also had a nurturing aspect. There are also fantastic stories in European folk literature, where an animal turns out to be human after all, and the plot of Janáček's opera *The Cunning Little Vixen* even puts the disjuncture between human and animal time on stage. This unusual family was at any rate a vestige of the old animistic religion that prevailed in many parts of the Malay archipelago, with its associated veneration of ancestors and faith of guardian spirits.

I was deeply impressed that such an immense engine of Mesozoic time could live—an itinerant piece of furniture—in a family house.

In the time of the Sriwijaya empire which ruled over much of Sumatra, estuarine crocodiles were a scourge of the basins of the Musi and Batang Hari rivers. Friedrich Martin Schnitger in his book *Forgotten Kingdoms in Sumatra* (1939) relates that a millennium ago, an Indian arrived in Palembang who claimed to be able to charm the crocodiles. This he did, and the crocodiles refrained from devouring a man who had been condemned to death and thrown into the river. The next day, the king asked the Indian to repeat his performance.

Once he had the crocodiles under his power, the king had the man seized and beheaded on the spot. The tenth-century chronicle relating the event concluded: 'And since that time the crocodiles of Serira (Sriwijaya) are entirely harmless'. Schnitger goes on to attest that throughout Sumatra the belief is still current that there is a special bond between humans and crocodiles. They are regarded as protectors and even magical kinds of vahana—able to raft people to distant and magical lands. Some of the riverine tribes in southern Sumatra even consider crocodiles to be their ancestors.

## AFTER EXTINCTION

It didn't take me long to commit to memory the rather beautiful Malay word for candle. Every evening in our hotel on the south coast of Papua, where it would get dark promptly at six in the evening and the emergency lights sometimes failed, I would walk to reception and ask 'Ada lilin?' And if I was lucky, the receptionist would be able to find me a candle. Although it was difficult to read by its light, it was sometimes more prudent to sit by the low lux of a paraffin candle with its guttering tow than under the sixty watts of a naked light bulb in what was after all one of the swampier regions of a humid great island notorious for its mosquitoes.

With the candle flickering in a small, stained saucer that had evidently served at some time as an ashtray, I sat on the veranda of my room in the Hotel Asmat, close to the small port of Merauke, and listened to the sounds of this small, isolated town on the Arafura Sea die away into the night. There was a frisson to be had, sitting in a wicker-chair at the end of the earth while a candle in its socket fitted and guttered, and the flame tore at the wick. We love company, as the philosopher Lichtenberg wrote, 'even it if is only that of a smouldering candle'. That must be why we light them in the grandest churches to soothe our grief about a loved one lost.

Behind me the hinterland stretched unimaginably flat and far to the north, almost as far as the Digul river. Nights were true blackout nights. Here a kerosene lamp would cost the average family many times more than we pay for electricity in the developed world. Candles have to be used sparingly too. With the decline of the candle modern humans lost the night, the regular occurrence at the end of each day of a nocturama in which things and bodies abandoned their solidity and contours. That is why night used to be a separate world.

I sat and watched the wick burn off, and the wax melt its own length down to a sludge of wax in the saucer in which the wick slumped, at imminent threat of drowning. Now there were no currents of air to deviate or harry the flame in its slow combustion except for the occasional movements of the pages of my notebook. In one of his last works, the French philosopher Gaston Bachelard meditated on the nature of verbs that describe change: 'to go out' can indicate passage from a space as well as the extinguishing of a noise or a heart, but its primary meaning is the guttering of a candle. 'The candle which goes out is a sun which dies.'

*Nirvana*: the Sanskrit word relates to the device used to snuff out a burning candle and prevent the wick from smoking. A quencher.


NEON SPLENDOURS OF JAYAPURA


The new Swiss Bel-Hotel in Jayapura, which dominates the waterline of Papua's capital, drove me to distraction with its piped recordings of birdsong on every floor including the breakfast suite. A taped recording of the real thing seemed to be the height of perversity in the home of the *cendrawasih*, those blue, orange and yellow birds of paradise, the incandescent promise of capturing one of which had sent Alfred Russel Wallace into transports of delight when he stopped off at present-day Manokwari in the 1850s. There is much traditional lore about this bird, which, because of its extravagant male tail plumage, was pursued as much by locals looking for feathery adornments as naturalists who adopted it as a model of strong sexual selection. In his notebook Wallace made a pencil sketch of the tail feathers, which end in a spiral of shimmering emerald, and speculates that the beauty of these birds would eventually be the cause of their 'disappearance': European hat-makers would see them off.

The piped birdsong at breakfast in the basement made me regret having checked into this incongruously swanky building: on previous visits to Jayapura I'd stayed in leaky but friendly guesthouses up in the hills—on the slopes of the fjords around the city, well away from the uninspiring centre of town. I had lain awake at night in those places and heard rain thundering on the roof, slopping into the gutters and sometimes seeping into the room itself—diluvial torrents. But it had to be said that the waterside setting of the Swiss Bel-Hotel was magnificent, with an unimpeded view across Humboldt Bay to the—by Indonesian standards—tiny capital city of two hundred thousand inhabitants; and guarding its approach the blue and red illuminated crosses that had been erected on the small rock islands in the bay. Jayapura straddles the slopes of several adjoining fjords, and from some angles you could see and hear the trucks straining to climb the Cyclop range to the south-east in order to deposit their cargo at the airport twenty-five miles away at Sentani. And the hotel's swimming pool was flush with the sea, so that at night it was possible to swim up and down the pool peering out into a kind of utter ink interspersed with brightly lit semiotic distractions.

In view of the recent unrest in the province, I allowed

myself a smile at the missing K in the neon-blue display of the BANK PAPUA, near the Hotel Matua, the other hotel in the centre of town, with its suggestion to docking sailors that their next port had been taken under the control of anarchists who wished to do away with the island. The emission of a sign. It reminded me that, years ago, on a trip through the eastern United States, I'd stopped at a motel in Georgia where the blinking blue message on the sign across the street read 'GOD LESS AMERICA'.

Then there was that drunken, impassioned, wayward novelist Malcolm Lowry, who took ten years to rewrite *Under the Volcano*, in which the soul's customary striving for salvation had turned into a petition for immediate damnation; and the fertile valleys and blossoming gardens of the Mount of Perfection had taken on corrupt and sere forms. Lowry had similar amusement at one time with a red SHELL sign that greeted him whenever he opened the door of the isolated squatter's shack (no water, no electricity, no heating) in which he lived on and off for fourteen years with his forbearing second wife Margerie Bonner on the inlet of Dollarton, north of Vancouver on the coast of British Columbia. One letter was extinct, the S.

This period marked the happiest phase of Lowry's life, as recounted in *October Ferry to Gabriola*. He and his wife had largely given up hard liquor for the simple life: swimming, eating crabs over a beach fire and the morning discipline of the typewriter.

One day the beach shack, to which they built a pier with their own hands, burned down, consuming a 1,000-page draft of a manuscript titled *In Ballast to the White Sea*, which represented nine years of work. Things persist although everything man-made sometimes seems beyond repair, and other things volatilise and disperse for ever. You can imagine Lowry wakening the morning after, and feeling how different it all looked: the greenness of the islet, the morning chill, birds chittering in a light rain, and then on the breeze the faintly acrid smell of their burned-out, charred lean-to. And across the bay, the fiery wink of the neon confounding the grainy blue-grey morning light.